KILL THE DUTCHMAN!

BOOKS BY PAUL SANN

Americana

Pictorial History of the Wild West (with James D. Horan)
The Lawless Decade
Fads, Follies and Delusions of the American People

Crime

Kill the Dutchman!
The Story of Dutch Schultz

Sports

Red Auerbach: Winning the Hard Way
(with Arnold Red Auerbach)

PAUL SANN

KILL THE DUTCHMAN!

THE STORY OF DUTCH SCHULTZ

PREFACE BY PETE HAMILL

A DA CAPO PAPERBACK

Library of Congress Cataloging in Publication Data

Sann, Paul.
Kill the Dutchman!: the story of Dutch Schultz / Paul Sann.
p. cm.—(A Da Capo paperback)
Reprint. Originally published: New Rochelle, N.Y.: Arlington House, 1971.
ISBN 0-306-80452-2
1. Schultz, Dutch, 1900 or 1-1935. 2. Criminals—New York (N.Y.)—Biography.
3. Racketeering—New York (N.Y.)—History—20th century. I. Title.
HV6248.S394S26 1991
364.1′092—dc20 91-18100
[B] CIP

This Da Capo Press paperback edition of *Kill the Dutchman!* is an unabridged republication of the edition published in New Rochelle, New York in 1971, with the addition of a new preface by Pete Hamill, and with some minor corrections. It is reprinted by arrangement with Howard Sann.

Published by Da Capo Press, Inc.
A Subsidiary of Plenum Publishing Corporation
233 Spring Street, New York, N.Y. 10013

Manufactured in the United States of America

I dedicate this book, too late, to Walter B. Lister. He was my City Editor on the New York *Post* in another time, long ago. He was so incredibly talented in his craft that after him none of us could be real good city editors; there was just no way, no way at all. He got the last interview with Dutch Schultz, because if he had to he could go out and get it himself. I wish he were around to read this book. Just Walter and a girl I knew in those days. He liked Birdye so much that he even considered giving me a day off for our honeymoon, but then he changed his mind. There was some kind of story breaking and he needed a reporter.

PAUL SANN
Greenwich Village, New York
7 March 1970

CONTENTS

PREFACE

For me, reading this book again is to plunge into two separate rivers of nostalgia. One is Paul Sann's longing for his youth as a newspaperman. The other is my own aching desire to relive mine.

Sann was my editor at the *New York Post* from the day in 1960 when I first walked into the old city room at 75 West Street and started to live my life. He was a lean medium-sized man with pouches under his eyes, a slit of mouth usually turned in an ironical grin, a cigarette always burning in his fingers, gray hair cut short and brushed straight back. When reading galleys or raw copy, he pushed his glasses up on his head and examined each word as if inspecting the defenses of an enemy. He had a taste for black gangster-style shirts and cowboy boots and good whiskey and was not immune to certain other bad habits: he gambled away many thousands on horses and football teams and the pitching of the Dodgers, Giants, Yankees, and Mets. He had a tough big city style that I first thought came from watching too much Bogart and later understood came right off the sidewalks of the harder New York of Prohibition and Depression. His tough exterior was, of course, almost entirely a sham, the artful defense of a man who acknowledges the ferocious subversive power of personal sentiment by denying its existence.

In fact, he loved many people and places and things: his wife and his children, Red Auerbach and the Boston Celtics, good writing, Sugar Ray Robinson, the American West, the music of Rodgers and Hart, the city of New York, beautiful women, homerun hitters, Smith Corona portable typewriters, and the New York Post.

He went to work for the Post when he was seventeen and stayed for half a century, mastering along the way all the skills of his imperfect trade. He was a great reporter, a fine writer in the punchy tabloid style, an ingenious composer of page one headlines, a surgically precise text editor. He added the intangibles of mood, spirit, attitude that infuriated some newspaper people but allowed others to flourish. And he had one other skill for which no Pulitzer is ever awarded but is the mark of a great editor. He had an excellent eye for talent. He wasn't afraid of hiring people who were smarter than he was (or seemed to be) or who had more obvious abilities. Second-rate editors always see young talents as threats. Paul Sann saw them as angels. And so he hired and helped nurture such writers as Murray Kempton, Nora Ephron, Jimmy Cannon, Larry Merchant, Anna Quindlen, Ernest Tidyman, Clyde Haberman, Warren Hoge, Milton Gross, Ed Kosner, Don Forst, Alfred G. Aronowitz, to mention only a few of the hundreds of talented people who moved in and out of his New York Post.

He was, in short, the greatest newspaperman I've ever known: tough, literate, intelligent, and profane—and extraordinarily generous. He produced two masterpieces. The *Post* was one of them, a flawed but stylish tabloid that went up against the products of the great Scripps-Howard and Hearst chains and survived.

His other masterpiece was this book.

It is, on one level, an homage to the Spirit of Gangsters Past. Dutch Schultz was a crucial part of the New York that Sann knew and loved when young. This was long ago, of course, before the Mob focused its rude talents on the peddling of heroin. In the days of the Dutchman, rumrunners were still socially acceptable and hoodlums were thought of as romantic, a feeling perfectly evoked in E.L. Doctorow's fine novel about the Dutchman, *Billy Bathgate*. Paul Sann was dead before Doctorow's book was published, but I think he would have liked it and quarrelled with it. In spite of all his other talents, Sann was basically a reporter, with a fidelity for factual truth; he would have argued against the artistic liberties that Doctorow allowed himself. That's why I'm happy that this book is once more back in print. If you loved *Billy Bathgate* (as I did), you can read this history and discover what *really* happened.

You will also hear the authentic voice of Paul Sann: skeptical, amused, sardonic, admiring. He at once celebrates the bad guys and judges them. He has enormous fun with the felonies of the era (which now have an odd innocence to them) and lovingly embraces the often arcane language in which those vanished gangsters expressed themselves. Much of the reporting here was fresh; Sann went back and found the documents and the survivors and gave the aging words a new life. He also uses his considerable literary intelligence to examine one of the most extraordinary accidental documents in our history: the last words of Dutch Schultz. These "ravings" (as they were called in the newspapers of the day) still have a Joycean energy and excitement to them. "Mother is the best bet," says the Dutchman, "and don't let Satan draw you too fast."

Doctorow used the dying words in his novel. They also inspired a book by William S. Burroughs. But Sann explains most of them without robbing them of their poetry. We can hear the Dutchman now, dying of peritonitis in the Newark City Hospital, his men Abbadabba Berman and Abe Landau already dead, the words flowing freely and splendidly. Even Sann, whose explanations fill a chapter, can't solve the mystery of the couplet: "a boy has never wept/nor dashed a thousand kim." All these years later, the words continue to astonish.

But this book doesn't astonish; it does something much more difficult. It illuminates. In the last years of the '60s, Sann sat down to write a book about one of the fabulous Jewish gangsters from an era that would die at Pearl Harbor. He did much more: he gave us the era itself, its attitudes, characters, and language, and made us understand how the big cities of America worked in the years between the wars. Reading it again, more than twenty years after its publication, I'm back in the old city room, about to rush out on a story, and I miss Paul Sann more than ever.

PETE HAMILL
New York City, May 1991

KILL THE DUTCHMAN!

"I suppose there ain't no wars around, so they have to put me on the front page."

—DUTCH SCHULTZ, July 1935

CHAPTER I

THE STAGE IS SET

COME THE TROUBLED AUTUMN THAT YEAR, DUTCH Schultz could no longer say that "there ain't no wars around." There was a war: the Kingdom of Italy, Mussolini's Italy, against Ethiopia. On the very day we're concerned with here, October 23, 1935, Il Duce's son-in-law, Count Galeazzo Ciano, proudly announced to the world that his aerial squadrons were dropping nothing heavier than ten-pound bombs on the tiny country of Emperor Haile Selassie. "We are anxious to do nothing to irritate the peaceful population," Count Ciano said. On the domestic scene that day, President Roosevelt was coming ashore at Charleston, South Carolina, refreshed by a three-week voyage in Pacific and Atlantic waters abroad the cruiser *Houston.* Across the depression-scarred landscape, there was relative tranquility.

The New York Stock Exchange was coming off a 3-million-share day, the heaviest trading in 15 months. Washington reported strong gains in the export sales of such items as cotton, metal and chemicals (Mussolini's purchases were way up). New York was cracking down on the loan-shark fraternity, waxing richer on the patronage of WPA workers whose checks were too slow in coming. The New Haven Railroad, in trouble then as now, filed a petition in bankruptcy. In Hollywood, Jackie Coogan was three days away from his 21st birthday and the $1 million fortune stored away for him during the 17 years since he had starred in *The Kid* with Charlie Chaplin, and there was mingled wonder and concern out there because the Charles Laughton–Clark Gable *Mutiny on the Bounty* had chalked up a final production cost of nearly $1.5 million ($20 million for Barbra Streisand's *Hello, Dolly!* in 1969). On the Broadway movie marquees, there were names like Richard Dix, Joan Crawford, Dick Powell, Ruby Keeler and Basil Rathbone. On the stage, Lunt and Fontanne were in *The Taming of the Shrew* and Beatrice Lillie and Ethel Waters were co-starring in *At Home Abroad,* while Jimmy Durante was coming in with Billy Rose's *Jumbo,* Gershwin's *Porgy and Bess* was starting its infinite career, *Three Men on a Horse* (revived in 1969, again with Sam Levene) was sending us all away laughing, and the Maxwell Anderson drama, *Winterset,* was tearing at our insides.

In the high drama at hand, a real-life affair opening on and off-Broadway on the same night, the assorted stars and supporting players assembled slowly over a period of six hours.

The headliner in the cast, Dutch Schultz, born Arthur Flegenheimer, came on stage first. It was six o'clock on an uncommonly warm and pleasant evening when the Dutchman, sole owner and proprietor of New York's biggest single policy combination, a $20-million-a-year operation, strode into the Palace Chop House and Tavern on East Park Street in Newark flanked by two of his bodyguards, Bernard (Lulu) Rosenkrantz and Abe Landau. Frank Fredericks, the bartender then on duty in the reformed speakeasy, said that the Dutchman and his helpmates walked the length of the 60-foot bar and went directly to the round table in the right-hand corner of the back room. None of the eight booths was occupied, and none of the other tables.

Herbert Green, the waiter, had the drinks served in about the time it took the three men to doff their topcoats and hats and sit down. King Lou, the chef, put up the steaks and French fries without waiting for Green to come into the kitchen with the order. The Chinaman had been on the job only three days but already knew the ritual that followed the arrival of the Schultz trio.

Now the other players started to drift into the Palace.

Michael (Mickey the Mock) Marks, a minor hanger-on of the mob, said he had come all the way from the Grand Concourse in The Bronx just to see Lulu Rosenkrantz about some walking-around money. There may have been a more pressing reason for this long excursion, however, because Marks left after a while and returned to the tavern sometime before 8:00 P.M. with a slender little auburn-haired item who was wearing heavy glasses. This was Frances Flegenheimer, born Frances Geis but known as Frances Maxwell in 1932 when she went to work as a hatcheck girl in New York's Maison Royal, one of the red-carpet speakeasies, and met the imposing Dutch Schultz. She was 18 then and a still-blooming flower out of Hell's Kitchen, daughter of a machinist. Now she was the Dutchman's wife of sorts and mother of his two known children. She had come to Newark from her apartment in Jackson Heights, Queens. The bartender, Fredericks, had seen her in the tavern four or five times in the past week but never knew who she was. On this night, in any case, Schultz spent the best part of an hour alone with the girl, who was modestly dressed in a brown velvet suit topped by the most expensive thing the Dutchman had ever bought for her, the silver fox neckpiece that marked her 21st birthday.

The pair had to break off at one point when the Dutchman had a visitor.

The new arrival was Max Silverman, a prosperous bondsman known to the New Jersey police because he had four arrests between 1922 and 1928 deriving from a certain sloppiness in his financial dealings. He was deposited at the Chop House at 7:40 by his Negro chauffeur, Alfred. Schultz, in a wrangle with the law over his carelessness about filing income tax returns in the time when he was the Beer Baron of The Bronx, recently had surrendered on a long-standing fugitive warrant out on him in New York and Silverman had posted his $50,000 bail.

Now the bondsman had come to the Palace, he would confide to the police later, to pick up some installment payments due on the fees of the Dutchman's high-priced New Jersey legal battery—$6,000 for Harry H. Weinberger, $2,500 for George S. Silzer, only a former Governor of the Garden State, and $2,000 for State Senator John E. Toolan. Silverman's mission, though, was something more than that of an errand boy. "I have been in constant contact with Arthur Flegenheimer," he would say when the detectives started talking tough. "I done this as my duty as a bondsman for several reasons, one of them being that Flegenheimer feared being kidnapped by federal men, in which event my bond would be declared forfeit." Besides, there was an equally pressing matter of "some money for myself, which Flegenheimer owed me." This item involved $3,500, but the chunky 43-year-old bondsman always insisted that he had departed the tavern without any fresh rolls of green. He said the Dutchman, an acquaintance for 17 years, had told him that he wouldn't have any cash until later that night or the next morning. He said this intelligence was so disappointing that he left the Palace in short order.

On the way out, Silverman bid a passing good-by to the only two people seated along the long bar—Beatrice, the manicurist from the barber shop in the Public Service Bus Terminal across the street, and a man he knew only as "Mikie" and had seen in the tavern on some of his earlier business visits there with the Schultz party. Silverman said he whistled for his limousine, parked near the terminal, at 8:10, and had Alfred drive him over to a night club on nearby Clinton Avenue.

Benny Birkenfeld, the night waiter, arrived at 8:00. Two new faces joined the round table after a while and Birkenfeld served them dinner. One of these men would never be identified. The other, already enshrined in literature and thus something of a celebrity in his own right, was the roly-poly funnyman of the Dutchman's circle, Otto Berman. Real name Biederman. Nicknamed Avisack by the gambler-financier of the underworld, Arnold Rothstein, when a thoroughbred of that name helped him put over a couple of betting coups. Called Abbadabba by his own preference because that had a spookier sound about it and he was not only one of the premier handicappers of his time but also a mathematical wizard with a computer where his brain was supposed to be. In Damon Runyon's *Little Miss Marker*, the movie that helped five-year-old Shirley Temple shove aside such grown-up female box-office draws of the Thirties as Greta Garbo and Janet Gaynor, there was a kindly horseplayer modeled after Abbadabba Berman. Runyon called the round man Regret in his chronicles of Broadway, naming him after the filly that astonished the racing world and ran off with the Kentucky Derby for the Whitney Stables in 1915.

But Abbadabba wasn't quite the lovable oaf that Runyon made out of Regret. He was in the Palace Chop House on that October night, the last night of his laugh-a-minute, bet-a-minute 46 years, because he was drawing a cool $10,000 a week to rig the pari-mutuel figures at select race tracks with last-minute bets so that the poor people of Harlem wouldn't take too much money out of the Schultz policy banks. Abbadabba had flown in with a delicious set of figures showing that in the preceding six weeks, with his split-second calculations shutting out the most heavily played numbers on any given day, the banks had taken down bets of $827,253.43 and paid out winnings of only $313,711.99—a magnificent house percentage for any gambling operation.

The Dutchman needed this kind of good cheer.

His overall take from policy and such relatively minor absorptions as the restaurant shakedown racket had dwindled alarmingly during his enforced absentee administration. The problem was even clearer than the needle beer that had launched his fortune: he had been operating more or less in the underground since January 1933, when the government first indicted him on taxes, and had been out of New York since his surrender in Albany late in November 1934 for the first of his two trials (one hung jury and one easy acquittal). Now the bookkeeping sheets spread on the gravy-stained white tablecloth in the tavern dining room showed a growing imbalance in income and cash outlays (among them an item of $9,000 a month listed as "ice" for the friendly policemen of New York) which would have produced a screaming panic in the board room of any legitimate enterprise. The six-week net that showed on the tapes from the mechanical adding machine, almost as good as the one Abbadabba had in his chunky head, projected a rather gloomy annual take for policy even with the game rigged: $6 million for a racket which was then raking in $65,000 a day, every day but Sunday, or more than $20 million for the year. Beyond the mob force and the inside help and the shares drawn by the army of runners and controllers on the streets of Harlem, simply listed as "niggers" by Massa Schultz, there was too damn much coming off the top. Thus there never was any question about the agenda for the Palace summit.

Jacob Friedman, co-owner of the Chop House with Louis Rosenthal, arrived at 8:50 to relieve Fredericks at the bar, and by then there was no one in the front at all and the party in the back had reduced itself to the four principals—Schultz, Rosenkrantz, Landau and Berman. Whether the fifth man left the scene altogether or withdrew to patrol duty outside the tavern would never be known for certain, although it would have made very good sense for Arthur Flegenheimer to have an extra gun or two on hand that night. He was in trouble.

Apart from his legal difficulties with the Federal Government, the Dutchman was at that moment badly out of favor with the more formidable shooting mobs. In his time of travail, he had turned into something of a wild man, sending shivers down the collective back of the underworld by openly announcing that he was going to kill Thomas E. Dewey, recently named by the Democratic Governor, Herbert H. Lehman, to supersede the policy mob's own handpicked District Attorney, William Copeland Dodge, and to do something about the city's rampant crime.

Dewey, a Republican and an ex-choir singer out of Owosso, Michigan, was a relatively recent but fierce antagonist. As Chief Assistant United States Attorney for the Southern District of New York, he had drawn up the tax indictment against Schultz, who would thereafter be very careful about surrendering for trial while his tormentor was still in that office. Now in his new role Dewey was beginning to poke around in the lush policy preserve after having built up a solid case in the restaurant racket which the Dutchman had set up back in July 1932 with an assortment of crooked union leaders and such strong-arm men as Jules Martin, Sam Krantz and Louis Beitcher. The take was estimated at $2 million a year, and it was pretty easy money.

This Schultz subsidiary sold both "protection" and sweetheart contracts. From the one-armed joints to such Manhattan establishments as Jack Dempsey's (well, the ex-champ couldn't take on the whole mob, could he?), Gallagher's, Lindy's, The Brass Rail and Rosoff's, the eateries were given a simple choice by the Dutchman's Metropolitan Restaurant and Cafeteria Association. They could pay "dues" to the MRCA, the scale varying according to what the traffic would bear, or certain bad elements in the town might drop stink-bombs on their premises during peak hours, such as lunch or dinner. That's how the "protection" worked.

On the labor front, the choice was just as straightforward. The MRCA could help its members negotiate "reasonable" contracts with Local 16 of the Hotel and Restaurant Employees International Alliance and Bartenders Union, more commonly known as the Waiters Union, or with Local 302 of the Delicatessen Countermen and Cafeteria Workers Union—or they could watch their receipts dip while picket lines kept the customers away. The MRCA happened to have three of the top leaders in each of these American Federation of Labor unions in its hip pocket, so there never was any difficulty arranging contracts that could be beneficial all around—except to the restaurant workers themselves, for they drew pitifully low wages in the process and also would find in time that $1 out of every $3 of their dues was finding its way into the mob's pockets instead of their own locals' bank accounts.

Dewey had William B. Herlands looking into the situation over a period of 14 months in an investigation that kept getting more intriguing all the time as Herlands began to hear more and more not only about Dutch Schultz but even about Jimmy Hines, the most powerful of the Democratic district leaders. The references to the Tammany wheel, whose name was being used by the Dutchman's plug uglies in the MRCA whenever anybody started talking back, furnished one of the early tips on the most absorbing of the city's underworld-political marriages. This one was going to get a lot more explosive as new sources opened up in later years. In the restaurant case, which put an assortment of crooked union leaders and Schultz musclemen behind bars, it was just an item of tantalizing interest.

The Hines-Schultz alliance really flowered in the policy racket, of course, and the first tentative peek into that festering sore had come about while the restaurant investigation was under way. What happened was that in either late August or early September of 1935 a son-in-law of a Harlem policy banker named Wilfred Brunder decided to drop in on the Special Prosecutor and tell him how the Bronx mob had muscled in on the numbers game. Dewey put Victor J. Herwitz on it, teamed with another helper of the racket buster's, Mrs. Eunice Hunton Carter, the only woman on the staff. Pretty soon Herwitz and Mrs. Carter, a Negro, were prowling around Harlem—and just as soon, naturally, the word went back to Schultz. It was then that the Dutchman started saying things like "Dewey's gotta go" or "We gotta knock off Dewey."

The roster of the more thoughtful Schultz contemporaries who did not like that kind of talk included some impressive figures: Louis (Lepke) Buchalter and Jacob (Gurrah) Shapiro, the Garment Center racketeers operating a national sideline which would come to be known as Murder Inc.; Charles (Lucky) Luciano, nee Salvatore Lucania, of the Unione Siciliana or the Mafia or the Cosa Nostra, pick your name; the Bug & Meyer mob of Meyer Lansky (from Suchowljansky) and Benjamin (Bugsy) Siegel; and New Jersey's Abner (Longy) Zwillman. This was the Big Six or the Syndicate—again it was a matter of taking the name you liked the best—and this loosely organized but harmonious conglomerate wasn't too crazy about the kind of heat that might develop if the independent and overly excitable Dutchman put the peerless Special Prosecutor on the spot.

For that matter, Schultz had problems with the hoodlum empire apart from his mind-blowing assassination plot. What with his tax troubles and all, he had been in the public prints too much; he was calling needless attention to the trade. Beyond this, there was a question in some of the better underworld minds whether he would stand up or start blabbing if Dewey nailed him. And finally there was a suspicion abroad that Schultz had done in his own long-time first lieutenant, the massive Abe (Bo) Weinberg—an item that would have made at least one Big Six dignitary most unhappy for a rather selfish reason. Weinberg, brooding about the way the policy racket's proceeds were being drained off to defray the Dutchman's extraordinary legal expenses, had been talking to Lucky Luciano about retiring his old buddy to some other field, possibly even a field of lilies. Schultz found out about this act of ingratitude and, fearing that the covetous Luciano might well be able to take over the lush Harlem game with Bo's help, reacted badly. In any event, Bo hadn't checked in with his beautiful blonde showgirl bride, Anna May Turner, since leaving their hotel room on September 9. "He must be dead," Miss Turner observed, "for nothing would keep him from coming to see me or letting me know where he is." She was so right; Bo must have been very dead indeed.

With all these minor irritations on his mind now in October, it follows that any table the belabored Dutchman occupied in any restaurant would have to face the door. The round table in the Palace could not have been more ideal for this safety-first purpose. The chair against the wall—always occupied by the boss himself—faced the narrow passageway from the bar. The chair to the left of that faced the swinging doors of the kitchen, which had an entrance from an alley outside. The chair on the right faced the window on the tavern's west wall, and the one opposite Schultz looked squarely into a rectangular mirror and thus commanded a second view of the opening into the room.

Out front, as the evening wore on, Jack Friedman had nothing but his housekeeping duties to keep him occupied. He said he didn't even know about the party in the back, a curious item at best since the waiter had been hustling drinks from the bar. One wonders if it hadn't occurred to Friedman after a while that the Palace Chop House and Tavern had fallen on evil times again just as the country, with the pump primed by the $5 billion WPA program and a host of other New Deal devices, made its upward turn from the recession that followed Franklin Delano Roosevelt's initial efforts to restore the economy shattered on Wall Street's Black Tuesday of 1929. Surely Friedman had to think back with some longing to the days, just two years before, when the place enjoyed a thriving trade as one of Newark's handier speakeasies. Consider the location: The Palace, facing the north side of the Public Service Bus Terminal, was just a couple of blocks from bustling Broad and Market Streets and no more than a brisk walk from Newark's Penn Station. And it was far, very far, from the nearest Prohibition agent. In those days, that long bar never seemed long enough.

Now it was a lonely oasis indeed.

Friedman ran a damp rag over the mahogany, adjusted three or four liquor bottles that seemed out of place to him, checked the register idly, and then started to walk to the back to settle down with a cup of coffee which the waiter, Birkenfeld, had brought out for him from the urn sitting ingloriously alongside the men's toilet in the back. Birkenfeld also had picked up some coffee for King Lou and now he was back in the kitchen.

Once Friedman glanced out the narrow window into Park Street, wondering where the people were. He said he didn't see anything, but there was a man in a green suit outside, perhaps out of the innkeeper's view. This man was leaning against the tavern and twirling a key chain with the figure of a white horse—from the whisky of the same name—on the end of it, or so the police were told later. The street was quiet, in any case, except for the scratchy sounds of the trio in the cabaret the Palace operated on the floor above the bar in the two-story building. It was pretty dead up there, too; the three-piece symphony happened to be entertaining a grand total of two couples, easily outnumbered by the help in the place.

It was about 10:15 when the 44-year-old Friedman got to the end of the bar and started to stir that coffee, and at that moment the high drama began.

"The front door opened suddenly," Friedman said later, "and a heavy-set man walked into the barroom and I heard a voice order, 'Don't move, lay down.' I could hardly discern his face as he pulled his topcoat up to hide it. I saw him place his hand on his left shoulder and whip out a gun from a holster. I didn't wait any longer. I dropped to the floor and lay behind the bar."

The heavy-set man, who had curly black hair and piercing brown eyes, packed 185 pounds of muscle on a wide five-foot-seven-inch frame. He was in his early thirties and good-looking in a tough kind of way. He was not alone. Right behind him—there was no way for Friedman to miss this dark and menacing presence—came a slightly taller man, obviously older, who kept his overcoat drawn around him but not buttoned.

This was a pair of skilled and sure journeymen in a trade which had attracted ever-increasing recruits going back to the bootleg warfare of the Twenties and was still luring them into the fold as Repeal kept turning the underworld down all those other rich streets.

The gunmen didn't need any directions from the terrified bartender.

They headed straight for the dining room.

For they had come to kill the Dutchman, once a package thief and burglar, then a helper on a beer truck, then a sometime shooter for Jack (Legs) Diamond, then a partner in a two-bit speakeasy in The Bronx, then the Beer Baron, then overlord of the Harlem policy racket, then Public Enemy Number 1 on the private list in J. Edgar Hoover's Federal Bureau of Investigation—and now, at the tender age of 33, evidently Public Enemy Number 1 on an even more formidable list.

"I don't know why anybody would want to shoot him."

—MRS. EMMA NEU FLEGENHEIMER,
Arthur's mother.

CHAPTER II
THE GUNS GO OFF

THE EXECUTIONERS MUST HAVE SUFFERED A FLICKERING moment of dismay when they stepped through that ten-foot passageway into the dining room of the Palace Chop House. Their information was that the man they wanted would be in the chair facing them—a perfect target under the bright orange-tinted light in that corner. He had been there every night for at least three weeks, conducting all his business there, seeing Frances Flegenheimer there, even entertaining select newspapermen there. He hadn't made that much of an effort, obviously, to keep his temporary command post in Newark all that secret.

But the Dutchman wasn't at the table.

It was no time to start asking polite questions, of course.

The gunman in front opened up even as he crossed the threshold and noted that his quarry was missing. He turned a .38-caliber pistol on the trio in the corner, firing across the room with a marksman's accuracy while his huskier confederate, just as sure, swept the table with the sawed-off shotgun he had brought in under his coat.

This part of the unequal shootout was over within seconds.

Even as he whipped out his .45 Colt to return the invaders'

fire, seven slugs ripped into Lulu Rosenkrantz, spraying his strong and compact five-foot-ten-inch frame from his chest and abdomen down to his right foot. The 36-year-old hoodlum must have had his back to the doorway, because one bullet went through his right wrist and two others landed in the right elbow and just above it, all from the rear. Withal, the hail of lead never dented the spanking new Essex County Deputy Sheriff's Badge—No. 74—which Rosenkrantz had acquired, ever so thoughtfully, when he took up residence with Dutch Schultz in the classy Robert Treat Hotel, just around the corner from the Palace. The brass potsy gave Lulu the right to carry his favorite shooting iron without being molested by the law, but this was one night when it wouldn't do him any good at all.

Otto Berman, the oldest of the trio and the one least suited for this kind of adversity because he was dragging around 220 pounds on a stubby little body, was hit six times. All the wounds—body, neck, wrist, elbow and shoulder—were on the left side, so Abbadabba, who was not armed, had to be in the chair in front of the window. He tumbled to the tile floor in a pool of blood and lay there, moaning.

Abe Landau, four years older than the taller Rosenkrantz on the ill-fated protection detail but in reasonably good trim at 180 pounds, must have been facing Abbadabba. The bullet which would do the most damage tore through his left shoulder from the back. Another one went through the upper left arm of the most dangerous of the Schultz gunners and a third tore a gaping hole through his right wrist while he was getting his .45 into action.

There were remarkably few wasted shots in that room. Two strays smashed the mirror. Four or five other bullets lodged in the sickly green walls, but they did not have to be strays, for five slugs went clear through Rosenkrantz's body, four went through Abbadabba's and all three went through Landau.

The Dutchman, of course, was on the premises—and he was not to be spared.

He had put on his light topcoat and grey fedora and stepped into the men's room just seconds before the twin messengers of death arrived, but the last bullet fired inside the Palace by the enemy had his name on it.

There was some talk afterwards to the effect that Schultz, in a twist of fate ideally ironic for the silver screen, where it would indeed turn up in due course, actually had been shot not by either of the assassins but by Lulu Rosenkrantz. This piece of melodrama stemmed mainly from the fact that Rosenkrantz, Landau and Berman all had been riddled by .38s or shotgun slugs whereas a .45-caliber bullet damaged their employer. And Rosenkrantz, as noted, was using a .45 Colt. The story that got around was that the Dutchman, a towering figure of bravery for this purpose, had heard the artillery and dashed out of the toilet to come to the aid of his beleaguered troops but the faithful Lulu, firing blindily in his terrible agony, mistook him for one of the raiders. The fact is that Schultz wasn't even armed, except for a cheap 3½-inch switchblade pocketknife, and he was wounded in the *pissoir*, not in the back room. Beyond all this, the professional who wielded the .38 when he was operating on the trio at the table happened to have a .45 as well, just for insurance.

Back in New York later, talking to his own set with a nice mixture of remembered split-second violence and understandable pride in his chosen craft, the professional said he had summoned up the presence of mind to go looking for the Dutchman after that hail of fire raked the other three. He said he kicked open the men's room door, found his quarry relieving himself at one of the two urinals and got off a shot with that spare .45 even as the desperately wounded Rosenkrantz and Landau were pouring lead his way.

The mute evidence in the Palace bore the man out.

Schultz was hit with a rusty steel-jacketed .45 slug that crashed into his husky body just below the chest, on the left, and tore through the abdominal wall into the large intestine, gall bladder and liver before lodging on the floor near the urinal he had been using when the door opened. Although his assailant talked of having fired only one shot, a second bullet missed and smashed into the peeling wall over the second urinal.

It was a rather awkward and undignified way for the Dutchman to catch it—with something other than a gun in his shooting hand—when his vaunted luck finally ran out.

Look back a moment: Schultz just happened to go the other way, minutes earlier, on the October morning in 1928 when his boyhood chum and bootlegging partner, Joey Noe, went on the spot outside Manhattan's Chateau Madrid. Schultz never even heard a shot fired in anger in the two-year war with a defecting playmate, Vincent Coll, that turned The Bronx and Manhattan into shooting galleries until a Tommy gun cut Coll into pieces in the famous drugstore ambush of 1932. Schultz suffered nothing worse than a superficial shoulder wound early in 1931 when he ran into a business rival, Charles (Chink) Sherman, in Manhattan's Club Abbey and the guns went off. And Schultz came out with nothing worse than a red face and a bad case of the shakes later that year in the celebrated Fifth Avenue shootout in which a detective killed his pal Danny Iamascia. Schultz ran that time.

Not this time.

This time he could neither run nor fight. The chances are that he didn't even know what had hit him. He just clutched his right side, the great hurt registering in his wide brown eyes, and stepped forward out of the toilet.

The Battle of the Palace was not over at that point.

The mechanic with the sawed-off shotgun had turned and fled through the bar even as his co-worker was tending to the primary target, but the man who shot the Dutchman wasn't quite in the clear. Abe Landau, with blood spurting out of a severed artery in his neck and a hole in his shooting arm, staggered after him pumping fire, and behind Landau, on rubbery legs, came the unbelievable Rosenkrantz. Their errant revolvers—bear in mind that Lulu had three wounds in *his* business arm—turned the Palace into something more like a saloon in a Hollywood oateater. The flying slugs shattered the cigarette machine and a whole flock of display bottles, smashed into the front window and splintered the wall over the front entrance without stopping the man the Schultz gunners wanted.

Landau somehow got all the way to the street, still pressing the trigger, while his quarry, finding that his confederate and their wheelman had sped off without him, ran west toward Park Place. He might have been scratched by one slug from the uncertain hand of the Dutchman's favorite bodyguard, but he was in no real danger. Landau was outside the tavern only a second or two when he began to waver, reeled toward a garbage can near the Military Park Diner a few feet away, and sat down on it like a guy who had one too many. His blue steel .45, the pride of Smith & Wesson, slipped from his hand and clattered to the sidewalk. The clip was empty.

Rosenkrantz hardly constituted a threat to the retreating

Wide World Photos

Dutch Schultz in 1934, the year before the guns went off in the Palace Chop House in Newark.

Wide World Photos

Bernard (Lulu) Rosenkrantz. Wounded seven times, this Schultz bodyguard kept firing at his assailants. Then, somehow, he found the strength to change a quarter and call for an ambulance.

United Press International

Abe Landau was Lulu Rosenkrantz's partner on the protection detail for the Dutchman. He was hit three times but got out his .45 and chased the assassin out of the tavern all the way into the street.

Newark Police Department

The Palace Bar and Chop House in Newark. Schultz and his men were gunned down in the back room.

Wide World Photos

In the morning, hours after the hired gunmen had done their work, the curious gathered at the scene.

enemy either. All spent, he collapsed to the tavern floor without reaching the door.

The Dutchman himself made his way to the middle of the barroom just as Jack Friedman, quivering on the damp boards alongside his ice container and remembering how the machine guns sounded when he was in the trenches in France during the war, dared to rise from his refuge.

"The first thing I noticed was Schultz," Friedman said. "He came reeling out like he was intoxicated. He had a hard time staying on his pins and he was hanging on to his side. He didn't say a cockeyed thing. He just went over to a table and put his left hand on it kind of to steady him and then he plopped into a chair, just like a souse would. His head bounced on the table and I thought that was the end of him but pretty soon he moved. He said, 'Get a doctor, quick,' but when he said it another guy gets off the floor. He had blood all over his clothes but he gets up and he comes over to me and he looked like he was going to cry. He throws a quarter on the bar and he says, 'Give me change for that,' and I did."

The early story, still ringing down the ages, was that the Dutchman himself, often identified as a very thrifty fellow, had changed the quarter to make the life-and-death call without staking the telephone company to an extra twenty cents. But the man who got off the floor had to be the amazingly strong Rosenkrantz, for Landau was outside on that garbage can then and Schultz was in that chair near the middle of the bar with the blood gushing out of his side. Rosenkrantz, a frightful sight, hung on to the mahogany while he waited for the change, kicked over a spittoon inside the bar rail when he turned unsteadily for the phone near the door, and then, sagging against the booth, managed to dial O with his good hand and gasp, "I want the police, hurry up." The call went from the operator to Patrolman Patrick McNamara, on the board at Police Headquarters. The cop heard a faint, faltering voice say, "Send me an ambulance, I'm dying," but the only sound that came back when he asked where the call was coming from was that of the receiver banging against the wood below the coin box. McNamara didn't have to press the question. He was just following routine. He had already had a call about the shooting in the Palace (today it's the Service Cleaners, perhaps an appropriate transition) from someone in the bus terminal, and there were other calls coming in even at that moment.

Now Newark would marshal all of its resources in a heroic battle to save the lives of the four bullet-riddled strangers in the town. Nothing would be spared in this effort.

"It is not true that the dying man is generally more honest than the living."

—NIETZSCHE

CHAPTER III

EMERGENCY CALL

ONCE PATROLMAN MCNAMARA WAS CERTAIN OF THE ADdress, he put the call—"shooting in tavern, 12 East Park, man wounded"—on the police shortwave and then dialed Acting Captain Tom Rowe, on night detective detail upstairs.

Rowe bounded out of his cubbyhole office into the squad room, where two of his men, Tim O'Leary and Jimmy Kelly, were discussing the day's report of a quick title defense by James J. Braddock, who had just come off the New Jersey relief rolls to take the world's heavyweight championship away from the hard-hitting but sometimes indifferent Max Baer. Now there was talk of a match between the big Irish boxer and Joe Louis, the stylish puncher from Detroit's Negro slums. The sports pages quoted Joe Gould, the Cinderella Man's manager, as saying that "Jimmy may not be the best fighter in the world but he's the gamest, he'll knock out Louis," and O'Leary wasn't too thrilled by that faint endorsement. "That's a helluva way for a manager to talk about his meal ticket," he was telling his sidekick just as Rowe, his topcoat over his arm, came in and said, "We got a shooting at the Palace Chop House. Let's roll."

Rowe raced his sedan out of Franklin Street into Broad, swung right with the siren screaming and made the seven blocks to Park Place, where it merges with East Park, in less than three minutes. But the Rowe team had been beaten to the scene by Sidney B. White, Chief Inspector of New Jersey's Alcoholic Beverage Control Commission, and a couple of prowl cars.

White had enjoyed what amounted to a bleacher seat for the action outside the tavern. Staying at the Robert Treat that night, he had found it kind of close in his room and gone to the window, facing south to Park Street, to let in some air. He had just noted the time, 10:17 P.M., and as he opened the window he heard what sounded like 15 shots and saw a man in a white chef's uniform (King Lou) and a man in a dark outfit (Birkenfeld) running out of the Palace's side door into an alley. Then he saw a third figure emerge from the tavern itself, duck into the alley next to the Military Park Diner, step out, crouch and wheel with some difficulty, as though he were wounded, and start firing in the direction of Park Place. This was Abe Landau, trying to bring down his fleeing adversary with a gun that might have been empty by then. White, from his safe perch, wasn't the only witness to the grim tableau on suddenly busy Park Street.

Elderly John F. Gaul, alighting from a trolley at the bus terminal on his way from a Knights of Columbus meeting, saw Landau get off at least one shot. Gaul watched in stage-struck horror until he felt a sting on his temple, reached up and found blood on his hand. He had been grazed by a stray shot either of Landau's or of Lulu Rosenkrantz's from inside the Palace, possibly a ricochet off the terminal wall. Marion Seaberg, 23, on the way home from her job in the RCA plant at Harrison, was crossing East Park and Park Place when Landau's quarry came running by, discarded some empty shells into the gutter, and sped on into Military Park across the way. I. Lindon Wilcox, a Public Service driver, saw two men trading shots when he turned into East Park for the terminal. Once inside, he found three bullet nicks in the rear panel of his bus. Wallace C. Wood, the cook in the diner, heard the shooting and went to the side window facing the tavern and saw Abe Landau collapse onto the garbage can. Louis Schwartz, an attendant in the parking lot opposite the terminal, saw the retreating gunman. Birkenfeld, the waiter, viewed the action from the alley and then hastened to the St. Francis Hotel down the block and called the police. King Lou, whose first instinct was to get behind the heavy wooden ice box and stay there when the guns went off, followed Birkenfeld into the areaway and crouched there, rooted in terror, until the first prowl car pulled up. Of all these people, not one could offer a useful description of the retreating gunman.

White, for his part, rushed from the Robert Treat to the tavern and found Landau sitting unsteadily on the garbage can. The wounded gladiator gave the name of Abe Frank (one of his aliases) and a made-up Newark address and said he was just passing by and got shot. Just at that moment, the two radio cars arrived and White asked Patrolman W. P. Duffy, in the first one, to call an ambulance. Then he went into the Palace with Sergeant Percy A. Stanton, encountered the badly mauled Rosenkrantz and Schultz, moved on into the back room, found Berman on the floor, saw the work sheets strewn on the table, picked them up with a handkerchief so he wouldn't obliterate any fingerprints the police might need for identification purposes, and then went back to Schultz.

The Dutchman, slumped in his bloodstained chair just below a poster extolling the virtues of something called Burnett's White Satin Gin, not one of the bathtub brands he had peddled, gave the ABC inspector the name of Flegenheimer and said he didn't know what had happened. White sensed that this was the only survivor who might be well enough to talk but couldn't get anything out of him. All Schultz mumbled was that he was in the toilet when someone came in and shot him.

Now Rowe was on the scene with his men and he took over the questioning. He recognized the man in the chair.

"You're Dutch Schultz, aren't you?"

"Yes," came the weak answer.

"Your real name's Arthur Flegenheimer, isn't it?"

"Yes."

"You're shot, aren't you?"

"Yes, and it's damn painful. I think they got me in the liver."

"No," the Captain said. "The wound's high. You got it through the chest."

"Well, get me off to a hospital."

"The ambulance is on the way. Who shot you?"

The answer came in the time-honored underworld phrase, faintly:

"I don't know who shot me."

Rowe detailed Timmy O'Leary to stand by the Dutchman and went on into the dining room, where Berman reached up a hand and murmured, "Help me, help me." Rowe told the fallen magic-maker of the numbers game that help was coming. Then he tried to find out who might have been responsible for all that mayhem. He got about as much from the crafty Abbadabba as O'Leary was getting from policy's overlord at that moment.

"You got a serious wound," the detective said to the

Dutchman. "Why don't you tell us who did it?"

"I don't know," Schultz replied. "I know I got bad cramps. Do something."

The chunky O'Leary turned to Jack Friedman, whom he had known going back to the speakeasy days, and asked him for a brandy. With his right hand holding a towel to his wound, Schultz took the jigger in his left hand and downed the drink. "Thanks," he said to the cop. "That feels good."

By now Landau had been sped off in the first arriving police emergency wagon and City Hospital's three ambulances—the total fleet of the creaking 49-year-old institution—were on the scene. Rosenkrantz was carried into the first one on a litter. Schultz, just five-feet-seven and a squat 175 pounds, was loaded into the second ambulance in the arm chair he had been in all that time and O'Leary went with him. The Dutchman's eyes kept closing on the speedy one-mile trip to the hilltop hospital on Fairmount Avenue but he wasn't out by any means. As the meat wagon roared into the driveway, he reached into his right-hand pants pocket, fished out a roll of bills and handed it to Bernard Alberg, the interne on the bus. "Here," he said, "you might as well have this as the state. Take care of me, buddy." The startled Alberg, holding a huge wad of absorbent cotton to the gangster's gaping side, said he would have to turn the money—it would add up to $725—over to his superiors. Schultz's other possessions—an expensive yellow-gold wristwatch and an oversized sapphire ring he wore on the little finger of his right hand, not to mention that little switchblade knife—were impounded by the police. The cash, ring and watch would be claimed in time not by one but by two women identifying themselves as the lawful-wedded wives of Arthur Flegenheimer.

Otto Berman was deposited in the receiving room alongside the Dutchman and Sergeant Arthur Jollimore, another member of Rowe's squad, tried to question him even as the doctors started their emergency treatment.

"Don't waste your time," Schultz called over to Jollimore. "He won't talk."

And Abbadabba didn't.

Indeed, Rosenkrantz, Landau and Berman would not so much as admit that they were helpmates of Schultz's until the cops were able to satisfy them that the Dutchman had confirmed that they were all his "boys."

Once Schultz was stripped and given a dose of morphine to kill the pain, Police Chief John Harris and his deputy, John Haller, undertook to question him again.

"What happened, Dutch?" Haller asked.

"All I know," said Schultz, "is that I saw fire and sort of lost track of everything. Now I've told you the truth."

"You haven't told us who shot you."

"I've told you everything I know. I don't know nothin'. I was in the tavern and some fellows came in shooting."

That "some fellows" was a cautious reference indeed. The man who shot the Dutchman used to boast that he had once been on the Beer Baron's payroll; even if he hadn't been, Schultz might well have known him, for he was one of the more celebrated killers of the time.

Harris and Haller tried a name on the Dutchman after a while, just to see if it would play. The name was Amberg. Actually, there were two Ambergs, Joe and Louis, called Pretty because he was so ugly, and they happened to be a pair of fairly fresh corpses on the hands of the New York police at the time. Pretty Louis had expired, indeed, on the very morning of the Palace shootout. All chopped up with a blunt instrument, either a hatchet or a hammer, he had been wrapped in a kerosene-soaked blanket and deposited in an old car set afire on a deserted street on the Brooklyn end of the Manhattan Bridge. Joe, 43, had preceded his 36-year-old brother to the grave just three weeks earlier. All dressed up for a golf date, he was lined up against a garage wall in Brooklyn's Brownsville section, spawning ground of Murder Inc., and shot to death. The unfriendly trio performing this mission also turned its artillery on the Amberg chauffeur, Morris Kessler, so he died just for being there.

The Newark cops mentioned the late Ambergs because there was a suspicion abroad that the hungry Dutchman had recently moved into the loan-shark racket and run afoul of the fearsome brothers. It made for an interesting piece of speculation in the wake of the Newark bloodletting but there was no substantiation for it. It is just as likely that an Amberg sideline, the narcotics trade, had got them in trouble with some of the other mobs.

In any case, the Dutchman didn't bite when the dirty name was tried on him.

"Let me alone," he said to Chief Harris. "You're killing me. I'm getting weak."

Lulu Rosenkrantz was even less helpful, if that was possible.

"Get the hell away from me," he said when Haller threw the usual question at him. "Go out and get me an ice cream soda."

It was hardly a moment for that kind of repast, of course—not for a man with seven bullet holes in him.

Now Schultz was moved to a vacant four-bed ward on the second floor of the hospital's North Wing, once again with Tim O'Leary to keep him company.

O'Leary, who retired from the force in 1964 and went to

work as a guard for the First National Bank of New Jersey, recalled 34 years after the Battle of the Palace that once he got upstairs he drew back with a start when he found himself standing by a window fronting on a row of old rooming houses. It had occurred to him that the word would be out by now that the Dutchman was still alive and that some fresh sharpshooters might be taking up temporary residence across the street.

O'Leary phoned this alert to his superiors downstairs, but it was hardly necessary, because the brass had remembered a night in Newark General, just five years earlier, when a trio of gunmen dropped in on a gentleman recovering from a bungled gangland ride. The patient, Dominick (The Ape) Paselli, 52 and in and out of police hands for a good many of those years, was suffering from nothing more than superficial wounds of the scalp and cheek when his guests arrived; he did not recover from the fresh leaden posies they were delivering. It wasn't a rap the cops had to take, because The Ape's presence in the private institution had not been reported to them, but they had it in mind nonetheless and now they had taken all the necessary precautions, inside Newark City Hospital and out.

Once O'Leary settled down on the side of the Dutchman's bed away from the window, he noticed for the first time that the gangster's black hair had touches of gray in it. He thought this was strange for a guy in his early thirties who had led such a high life up to that night but he didn't dwell on it. Schultz, waiting his turn in surgery, seemed fairly alert and wasn't complaining, so the cop started talking to him again.

"Anything you want me to get for you?"

"I want a priest," said the Dutchman, who was the son of

a German-Jewish immigrant couple and had listed his faith as Hebrew on his hospital pedigree.

"You asked for Father McInerney when you were down in the emergency ward," O'Leary said, referring to the Reverend Cornelius McInerney, a chaplain at Essex and Hudson County prisons, "and it's been taken care of. The Father is probably on the way. You know him?"

"Yes. He's my friend."

"Why don't you tell me who shot you now?"

"I don't know."

"You got a family you want me to call?"

"Yes, a wife."

"Where?"

The Dutchman gave the detective a vague address in North Jersey, either out of approaching delirium or guile. O'Leary knew there was no such address and tried the familiar question once more.

"Tell us who did it. We'll go get the guy. Don't you want us to do that?"

"I don't know who shot me," the wounded man murmured. "It was somebody that didn't like me, I guess."

Well, that was the heart of it.

Even at that moment, as the clock moved toward midnight, the "somebody" who didn't like Dutch Schultz—and of course it was more than one somebody—had a second shift of torpedoes going to work across the river in Manhattan. This time the guns would be pointed at the heart or the head of the pint-sized tough guy who had been delegated to keep an eye on the New York end while the Dutchman was trying to stand off both the law and his business enemies from what he had mistakenly considered a safe distance.

"It's gotta be one of them coincidences."

—MARTY KROMPIER, when he was told that Dutch Schultz had been shot the same night.

CHAPTER IV

MANHATTAN: A CLOSE SHAVE FOR MARTY

LITTLE MARTY KROMPIER WAS A BIG MAN ON NEW YORK'S Broadway once the collective ruin of the Lawless Decade gave way to the hopefully more sedate Thirties. The policy racket's $65,000-a-week payroll, scooped up in the Palace Chop House following the shooting orgy there, listed the glib and dandy Krompier as the third highest toiler in the Dutch Schultz vineyard. He was down for $1,500 per against the $1,875 bounties drawn by the top resident guns, Lulu Rosenkrantz and Abe Landau.

Now if $1,500 a week, every week, seemed rather high in the wake of the Great Depression (how many corporation executives got that much?), consider Mr. Krompier's multiple responsibilities in the highly diversified Schultz operation.

He was the chief enforcer and Keeper of the Peace in the policy business, while Rosenkrantz and Landau occupied themselves more exclusively with the personal health and well-being of the Chairman of the Board. Little Marty was the man the Dutchman sent around whenever the native policy bankers of Harlem, Negro and Puerto Rican and Cuban, grew emboldened and demanded a larger share of the take from their white master. He was the Dutchman's ambassador to the satellite industry that was shaking down some 240 New York eating places; he settled the internal disputes between the Schultz hirelings and the occasionally recalcitrant union official or restaurant owner. He was in the Schultz inner circle, along with the brothers Weinberg, Bo and George, that helped Jimmy Hines install Bill Dodge as District Attorney in 1933 so that the law would not deal too harshly with the small fry of the numbers game when the honest cops showed up and arrested them (Krompier knew what to do about cops like that; once he had a couple of them moved off the Broadway beat just for harassing Marty Krompier). Going back into the more leisurely bootlegging days, he was at Schultz's side in the 1931 Club Abbey battle which retired Chink Sherman to a hospital for an extended period of recuperation.

In his spare time, Krompier looked after the interests of his employer in the boxing industry in the shadow cast by Owney Madden, who had managed to pick up a world's heavyweight title with the most ungainly glass-chinned tiger of them all—Primo Carnera. For Schultz, Krompier was entrusted with the care and feeding of an Italian gladiator rechristened Nathan Mann, who at a mere five-ten and 180 pounds just didn't have the brawn to go all the way with the big boys. Mann's proudest achievement was a win over Bob Pastor but then he ran into Joe Louis (KO, three rounds) and it was all downhill after that. Except for Mann, who after all did get out of boxing's "underneath" into main events in Madison Square Garden, Krompier produced no true gems for the Dutchman in the fistfight racket. This was the only known area in which this $1,500-a-week executive had failed the front office.

So it was that on the night of October 23, 1935, Marty Krompier was in New York minding the store while Lulu Rosenkrantz and Abe Landau were in Newark guarding the body.

It started out like a quiet night.

The Krompier social schedule called for a fast trip uptown with his brother Jules and Sammy Gold, a bookmaker pal, to take in an evening's boxing at the New Park Casino, a hole-in-the-wall club where some chattels from Krompier's own Lenox A. C. were going on display. And then, the accustomed pre-midnight visit to the Hollywood Barber Shop, next door to the Palace Theater in the subway arcade at Broadway and 47th Street. The fastidious Krompier always stopped there for a quick shave before setting out on his late rounds along the Great White Way. The shop was a congenial way station whether a man needed tonsorial attention or not. On this night, Walter Winchell had been there just ahead of Krompier. So were Abe Bronson, manager of vaudevillian Willie Howard, and Harold Scadron, proprietor of light heavyweight champion Bob Olin. Monte Proser, press agent and night club operator who had handled a couple of the Dutchman's Broadway joints, was playing the pinball machine near the coat rack when John (John the Barber, of course) Sideri patted the last sprinkle of after-shave lotion on Krompier, applied a touch of talcum to the back of the neck, and said, "OK, Marty, all done."

Krompier bounded up and reached for his coat. The barber idly dusted the chair. Jules Krompier waited in the corner. Sammy Gold stood to Proser's right, watching the pinball game. The Negro attendant ran his whiskbroom over Krompier's threads and then drew the green shade—the closing signal—on the door.

It was 12:01 A.M., and at that moment the door burst open violently and a late arrival stood framed in it coldly surveying the scene with a .38-caliber pistol pointed at the man nearest to the coat rack.

This was just about 100 minutes after the guns had gone off in Newark. Upstairs on Broadway newsboys at that moment were hawking replate editions of the *Daily News* and *Mirror* with the first sparse details of that gory saga of the post-Prohibition gangland wars.

The gunman in the Hollywood doorway had the help of a passing B.M.T. express on the level below to muffle the sound of his labors. His first shot went into the ceiling—perhaps because he was a trifle more nervous than a professional killer is supposed to be, perhaps to give the Negro attendant time to jump away from the target.

The next four bullets hit Marty Krompier with a degree of accuracy that might have killed any other man—one in the chest, one in the belly, one in each arm. Two other slugs, in the left arm and side, apparently strays, felled Sammy Gold. Nobody else was wounded but the gunman had three confederates arrayed behind him in the arcade and the lead thrown in those burning seconds suggested that one of his restless playmates had gotten off a few shots for insurance purposes. This theory was backed up when a still-warm .38 was retrieved near the barber shop door with only four spent shells in it; the lead gunner had emptied his revolver.

As the raiding party turned and fled, Krompier toppled toward Proser, clutching the press agent's suspenders and gasping, "They got me." Proser, with his pants starting to fall, reached down in time to keep the badly wounded hoodlum's head from banging against the linoleum floor. Minutes later, the police were on hand, along with a quickly gathering band of reporters who had been roaming the midtown haunts to find Krompier and, hopefully, solicit his informed comments on the bloodbath across the river. With more experienced help at hand, Proser adjusted his trousers and went to the wall phone to dial Walter Winchell at the *Mirror* office nine blocks away. "You blew it, pal," the breathless press agent told the man who invented the Broadway gossip column. "They just shot Krompier in here." Winchell, of course, raced back to his favorite tonsorial parlor to cover the story.

The four-man firing squad made an easy escape.

Two fled by way of the B.M.T. platform and two others went upstairs into Broadway and walked away. Nobody saw anybody running—and nobody in the blood-splattered barber shop, where Krompier had now been installed in his favorite chair to await the ambulance, was very helpful about describing the intruder in the doorway. Proser, for his part, said that while he faced the guy head-on it might as well have been "a six-foot brunette with a machine gun in one hand and an automatic in the other." In more recent years a producer of stage and night club shows in New York and Las Vegas, Proser now says he wasn't just kidding when he offered police that garish description. "I didn't want to get mixed up in anything like that," he said, "because I knew the mob scene too damn well. Anyway, I couldn't have described the character with the heater if I tried. It all happened too fast—and my pants were falling down besides."

Krompier, a frightful sight, greeted the first police arrivals with something none of the men in blue had ever expected to hear from those familiar lips: "Do something for me, do something for me." The cops stanched his wound with towels until the ambulance got there, but their old adversary wasn't going to do much for them. Did he have a good look at his assailant? "Sure. I'd know him if I saw him again." Okay, had he ever seen the man before? "No, I don't know him. I'd know him if I saw him again." Didn't he know what had happened to Dutch Schultz over in Newark? Was there any connection between the two shootings? "How do I know? It's gotta be one of them coincidences." The cops turned to Gold, stretched out alongside the adjoining chair. Did he know the gunman? "No, I never saw him before." Did he know Dutch Schultz? "I wouldn't know him if I fell over him." This might have been true. The police had nothing to link Gold, who always insisted that he was a commission merchant and not a guy who handled bets for a living, to the mob.

In Polyclinic Hospital, only four blocks from the barber shop and across the street from one of his own regular business stops, Madison Square Garden, Krompier had to suffer some more interrogation while a team of surgeons was being assembled for the dubious task of trying to save his life. The gangster cut the detectives short: "I can't tell you anything now. I can take it—can't you see I can take it?—but I'm taking enough now with the terrific pain."

In a criminal career dating back to 1918, marked by one youthful reformatory sentence for petit larceny and some quick discharges for such items as homicide, assault, grand larceny and violation of the Sullivan Law (no weapons, fellas), Krompier had been over some rough spots but this was the first time he had felt any lead coming at him.

The doctors called for blood and the cops obligingly sent over Krompier's brother Jules, then in custody as a material witness in the Late Late Show at the Hollywood. Another brother, Milton, came down from The Bronx and furnished a second transfusion. Natie Mann gave his blood, too, and then the surgeons went to work. The prognosis was all bad:

the slug that entered Krompier's abdomen had ripped his insides apart before settling so deeply in the intestines that it couldn't be recovered. It was the same kind of wide-ranging wound that had proved fatal to Senator Huey P. Long, the Louisiana Kingfish, cut down by an assassin's bullet in the state capital at Baton Rouge just a month earlier. In Polyclinic, the word was that Mr. Schultz's jack-of-all-trades could not possibly live to see another sun light up the town.

The hardy gangster fooled them all, hanging on through a series of operations which proved so remarkable that the Polyclinic team eventually would receive a letter of commendation from the medical faculty at Johns Hopkins University in Baltimore. But while Sammy Gold was discharged within good time, recovered, Krompier was to be a guest of Polyclinic's for nine weeks—under round-the-clock guard all the way lest anyone come in and try to rob the doctors of their triumph.

Over this long stretch, in agony all the way, the man in the hospital gown developed a more or less general answer for the detectives who kept dropping in with that old nagging question.

"Tell us who shot you, Marty."

"I can't. The doctor has ordered me not to talk."

One day the patient did talk—to Detective Samuel Orbach, a familiar face from the Broadway beat.

"Who did it, Marty?"

"It's a swell day, isn't it? It must be warm outside."

Krompier sampled his final hospital lunch on New Year's Day. Then his brother Milton helped him into a fur coat that was too long for his five-foot-seven-inch frame and with the gangster's left arm dangling at his side and only partially

United Press International

Marty Krompier, the $1,500-a-week Schultz lieutenant shot up on the Manhattan end of the 1935 bloodletting, is shown outside Gamblers Court in 1947 after he beat a bookmaking charge.

useful (he would demonstrate this to a jury eight years later to beat a charge that he had lugged two heavy boxes of stolen rhinestones into a Fifth Avenue jewelry store to trade them in for cash), led him from his third-floor room to a waiting limousine.

But that wasn't the end of the Polyclinic chapter.

Five hours later, at 6:00 P.M., three sharply dressed men who looked as though they might have come right off the set of a Jimmy Cagney underworld melodrama approached a nurse who was sitting at the midtown hospital's third-floor reception desk making an entry in a patient's chart. Two of the visitors stood back a step or two. The third—and he had a scar on his right cheek, naturally—approached the young nurse and this colloquy ensued:

SCARFACE: *Where's Krompier?*

NURSE: *Who are you?*

SCARFACE: *That's who I am* (producing a gold shield).

NURSE: *You'll have to go to the information desk downstairs.*

Just at that moment, a uniformed patrolman who had been checking on a routine accident case on the floor emerged in the far end of the corridor and one of the trio spotted him. "Come on, let's go," he whispered, "here comes a cop." With that, the misguided movie-style trio (didn't they know that Krompier would have had some delegates from the Police Department for company if he was still in the hospital?) fled down a stairway.

It remains a sound assumption that those three men had come to Polyclinic to finish the job on Marty Krompier, and it flows from that dreary fact that the little vice president of the Dutch Schultz conglomerate was a very lucky man indeed. But, then, he had known that long ago in October, because once he satisfied everybody that he wasn't quite ready to go he began to hear the rest of the Newark story . . .

"Let them come. I'm not afraid of anybody."

—DUTCH SCHULTZ, dying.

CHAPTER V

"AS YE SOW..."

WHEN THE AMBULANCES ROLLED INTO NEWARK CITY HOSPITAL with that badly mauled dinner party from the Palace Chop House, the two internes on surgical duty, Edward J. Yorke and Royal A. Schaaf, had 14 minutes to go before signing out on a 48-hour weekend break. Instead, just after midnight, they formed the nucleus of a 20-man operating team which would go to work in relays for the next 27 hours and 20 minutes in a heroic but vain effort to reverse a judgment made by some professional men in another calling.

While it surely did not occur to the medical fraternity, the incidental stakes for Newark were rather high: if all four victims died, New Jersey's largest city would acquire the unhappy distinction of having served as host for the second largest multiple gangland execution in the nation's history. The St. Valentine's Day Massacre in Al Capone's adopted Chicago, just six years before, came quickly to mind as the lights burned through the long night at Police Headquarters. In that panorama of death, five card-carrying members of the Bugs Moran gang and two casual visitors had been lined up against a garage wall on North Clark Street and cut down in the withering fire of two machine guns and two shotguns. There was no suspense at all in arriving at the casualty toll in that one. It was just a matter of counting seven bodies.

In Newark, it was a cliff hanger from the start.

The first to go was the oldest and surely the man the enemy cared the least about, Otto Berman, the mob's Abbadabba and Damon Runyon's softhearted Regret.

Nobody was more amused than Runyon, by the way, when the first stories out of the Newark abattoir described Berman as a plug ugly who was one of the Dutch Schultz bodyguards. In *The Bloodhounds of Broadway,* where he made his debut as a Runyon character, Abbadabba was introduced with this mild description:

"Generally, he is talking about nothing but horses, and how he gets beat three dirty noses the day before at Belmont, or wherever the horses are running. In all the years I remember Regret, he must get beat ten thousand noses, and always they are dirty noses to hear him tell it."

Regret also turned up in *Guys and Dolls, Blue Plate Special* and *Money from Home.* Runyon sometimes identified him as a reformed gunbearer for Arnold Rothstein and Legs Diamond, but that was just local color. The sports writer-turned-author knew the blue-eyed Berman well, so well that when the end came in Newark he rushed right into print to set the record straight on the strong-arm bit. "He would have been about as efficient a bodyguard as a five-year-old child," Runyon wrote in Hearst's New York *American.* The closest the round man had ever come to physical force—on the record, in any event—was in a case of attempted rape back in 1916. It was his only arrest, and Berman beat it.

For a high roller who had touched the tightfisted Dutchman for $10,000 a week for a while, all tax-free, and who was once credited with handicapping 28 winners in 29 races, Berman departed the high life in such penury that no one could ever again dare to challenge the item of foolproof wisdom which holds that all horseplayers die broke. There was $87.22 in his pockets when they carried him into the hospital, and all his known estate added up to was $7,000, strongly suggesting that there were days when Abbadabba had 28 *losers* in 29 races.

Berman, also known to the police as Dutch Otto, passed from the scene at 2:55 A.M. on October 24, just about four and a half hours after those uninvited guests had dropped in on the money counters in the Palace.

The next to go, as the autumn sun lit up the ragged Newark skyline at 6:30 A.M., was Abe Landau, who had all but bled to death through that severed artery in his neck even before they got him on the operating table. Landau, who went back to Schultz's early bootlegging days in The Bronx in 1929, had $344.10 on his person when they brought him in, and there was no evidence that he had left much more than that behind. And for a life of crime dating back at least to 1916, when he was 21, he passed from the scene with a rather skimpy police record. He paid a $2 fine for disorderly conduct in 1916 and served a sentence in the pen for felonious assault in the same year but then managed to stay out of the law's grasping arms until 1934, when he beat a homicide rap growing out of the sudden death of a fledgling Schultz rival in The Bronx. One of the nicknames the police had down for Landau was The Misfit, but it's rather hard to figure out what he had done to earn it. With the Dutchman, he always ranked very high: dependable, sure, loyal. On the nights when the guard detail came down to one man, even while Bo Weinberg was alive and well, it was a good bet that Landau would be the guy walking beside the policy magnate.

While the first two checkouts occurred in plenty of time to

spruce up the Newark story for the early afternoon editions, Schultz and Lulu Rosenkrantz were to hold on a good deal longer.

The high drama, of course, centered around the third-floor recovery room which would be the Dutchman's last sanctuary from his enemies both inside and outside the law. On a bench in the corridor, a lonely deathwatch gathered early in the day—the gangster's mother, Mrs. Emma Neu Flegenheimer, and his sister Helen and her husband, Henry Ursprung, called Peanuts because he had charge of the vending machines in the Schultz speakeasies before his brother-in-law found him a minor job in the policy business.

Father McInerney, the priest Schultz had sent for, stayed with the family much of the time. While it was never quite clear how the Dutchman had come to know the cleric, it is possible that they had met in the Hudson County Jail when Schultz was tossed in there after his surrender on the tax warrant. That institution happened to be on the McInerney rounds as a chaplain. Schultz, with his flair for liberal postures, said only that he had come to know and admire Father McInerney after learning that he had set up his parish in Livingston at a time when Ku Klux Klan elements supposedly were making that New Jersey town a little uncomfortable for Catholics.

Mrs. Flegenheimer had heard about the shooting on the radio in her Bronx apartment not long after it happened, and in the morning she had a call about it from a girl she had never met or talked to and could have known of only through the newspapers, Frances Flegenheimer. Arthur had never told his mother about setting up housekeeping with Frances. Was it because the girl was a Catholic? Was it because she was only 18? Was it because he had another wife somewhere?

These questions would never be answered, surely not by the Schultz side of the family.

The aging Emma Flegenheimer, indeed, professed to know as little about her son's flashy career as the affairs of his heart. Under gentle questioning by Newark's Deputy Director of Public Safety, Avitus J. Dougherty, she insisted that she had never been aware of her son's eminence in the underworld, despite his ample press notices over the preceding four years. "Arthur never told me anything about his business," she said. "I don't know why anybody would want to shoot him." She said she had seen him on October 15—she didn't say where—and that "he seemed very happy then."

And what about the immense fortune that had poured into Arthur's king-sized pockets? Had any provision been made for his mother? Mrs. Flegenheimer, left with the children when they were young, her husband having either vanished or died, said she was the beneficiary of a $2,500 insurance policy on her son's life—for which she had paid the premiums—and that she had no knowledge of any other funds. A bank account containing $5,000 did turn up, but it is doubtful whether much of it was left to cut up after Mrs. Flegenheimer and Frances went to court over its disposition.

In the hospital, Frances Flegenheimer was not nearly as much in evidence as the Dutchman's family. She was otherwise occupied most of the time because the police thought she fit the description of the "mystery woman," now very large in the headlines, who had visited Schultz in the Palace a couple of hours before the shootings. The theory at first was that this woman may have led the firing squad to the scene. This was quickly discounted once the authorities had Frances in custody and she admitted, after balking, that she was the one in the tavern. She said that a "man in green" had led her to Arthur—the only name anyone around him ever used, by the way—but she said she had no idea who the man was.

Alternately hysterical, weeping and defiant under the incessant interrogation, the girl said she left the tavern before nine o'clock because Arthur had urgent business there and had suggested that she go to the 30-cent movie around the corner, the Terminal, and come back afterwards. She said she returned sometime after eleven, saw the crowd outside the Palace, thought there had been a raid or something, and elected to go back to New York, And then? She said that when she got off the Hudson Tubes in Manhattan she bought a tabloid, read about the shoot-'em-up in Newark, proceeded to Jackson Heights, tucked herself into bed for the night, arose and called Arthur's mother around 9:30 A.M., and then made haste for the hospital.

Deputy Chief Haller wasn't exactly delighted with that story.

"She says she did nothing to get in touch with anyone until 9:30 the next morning, although she knew her husband was near death," he said. "Her actions were contrary to all that might be expected of a wife—even a gangster's wife—unless she isn't telling the truth."

There would be more in that vein, much more, but first the situation up on Fairmount Avenue turned extremely grave.

To go back a step, Abbadabba Berman's quick departure had reduced the battlefield party just enough to accommodate it perfectly to the little hospital's facilities: three operating rooms and three patients requiring emergency surgery. Once Abe Landau expired, Lulu Rosenkrantz, even though his case was deemed hopeless on the face of it, drew off the major medical talents because there was so much to operate on. And then Dr. Schaaf turned to an exploration of the devastated Schultz interior with the equally weary Dr. Yorke and Dr. Charles J. Calasibetta, the senior resident interne in surgery, who himself had been on duty since 8:00 A.M. the day before.

Dr. Calasibetta, now on the Medical Examiner's staff in Newark, recalls that October 23 happened to be a rather lively day even before the stretcher bearers started arriving from Park Street. He had handled a ruptured appendix, a perforated ulcer and an assortment of accident cases—a fair order for a surgeon-in-training drawing a skinny $20 a month by way of a paycheck. He recalls that the operation on the Dutchman, some 90 minutes, readily revealed the damage to the spleen, stomach, colon and liver but did not bare the full course of that rusty .45 slug. The penetrations of the posterior wall of the stomach and the gall bladder escaped the weary, hurrying medical sleuths. Dr. Yorke, who eventually moved on to California, confirmed this. "We were quite surprised at the autopsy table," he told the author, "when we noted what we had missed in surgery."

Dr. Harrison S. Martland, the Medical Examiner then and in years to come so rich in honors that the Medical Center which replaced the old City Hospital in 1955 would be named for him, made the same observation, perhaps more wryly, when he performed the autopsy. There's no suggestion of negligence here, of course, because an army of surgeons might well have been unable to pin down the wild, erratic journey of that one zigzagging bullet. Then there's a question as to whether it would have mattered anyway. Schultz, hemorrhaging internally, also was being assailed by the worst possible enemy—peritonitis—before they got him on the table. This was ahead of the time of sulfa and penicillin, so the patient very likely had little chance against the inflammation even though he seemed to weather the long operation itself.

Dr. Calasibetta recalls that once the Dutchman was in the Ward 6 recovery room and out of the ether he showed early signs of a rally. "He coined his own name for the morphine," the doctor said, "and whenever he wanted another shot he would manage a smile, somehow, and say, 'How about another bon bon, Doc?' It was hard to turn the man down but in his shape the narcotic didn't help enough anyway."

As the day wore on, Schultz, at the outset the healthiest of the ill-fated quartet except for a single gallstone, began to sink rather rapidly. At 2:00 P.M., he called for Father McInerney, who had left the hospital briefly. The priest came back within half an hour and spent a few minutes with the dying man. When he came downstairs, the reporters asked him why he would minister to the Jewish Schultz.

"Because he sent for me," Father McInerney replied.

"What for?"

"He wants to die a Catholic."

"Will he die in the faith?"

"Yes. I baptized him and gave him the last rites of the church."

Even at that moment, another kind of farewell, drawn from the New Testament, was being delivered to the hospital's reception desk by a Western Union messenger. "As ye sow, so shall ye reap," said the wire. It was signed "Madam Queen of Policy," and it had come, of course, from Harlem's Mme. Stephanie St. Clair. This flamboyant figure, sometimes called the Tiger from Marseilles, truly had fought the Dutchman to the death. She not only had refused to yield her numbers bank to Schultz when he was on his triumphal armed march through the Negro community but also had gone to the Mayor and the District Attorney to protest the white mob's

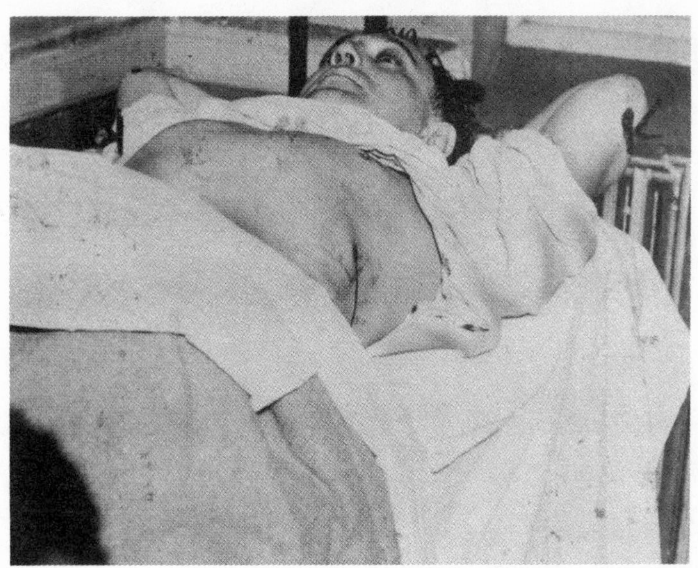

Wide World Photos

Dutch Schultz in the emergency ward at Newark City Hospital. Only one bullet hit the Dutchman, just below the chest, but it would prove fatal.

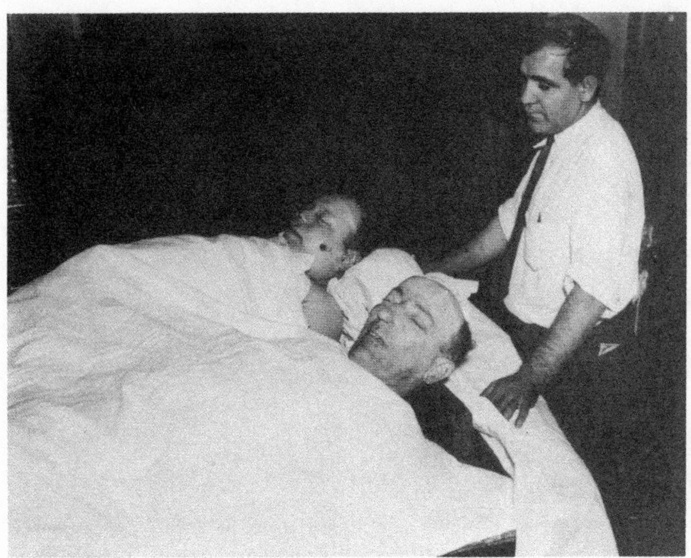

United Press International

Abbadabba Berman (left) and Abe Landau were the first to expire in the Newark shootout. They're shown in the morgue.

United Press International

Stephanie St. Clair, who liked to be known as Madam Queen, stood Schultz off when he tried to take her piece of the policy racket in Harlem. She shed no tears when he died.

incursion into the multimillion dollar penny-ante game. That's the way Madam Queen played it; she didn't care if the whole town knew she was in policy so long as the white folks in the seats of power knew what the Dutchman was pulling off.

The St. Clair wire furnished nothing more than a grim tidbit for the army of newspapermen on the scene, held at bay most of the time in the hospital's oval driveway, but the heavy curtain around the dying moments of Arthur Flegenheimer was about to be penetrated.

A young reporter on the Newark *Evening News* staff, Harry Burke, who had the hospital on his beat and knew every corner of it, found a way to get around the wooden police barricades set before the elevators and the stairwell leading to the Dutchman's ward. Acting like a stray visitor, Burke slipped upstairs by way of a back staircase. He knew the nurse in charge on the third floor, Peggy Zartler, but he had an idea that he could do better with 20-year-old Mary Crawford, who had just finished her nurse's training in the same class with Kathleen Barneo, the girl who was shortly going to become Mrs. Harry Burke. Everything was going for the kid reporter that day. He found Mary Crawford at the big desk in the center of the floor, writing an entry into a less celebrated patient's chart. She had been in and out of the Dutchman's room helping Miss Zartler and the other nurses and she told Burke that the gangster appeared to be in delirium and was mumbling much of the time. She said that detectives working in relays had their ears to Schultz's lips but couldn't make any sense out of what he was saying. She had picked up a few things, though.

Burke slipped downstairs to the free phone in the emergency room and passed this intelligence on to his City Editor,

Lloyd Flemly, not failing to include the more vivid samplings plucked from the Dutchman's prose on Miss Crawford's quick trips to the sick room. Some of these valedictory utterances were explicit enough—"Journey's end. This is my death." And some weren't—"Let them come. I'm not afraid of anybody. I won't run. They're a bunch of fakers anyway."

When the *News* hit the streets early in the afternoon with these absorbing morsels, the police decided that it might be a good idea to supplement the scribblings of the detectives crowded around the bedside with a full stenographic record of the last words of Arthur Flegenheimer. Francis J. Long, the male secretary of Police Chief Harris, was ushered into the cramped 10-by-15-foot room at a moment when the patient's temperature had soared to 106 and he had been jabbering on and off for hours.

Long caught what he could. Sergeant Luke Conlon, head of the Newark Homicide Squad, stood alongside of him, dropping in questions now and then in the hope that in his extremity the dying racket overlord might let something slip that would either lead the local cops to the execution squad or perhaps tell the New York police some things they didn't know about the increasingly more affluent gangs in that playground. Up to that moment, an unofficial and possibly conservative estimate had put the roster of the New York dead in the underworld warfare since Repeal at 78. Dutch Schultz had to know about a goodly portion of those casualties, not to mention the sizeable band that had fallen earlier in his own two-year strife with Vincent Coll. Would his feverish rantings clear some unsolved murders off the books?

Francis Long took up his place near the bedside at 4:00 P.M. What he was able to make out, just the way he transcribed it, typing errors and all, follows. While much of it appears to be an incoherent jumble, the chapter which comes after the Dutchman's swan song will discuss the real identity of some of the men he was talking about and offer some insights into what he may have been trying to say on the way to his private hell.

"A boy has never wept . . . nor dashed a thousand kim."

—DUTCH SCHULTZ on his deathbed.

CHAPTER VI

THE LAST WORDS OF DUTCH SCHULTZ

October 24, 1935

Statements made by Arthur Flegenheimer (alias "Dutch Schultz") in the Newark City Hospital on the above date between 4 P.M. and 6:00 P.M.; from stenographic notes made by F. J. Long, Clerk-Stenographer, Newark Police Department.
George, don't make no bull moves.
What have you done with him. Oh, Mamma, Mamma, Mamma!
Oh, stop it! Stop it!...Oh, Oh, Oh, Sure, sure, Mamma, etc.
("Schultz" at this time was irrational, suffering with a fever of about 106 degrees, with a gunshot wound. Sergeant Luke Conlon, Detectives from Newark Police Headquarters and from the Prosecutor's Office were at his bedside. One of the officers had a newspaper)
"Schultz" noticed the newspaper and said: Has it been in any other papers? (Then, relapsing into irrationality) Now listen, Phil, fun is fun. Aha....Please! Papa! What happened to the 16? Oh, Oh... He done it? Please.. please..John, please. Oh, did you buy the hotel; you promised a million...sure. Get out!

I wish I knew. Please make it quick; fast and furious; please..fast and furious. Please help me get out; I'm getting my wind back, thank God! Please, please; Oh, please. You will have to, please....tell him, "You got no case." You get ahead with the dot and dash system. Didn't I speak that time last night. Whose number is that in your pocketbook, Phil? 13780. Who was it? Oh!...Please, please.. Reserve decision; police, police; Henny and Frankie....Oh, Oh; dog biscuit, and when he is happy he doesn't get snappy....Please, please do this! Henny, Henny; Frankie! You didn't meet him; you didn't even meet me; the glove will fit what I say....Oh, kayiyi, kayiyi! Sure, who cares? when you are through! How do you know this? Well then...Oh, Cocoa; no... thinks he is a grandpa again and he is jumping around. No; Hoboe and Poboe I think mean the same thing.
Question by Sergeant Conlon: Who shot you?
Answer: The bos himself.
Q: xxx He did?
A: Yes: I don't know
Q: What did he shoot you for?
A: I showed him boss; did you hear him meet me? An appointment; appeal stuck. All right mother.
Q: Was it the boss shot you?
A: Who shot me? No one.
Q: Was it bow-legs?
A: Yes, he might have shot me; it wasn't Robeck (?) or the other guy; I will see him; I never forget and if I do I will be very careful.
Q: Was it bow-legs who shot you?
A: I don't know who shot me, honest to God! Suppose you help me get up now, like a swell fellow.

Q: We will help you.
A: Will you get me up? O.K., I won't be such a creep. Oh, mamma, I can't go through with it, please. Oh...and then he clips me; come on, xxxxxxxxxxxxxxxxcut that out, we don't owe a nickel; fold it! Instead, fold it against him; I am a pretty good pretzeler....Winifred... Dept. of Justice; I even got it from the Department, sir. Please, stop it; say listen, the...last night.
Sergt. Conlon: Now, don't holler.
A: I don't want to holler.
Q: What did they shoot you for?
A: I don't know sir; honestly I don't. I don't even know who was with me; honestly. I went to the toilet; I was in the toilet and when I reached the.....the boy came at me.
Q: The big fellow gave it to you?
A: Yes, he gave it to me.
Q: Do you know who that big fellow was?
A: No.
Schultz: See, George, if we wanted to break the ring. No....please; I get a month. They did it. Come on: cut me off and says you are not to be in the beneficiary of this will. Is that right? I will be checked and double-checked and please pull for me.
(One of the detectives) We will pull for you.
Schultz? Will you pull? Will you pull? These native children make this and sell you the joint. How many good ones and how many bad ones! Please, Joe. Please! I had nothing with him; he was a cowboy in one of the.... seven days a week fight. No business, no hang-out; no friends, nothing; just what you pick up and what you need.
Sergeant Conlon: Who was it shot you?

Schultz: I don't know. No; don't put anyone near this check; the check. You might have; oh, please. Please do it for me. Let me get up, sir, heh? That is Connie's, isn't it? Uh heh. In the olden days they waited and they waited. Please give me my shot. Please. Oh...Oh...It is from the factory. O.K. Sure, that is a bad...well, Oh, go ahead; that happens for crying; I don't want harmony: I want harmony. Oh, mamma, mamma. Who give it to him? Who give it to him? Tony?
Let me in the district; ....fire
...factory that he was nowhere was near. It smoldered. No, No! There are only ten of us and there are ten million fighting somewhere in front of you, so get your onions up and we will throw up the truce flag. Oh, please let me up; Leo, Leo! Oh, yeh! No, No; I don't....please! Please shift me. Police are here; communistic ....strike....baloneys....Please; honestly it is a habit I get; sometimes I give it and sometimes I don't. Oh, not; I am all in; say.... That settles it. Are you sure? Please, he eats like a little sausage baloney maker. Please, let me get in and eat. Let him harrass himself to you and then bother you. Please.... Don't ask me to go there; I don't want to. I still don't want him in the path. Please, Leo, Leo; I was looking for something. Meet my lady, Mrs. Pickford, and I am sorry I acted that way so soon, already. Sure, it is no use to stage a riot. The sidewalk was in trouble and the bears were in trouble and I broke it up. Please; Oh, mamma! No knock to her, she didn't know. Look; that is it. She let her go the opposite. Oh, tell me. Please; put me in that room; please keep him in control; my gilt-edge stuff, and those dirty rats have tuned in.

Please, Mother, Mother, please, the reaction is so strong. Oh, mamma, mamma, please don't tear; don't rip; that is something that shouldn't be spoke about; that is right. Please get me up my friends; I know what I speak of. Please, look out, the shooting is a bit wild, and that kind of shooting. Saved a man's life. Oh, Elmer was. No, everything frightening; yes, no payrolls, no walls, no coupons. That would be entirely out; pardon me; Oh, yeh! Oh, I forgot I am plaintiff and not defendant. Look out, look out for him. Please..and he owes me money; he owes everyone money. Why can't he just pull out and give me....control.....all right, please do. Please, Mother! You pick me up now. Please, you know me. Oh, Louie, didn't I give you my door bell? Everything you got, the whole bill. And did you come for your rest in the doctor's office, sir? Yes, I can see that. Your son-in-law, and he isn't liked, is he? Harry, does he behave? No; don't you scare me; my friends think I do a better job. Oh, police are looking for you all over; please be instrumental in letting us know. That wouldn't be here; they are Englishmen and they are a type I don't know who is best, they or us. Oh, sir, and get the doll a roofing. Please. You can play jacks, and girls do that with a soft ball and do tricks with it. Please; I may take all events into consideration; no, no. And it is no; it is confused and it says no; a boy has never wept...nor dashed a thousand kim...Did you hear me? Now leave it or take it. No, I might be in the playing for I know. Come on over here; come on over. Oh, Duckie, see we skipped again.

Question by Detective: Who shot you?
A: I don't know.
Q: Was it the big fellow?
A: I don't know.
Q: When you were coming out of the Toilet?
A: I don't know. Pick me up. No, no, you have got to do it as I see it. Please take me out of the bed.
Q: The doctor wants you to lie quiet.
A: That is what I want to do. I can't come; express office was closed. Oh, mamma, mamma. Please, please...
Q: How many shots were fired?
A: I don't know; none.
Q: How many?
A:Two thousand; come on, get some money in that treasury; we need it; come on, please get it; I can't tell you to. You are telling the truth, aren't you, Mr. Harris. That is not what you have in the book. Oh, yes I have. Oh, please, warden. Please. What am I going to do for money. How is that; how do you like that? Please put me up on my feet, at once. Thank you, Sam, you are a boiled man; I do it because you ask me to. Did you hear me? I would hear it, the Circuit Court would hear it, and the Supreme Court might hear it. Come on, pull me up, sir. All right. Cam Davis. Oh, please reply. N.R.A. If that aint the payoff. Please crack down on the Chinaman's friends and Hitler's commander. All right, I am sore and I am going up and I am going to give you honey if I can. Look out. We broke that up. Mother is the best bet and don't let Satan draw you too fast.
Question by Detective: What did the big fellow shoot you for?

A: Him? John? Over a million, five million dollars.
Q: You want to get well, don't you?
A: Yes.
Q: Lie quiet.
A: Yes, I will lie quiet.
Q: John shot you; we will take care of John.
A: That is what caused the trouble. Look out. All right, Bob. Please get me up. Come on, John, get me up. If you do this you can go on and jump right here in the lake. I know who they are; they are French people....Malone.... All right; look out, look out! Mamma, mamma ....Oh, my memory is gone. A work relief.... police. Who gets it? I don't know and I don't want to know, but look out. It can be traced. That is the one that done it, but who had that one; oh, oh, Mamma, please let me get up. XXX He changed for the worse. Please, look out; my fortunes have changed and xxxxcome back and went back since that. It was desperate Ambrose, a little kid. Please; look out....Look....Mike ....Please, I am wobbly. You aint got nothing on him, but we got it on his helper. Please ....
Q (Detective): Control yourself.
A: But I am dying.
Q: No you are not.
A: Move on, Mick and mamma. All right, dear, you have got to get it.
(At this point the nurses changed the dressing, 4:40 P.M., and "Schultz" asked for a drink of water which was given to him. When one of the nurses was taking off one of his garments he said, "Look out for my xxxxxring.")
Mrs. Flegenheimer was brought in.
Mrs. Flegenheimer: This is Frances.

"Schultz": Then pull me out, I am half crazy. They won't let me get up; they died my shoes, open those shoes here. Give me something; I am so sick. Give me some water, the only thing that I want. Open this up, break it so I can touch you. Dannie, will you please get me in the car. Now he can't butt in. Please, Nick, stop chiseling.

(Mrs. Flegenheimer left the room).

Question by Detective: Who shot you?

A: I don't know; I didn't even get a look. I don't know. Who can have done it? Anybody. Kindly take my shoes off.

Q: They are off.

A: No, there is a handcuff on them. The Baron does these things.

(Schultz): I know what I am doing here with my collection of papers, for crying out loud. It isn't worth a nickle to two guys like you or me, but to a collector it is worth a fortune; it is priceless. I am going to turn it over to .....Turn your back to me, please, Henry. I am so sick now. The police are getting many complaints. Look out. Yey, Jack; hello Jack. Jack, mamma. I want that G-note. Look out, for Jimmie Valentine, for he is an old pal of mine. Come on, Jim, come on Jimmie; oh, thanks. O. K. O.K. I am all through; I can't do another thing. Hymie, won't you do what I ask you this once? Look out! Mamma, mamma! Look out for her. You can't beat him. Police, Mamma! Helen, Mother, please take me out. Come on, Rosie. O.K. Hymes would do it; not him. I will settle.....the indictment. Come on, Max, open the soap duckets. Frankie, please come here. Open that door, Dumpey's door. It is so much, Abe, that....with the brewery. Come on. Hey, Jimmie! The Chimney

Sweeps. Talk to the Sword. Shut up, you got a big mouth! Please help me up, Henny. Max come over here....French Canadian bean soup....I want to pay, let them leave me alone....

The closing line came on the stroke of 6 P.M. Then the Dutchman fell into a deep coma. The stenographer was withdrawn and finally the police themselves left the overcrowded little room. Toward the end, the deathbed vigil reduced itself to Dr. Earl Snavely, Superintendent of the hospital, Dr. H. A. Strasser, Dr. Calasibetta and a nurse, Mae Clarkson. At 8:20, sensing that the end was at hand, Dr. Snavely gave the word to let Frances Flegenheimer come in and say her farewell. She went to the bed, bent over and whispered, again, "Arthur, this is Frances." There was no response and she withdrew, sobbing. About fifteen minutes later the patient appeared to mumble something and Miss Clarkson thought he was asking for water again. Even as she turned to get it, however, Dr. Calasibetta was checking the pupils of Schultz's eyes and putting his stethoscope to his chest. Then the doctor looked up at his colleagues and said, "It's all over." The death certificate put it at 8:35 P.M. Someone drew the sheet up over the Dutchman's head and Dr. Snavely went out into an adjoining room where the next of kin now waited. He went directly to the bent little woman in there and she arose. "Mrs. Flegenheimer, your son has died," the hospital chief said, and the Dutchman's mother collapsed into the arms of her daughter and son-in-law. Revived in a few moments, she was taken to the bedside, where she prayed in silence for 15 minutes. Then she was led downstairs, where she collapsed again outside the hospital even as Helen Ursprung was pleading with a swarm of reporters, "For God's sakes, can't you stop pestering us?" Then Henry Ursprung lifted Mrs. Flegenheimer into his arms and carried her to an old sedan parked in the driveway.

If there was any small consolation left to them it was nothing more than that their Arthur had cheated the enemy out of something like 20 hours or so.

"A thing long expected takes the form of the unexpected when at last it comes."

—MARK TWAIN

CHAPTER VII

WHAT THE DUTCHMAN WAS SAYING

RAVAGED BY THE PERITONITIS TEARING THROUGH HIS BODY, the one thing Dutch Schultz was able to make utterly clear and explicit was that to him, like any average American boy, mother was good ("Mother is the best bet") and the devil was bad ("Don't let Satan draw you too fast"). The Dutchman had some acquaintance with Satan, evidently, before the call came from the lower depths; he had established no connections going the other way—upstairs. Now what was he saying beyond these homilies?

When he said "George, don't make no bull moves," he had to be talking about George Weinberg, office manager for the policy racket, the administrator who kept the wheels turning in the numbers banks once the Schultz takeover started in 1931. The Dutchman had a bad time with George less than two months before the assassins caught up with him in Newark. He had to tell George that his brother Bo wouldn't be around any more. He may have conveyed the bad news in a rather crude way, too, like "George, we hadda put a kimono on Bo." George had been around the mob long enough so he wouldn't need an interpreter for that kind of underworld lingo. He would have taken it to mean that his big brother, who had brought him out of a no-account life into the relative affluence of the Dutchman's inner circle, had been encased in a cement shroud and dropped into the swirling currents of the East River.

How Bo died was something else. George said he never really knew. One story was that Schultz had summoned Bo to a midtown hotel and personally performed the execution with the .45 he always had tucked into his shirt-waist for indoor business conferences. The other, told by Dixie Davis, was that Lulu Rosenkrantz and a helper named Sam Grossman picked Bo up one night when he had a load on and they had him between them in a car when Lulu's little howitzer went off. It could have been an accident, the counselor said, adding a touching epitaph from the Dutchman. "We will miss good old Bo," Davis quoted his tenderhearted employer.

Be that as it may, when the weaker George was advised of the death in the family he had to consider, naturally, whether he should remain on the payroll of that sorehead Schultz or offer his limited racket experience to some lesser cartel. Well, there was no "bull move." The Dutchman had cooled George off nicely, because George was still very much on the scene and engaged even then, as the boss lay dying, in a vain effort to hold the policy empire together with the eager help of Dixie Davis.

The next name in the Dutchman's jumbled dialog with himself is Phil. "Now listen, Phil, fun is fun." This is perhaps harder to trace than the reference to George, but there was a Phil among the Dutchman's business associates along the scarlet way—Phil (Dandy Phil) Kastel, the New Orleans slot machine partner of Frank Costello. Going back to the time when the Congress, under the inspiration of such bluenosed stalwarts as Representative Andrew J. Volstead of Minnesota and the acid-tongued Bishop James Cannon Jr., ordained that America should be dry, the speakeasies which cluttered the landscape generally kept a few one-armed bandits on hand to wean away any stray pieces of silver still jingling in the pockets of the lawbreakers on the premises.

Schultz always had slot machines in his watering places and even kept some handy in his legal, undercover night club operations after the Eighteenth Amendment was stripped from the books in December 1933. He kept them, that is, until the noisy Mayor LaGuardia arrived on the scene and advised his somnolent police force that he didn't care for slot machines because they hardly ever paid off and in some places, like candy stores, school children were putting their lunch nickels in them. The Dutchman's slots, like most everybody else's who loved peace better than war, had to come from the Kastel-Costello supply depots. The "fun is fun" reference suggested to the more studious New York detectives that Schultz at some point had tried to cut a corner or two on Dandy Phil and heard some bad language in return. And Dandy Phil was the type who didn't have to make idle threats, because the quietly efficient Don Francisco Costello had an army of beautifully disciplined Mafia soldiers at his command in those days.

Once Phil departed the deathbed incantation, mother's boy, still adhering to the familiar form, introduced "John" to the thoroughly absorbed audience in that less than plush hospital ward. "John, please . . . did you buy the hotel; you promised a million . . . sure." Now there was only one John in the Dutchman's social circle with whom he could kick around so much green—Johnny Torrio, formerly resident in Chicago but lately something of a combined elder statesman and financier for the New York rackets.

Torrio was the little underworld professor from Brooklyn who took Alphonse Capone out of New York's Five Points Gang in 1920 and made him his understudy in the Windy City racket playland. Outside his Gold Coast apartment on a brisk January day in 1925, Torrio fell before an assortment of garlic-tipped bullets presumably directed at him by loyal heirs of the North Side's recently assassinated Dion O'Banion. Too tough to die, Torrio was sufficiently recovered within ten days to cast a hard eye on a collection of suspects and tell the police, casually, "I wouldn't lay the finger on." Then, since the Chicago streets had turned so unsafe, he elected to pay the State of Illinois nine months he owed on an old pinch in a brewery raid. And then, apparently dejected over the failure of his efforts to bring all the bad men of Carl Sandburg's "stormy, husky, brawling City of the Big Shoulders" together under one bulletproof shelter, turned the scepter over to the promising Capone and departed for the native Neapolitan acres in Italy.

Now Torrio was back, an adornment of the Manhattan scene, and the police believed that the Dutchman, squeezed for cash when the policy net started to shrink, might have been compelled to go to the man who had stepped into the murdered Arnold Rothstein's shoes as a bankroller for suddenly depressed mob operations. Of course, Torrio would disdain any suggestion that he had ever done any business, financial or otherwise, with the likes of any such punk as Arthur Flegenheimer. Just the same, the Dutchman in his semi-conscious raving was evidently referring to a million-dollar hotel deal—and John Torrio might well have been the man he had to see if he was thinking about following the lead of so many post-Prohibition racket guys and adding some legitimate investments to his tattered portfolio. The theory about a hotel deal drew further support from a letter found among Schultz's effects. Signed by an Al Jennings and sent from Bridgeport, where Schultz had spent much time between his two upstate trials and his unfortunate sojourn in New Jersey, this letter regretfully advised the Dutchman that negotiations for the purchase of a hotel, not named, had fallen through.

Schultz definitely was involved with the old Chicago terror in at least one other large financial operation. In January 1933, the New York Department of Insurance petitioned the state's Supreme Court for an order to dissolve a new giant in the bonding field, the Greater City Surety and Indemnity Company. Why? It turned out that Messrs. Torrio (1,667 shares) and Schultz (833 shares) were two-thirds owners of the company and in a dandy position to corner the market on bail bonds, since they happened to be so well acquainted among the people in town who needed bail the most. Besides, the Insurance Department had detected some hanky-panky in the handling of the company's funds.

Three years later, once Tom Dewey aired all that dirty linen during Jimmy Hines' trial for protecting the policy racket, Dixie Davis shed an appropriately garish light on the Torrio-Schultz adventure in bail bonds. Davis said it was the Dutchman who first spotted the marvelous possibilities in the bonding business but that the absolutely immoral Torrio presently summoned him to a moonlight gathering in a coal-yard shack off the East River and advised him that he (Torrio) simply had to have a piece. Davis said that Schultz, suitably aware of his insistent visitor's awesome credentials, coughed up $70,000 worth of stock in the bonding company rather than chance any unseemly argument. In this connection, the counselor deposed that even when his own artillerymen were on hand the Dutchman invariably showed Mr. Torrio an inordinate amount of respect. This was as it should be, inasmuch as the whole underworld community, except perhaps for those hotheads who took the shots at him in Chicago, tended to bestow a very special deference on Johnny Torrio; when his time came in 1957, he died in bed. Heart, you know. He was 75 years old and very likely pretty bitter about things by then. With his busted protégé Capone babbling away after his income tax adversities put him in Alcatraz, Torrio in 1939 had suffered the indignity of a 2½-year prison sentence and a cash outlay of $177,352 to settle an old tax bill.

"John," in any case, momentarily departed from the Dutchman's swan song as suddenly as he had arrived. "Phil" came back in an utterly meaningless reference, followed by some much less glittering names. "Reserve decision; police, police; Henny and Frankie." And after that a passing reference to "dog biscuit"—underworld argot for money—and then, "Henny, Henny; Frankie! You didn't meet him; you didn't even meet me." The Henny who came to mind was the Dutchman's brother-in-law, Henry Ursprung, but he was a minor hand in the operation, just family, really. Schultz more likely was referring to Henry (Sailor Stevens) Margolis and Frankie Ahearn, two allies from his early beginnings on the Bronx beer run. Margolis and Ahearn, in fact, had been indicted with him on the original 1933 tax rap, presumably in the hopes that they would do some singing and help the government make the case stick, but there wasn't the barest chance of that happening. This pair just dropped from sight with the Dutchman, not even bothering to show when he surrendered to stand trial, and they were still among the missing when Schultz caught that bullet. They went legitimate in a Bronx restaurant operation after the smoke cleared. They're still in it.

When Sergeant Conlon put in that very tired who-shot-you

question, Schultz came back with "The boss himself." Why? "I don't know sir; honestly I don't." Who could the boss have been? In the underworld of the early Thirties the gentleman who bore that common appellation happened to be Lucky Luciano. He earned the high title when he made his way to the top of the Eastern branch of the Unione Siciliana, precursor of the Mafia and what Joe Valachi would tell us later was really the Cosa Nostra ("Our Thing"). But if the dying man was trying to say that Luciano had shot him, it was a bum steer because the sharpshooter in the Palace—and Schultz could indeed have known him by sight, as noted earlier—met the description neither of "the boss himself" nor of the immediately following reference to "the big fellow." The actual killer was just that, a killer, one of the best in the Murder Inc. stable, as the record would bear out six years later.

Going on without prompting now, Schultz mentioned "the ring" and something about "if we wanted to break [it]." Here, he could have been talking about the rival Italian mobs, bearing sealed-in-blood Mafia credentials, which had started to cast soulful looks at his numbers barony once his troubles with the government began to distract him. We have noted that toward the end Bo Weinberg had sat down with the enemy, in this case Lucky Luciano, to talk about a takeover. Joe Valachi, a Cosa Nostra soldier in good standing then, confirmed this.

From "the ring," Schultz's ravings turned, curiously, to the vibrant politics of the Thirties, something about "communistic . . . strike . . . baloneys." What this established, other than the true-blue Americanism of the mobster, never was clear. It could have been a reference, however, cloudy, to some of the troubles Schultz encountered from honest elements in the unions when his hired strong-arm men began to set up sweetheart contracts for the restaurants on his protection rolls.

If the Dutchman's mention of the Communists did happen to be purely political, it may be said that he at least balanced it with a passing rap at the Nazis. This came in a sentence which said, "Please crack down on the Chinaman's friends and Hitler's commander." Schultz, of course, had no enemies in the German madman's inner circle. The "Chinaman," on the other hand, had to be Chink Sherman, who had led the enemy force in that Club Abbey battle. Schultz had other troubles with that bum, some quite recently, but at the moment of his oration Sherman happened to be dead, sealed away in a homemade limestone grave on a farm near Monticello in the Catskills, and nobody on the side of the law knew it. Did the Dutchman know?

Now "John" came back into the deathbed scene.

Sergeant Conlon wanted to know "what did the big fellow shoot you for?" and got this answer: "Him? John? Over a million, five million dollars." So the price was going up, but bear in mind that Uncle John Torrio could deal in that kind of scratch too; he was a high roller. Schultz did not bite, however, when Conlon once again asked about the hand that held the gun—"John shot you; we will take care of John." This was most unlikely, actually, because Mr. Torrio had never been known, not even in the bygone Chicago days, as a man who would deign to carry out his own murder missions; there were always hired hands for that.

What else was Schultz saying? Apart from the pure poetry of those two splendid and ever-mystifying lines—"a boy has never wept/ nor dashed a thousand kim"—his ravings did furnish a kind of underworld glossary for the uninitiated. "Dog biscuits," as noted, was the coin of his realm and the "sidewalk" was a reference to his freedom to carry on his trade; he had once said to Dixie Davis, while he was on the lam, "If I don't make the sidewalk soon, this racket will go to pieces." He was referring to the numbers game there. "Get the doll a roofing" probably meant that he wanted someone to take care of Frances—or was it some other love of his life? When he said "onions" he meant girls, too. The phrase, "I am a pretty good pretzeler," seemed rather obscure but it turned out that "pretzel" was the Dutchman's word for a German. Comedian Joe E. Lewis, who played in Schultz-owned joints in his time, recalled that the gangster often said, "I ain't a bad pretzel."

While the mention of a "cowboy in one of the . . . seven days a week fights" also seemed wholly obscure, Craig Thompson and Allen Raymond, in their excellent book, *Gang Rule in New York*, recalled in 1940 that Schultz may have been calling up a scornful remembrance of another old foeman, the late Legs Diamond. Thompson and Raymond said that when the celebrated Clay Pigeon of the Underworld finally departed in 1931 and the cops asked Schultz why anyone would want to shoot that guy for keeps the Dutchman treated the question with contempt, dismissing Diamond as a "cowboy."

When the line "Talk to the Sword" came up in the dying man's farewell there was no doubt that he was talking about himself. He was "The Sword"; he had used the expression quite commonly in the conduct of his affairs. "Come on . . . open the soap duckets" was another allusion to money in the lexicon of the dying man, and when he spoke of "The Chimney Sweeps" right after that he was using one of his pet phrases for the Negroes he had to keep in his employ after his takeover of the numbers game. There was a more explicit racial reference, noted earlier, in the expense sheets found on

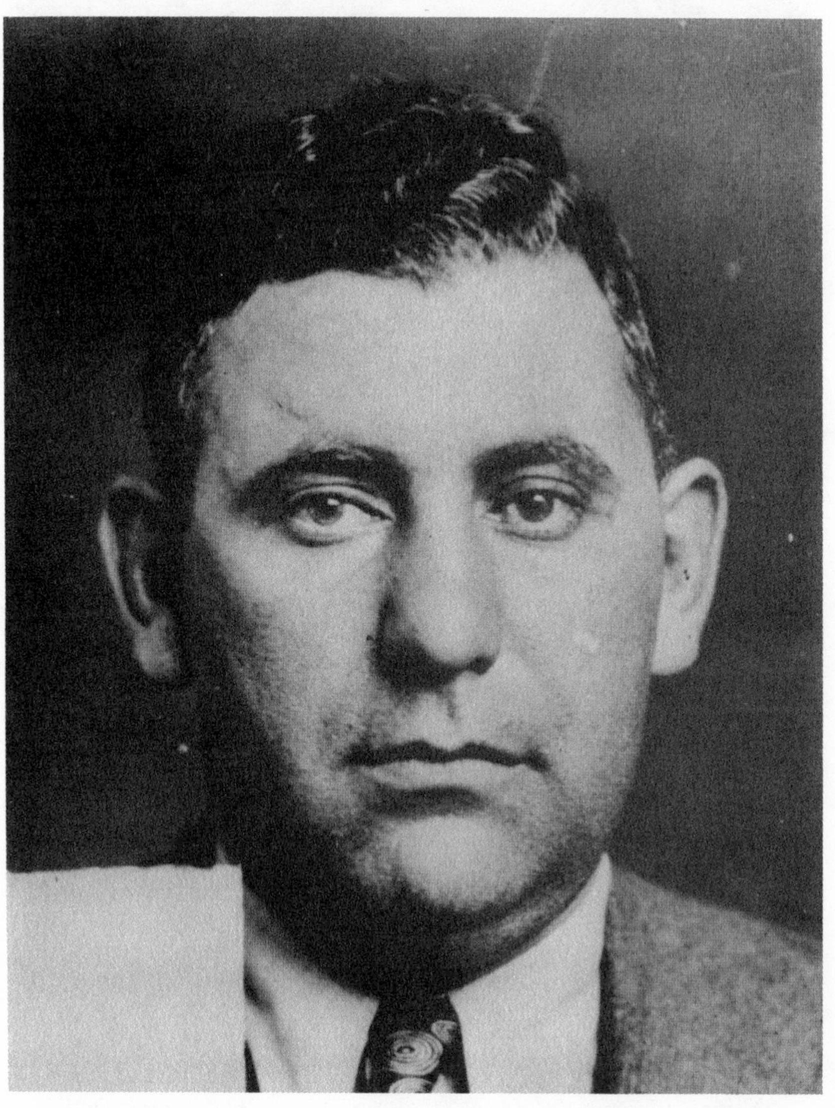

United Press International

Abe (Bo) Weinberg was Dutch Schultz's No. 1 strong-arm man in policy until he started to deal with the enemy—in the person of Lucky Luciano. After that Bo went on the spot. The murder was never solved.

Wide World Photos

Johnny Torrio (center), back in New York after deserting his Chicago racket kingdom because somebody tried to kill him, figured in the dying ravings of Dutch Schultz. The two underworld figures, hardly compatible, had done some business together not long before the Dutchman was slain.

that table in the Palace. It said, "niggers, $9,000"—a suggestion, no doubt, that the Dutchman never quite relished paying policy's hired hands their share, however piddling it might be against the towering sums they were feeding into his accounts.

When you put it all together, you have something of an autobiography dictated by a man who tended to touch all the high spots but was rather casual about last names, dates and places. The head of Newark Junior College's English department, Professor Leo Lemchen, used the Schultz ravings in class in 1940 as a piece of American folk literature, borrowed from the James Joyce stream-of-consciousness technique in fiction. "Schultz," said Lemchen, "told his life story in these mutterings, and left behind him a clear picture of the character and outlook of a type which played an important part in the American theme. It is a complete self-portrait." But the Professor wasn't too high on the author. Taken in its entirety, he put the deathbed jumble down as the work of a "fear-ridden weakling" who had a "bullying, cruel and crafty nature. While the babblings seem not to make sense, one gets a glimpse of a man's mind laid bare. The gangster alternated threats to associates . . . with piteous appeals to 'mamma' to help him."

When Schultz said "my . . . gilt-edge stuff, and those dirty rats have tuned in," it sounded to Lemchen like a piece of bitterness from a domineering feudal lord whose serfs were demanding a bigger slice of the action.

The last soliloquy—or the police role in it, in any case—also brought some tart comment from Dr. Bruce Robinson, psychiatrist for the Newark Board of Education. The doctor thought the police had blown it. He said that when Schultz pleaded continually for his mother ("Please, Mother! You pick me up now. Please, you know me.") the room should have been cleared of the law and a woman produced, any woman the dying man might have accepted as his mother in a moment when he was apparently retreating to his own childhood. Then, according to Dr. Robinson, Schultz might really have spilled some secrets, whereas he was never going to tell the cops anything. "He was always on the defensive against the police," the doctor said, "and I don't think he sank so far into unconsciousness at any time as to give them a chance to break down that defense."

The doctor may have had a point.

The fact is that when the Dutchman uttered his closing line on that black evening—"I want to pay, let them leave me alone"—he was leaving the police quite empty-handed. With the end at hand for their briefly talkative captive, they didn't have much to go on. The real saga of Arthur Flegenheimer would take almost three decades to unfold. First, some intriguing items of that last night's business had to come out. Then the untold story of the Dutchman in the policy racket would be brought out by Tom Dewey in the process of sending Jimmy Hines off to Sing Sing. Then, in 1941, some of the missing details of the Massacre on Park Street, including the names of the torpedomen, would come out. And finally, 21 years after that, Joe Valachi would fill in the last missing strokes and make the canvas, dipped in crimson, complete.

"Well, I'd do it again. I was proud of him and I'll be proud to tell my children about their father."

—FRANCES FLEGENHEIMER

CHAPTER VIII

ORDEAL FOR FRANCES

ONCE DUTCH SCHULTZ EXPIRED, TO BE FOLLOWED AT 3:20 the next morning by the all but indestructible Lulu Rosenkrantz, the spotlight turned on the woman—one of the women, surely—that he left behind.

Frances Flegenheimer faced a most difficult time mostly because the Newark authorities couldn't understand why she hadn't turned right around and come back to those soiled precincts when she picked up the *Daily Mirror* in Manhattan and discovered that her one true love had suffered a rather serious bullet wound.

Deputy Police Chief Haller had a long session with the redhead on the afternoon of October 24 and simply could not be persuaded that she had gone off to bed, like any square wife on any square night when hubby was out of town, after reading the bad news. Haller thought that everything about Frances Flegenheimer was "highly suspicious." He didn't even care for the way the 21-year-old carried off the role of the grieving widow, not even when the tears welled up in those blue-gray eyes. The hard-boiled Chief never thought there were enough tears. To him, the girl was "more angry than sad."

That was harsh, to be sure, but Frances had furnished the basis for it with her own fibs. She initially denied having been in Newark at all when the guns went off, saying she had last seen her Arthur at the Robert Treat on the preceding Sunday. Haller wasn't buying that. He had no less than three witnesses who could place her in the Palace some two hours before the shooting. He brought in one of them, Frank Fredericks, and the bartender took one look and said yes, that was the woman who came in to see the Dutchman. It was only then that Frances Flegenheimer decided that a little more candor might be in order.

"I shall tell you the truth," she said, but there was a fast qualification:

"Why should I be mixed up in this thing? Just because I am married to this man? I don't want to be mixed up in this thing."

The Essex County Prosecutor, William A. Wachenfeld, was in this particular session at Police Headquarters, and under his softer questioning Frances finally told her story about seeing Schultz, getting packed off to the movies, returning to the tavern at 11:20 P.M. and departing for home when she saw the crowd outside.

"I thought it was a raid," she said.

Who else was in the Palace while she was there?

Just Lou (Rosenkrantz) and Arthur, she said. No one else? Well, a man named Mike, in a light suit, took her to Arthur in the back room. What about Landau and Berman? Lou was the only one she saw with Arthur. Did she know Marty Krompier? "I don't want to answer any questions."

Here there was a break for another vain trip to the bedside but later that evening, indeed at the very moment that Dutch Schultz was being pronounced dead, Haller had the girl in for another question-and-answer period:

Q. Have you any desire to aid the police?
A. I don't know of any men.
Q. Aren't you interested?
A. I can't see how I can be of help. The first time I lied.
Q. Do you know Marty Krompier?
A. Maybe I do and maybe I don't.

This sort of thing prompted the District Attorney to decide that Frances ought to be detained as a material witness and, while an attorney from the Dutchman's legal battery protested that the whole proceeding was "un-American and inhuman," she was held the next day in $10,000 bail. Three of the other material witnesses, Jack Friedman, Ben Birkenfeld and King Lou, were let out on $1,000 bonds.

For Frances Flegenheimer, now looking badly frayed in her role as the child bride of Dutch Schultz, the worst was yet to come. She had that last visit with Arthur 15 minutes before the end and her tough guy's terrified, small boy's pleading (". . . pull me out, I am half crazy. They won't let me get up; they died [*sic*] my shoes") would sound in her ears forever. She was back on Haller's grill before Arthur died but it was 10:30 P.M. when she learned that she was going to be arrested and 2:00 A.M. before she was finally told that she wouldn't have to go to the hospital any more. "I'm all right," she sobbed then. "He's gone. Gone." Then she broke down and someone produced a blanket and a pillow and they let her stretch out on a desk. In the morning, a court appearance, with her auburn tresses in terrible disarray, her face covered by a handkerchief to foil the cameramen—and a bombshell.

"I wouldn't be surprised," Haller told the reporters after the hearing, "if another woman appears to lay claim to the title of Mrs. Schultz."

It was an indelicate way to put it at best but Haller, stubbornly clinging to the notion that Frances may have led the executioners to the Palace, even unwittingly, wasn't stopping there. He conceded that the girl was the mother of the Dutchman's infants—Anne Davis Flegenheimer, named for the Schultz mouthpiece and born on June 26, 1934, and John David, born the preceding July 25 while Schultz was on trial upstate—but he observed that there was an interesting exchange of correspondence among the items picked up in the gangster's suite at the Robert Treat. He was talking about a packet of missives bearing the salutation "Poppy" and signed "Mommy." Without producing any texts for the more dedicated historians, Haller read from one small sample: "Poppy, I am so lonesome for you. Wish I could come East and join you. We are looking forward to a reunion. Mommy."

The Chief's saucy recitation didn't end there.

"One letter," he went on, "had a picture of a woman and two children, but the woman was not this Mrs. Schultz and the children appeared too old to be hers."

This morsel, the icing on the cake for the Roman feast the newspapers were enjoying while the Dutchman's remains were in storage in the Newark morgue, needed no qualification. The Chief said that Frances Flegenheimer had been treated to the dubious pleasure of a peek at the photo and had agreed that the children in it were nothing at all like the ones she had brought forth for her Arthur.

Was there any lingering doubt about the possible existence of another Mrs. Arthur Flegenheimer? The unchivalrous Haller's communiqué also included the revelation that Frances Flegenheimer had never been joined to the broken-nosed Romeo in any civil marriage ceremony; all the girl had, or said she had, was a "letter of contract" formalizing her union with the guy.

This item never was explained, even when the tight-lipped Frances sat for two lengthy interviews in 1938 with Maureen McKernan, one of the legendary women reporters, then on the New York *Post*. Frances just wouldn't talk about it. She did say that she had met Arthur in 1932 at the Maison Royal, one of the stops on his night-crawling rounds. She said she was impressed with his good English, his good manners, his quiet dress and his unassuming ways. She said it was love at first sight, like it happened the first time he handed her his $4.95 fedora and looked into her limpid eyes. She said the union took place three months later and had always been harmonious in the three years before that pistol broke it up. She told Maureen McKernan that her proudest possession, and she was wearing it at the time, was a gold bracelet from Arthur bearing such charms as a wine glass, a whisky bottle, a head of Christ on a medal—and a miniature revolver. She said she would always treasure the bracelet because "Arthur said it represented his life and interests," which made one wonder why the Dutchman hadn't added a bottle of beer or a gold policy slip or two to the little trinket.

But then Frances didn't care for the image of Arthur as a plug-ugly and an unlettered hoodlum. She said he loved the better things in life, like the printed word; she said she had finished reading Hervey Allen's jumbo-sized best-selling *Anthony Adverse* to him at the Robert Treat just a few nights before the end. That gargantuan project, the ultimate test for any pair of lovebirds holed up in an unfamiliar bed, should have cleared up any question about all the cozy hours the happy couple had spent together in Newark in those last weeks.

Did Frances Flegenheimer have any regrets?

No. She said she was proud of Arthur and would be proud

to tell the children about him. "He used to say that the Prohibition law was made by racketeers and that he was doing a public service providing liquor for people who wanted it. He said he and his kind were victims of a vicious law." And the policy racket? Frances skipped it.

While the *Post* interview did not touch on the "letter of contract" bit, it is entirely conceivable that the Dutchman, out of his vast store of legal knowledge, all acquired the hard way, knew that a man also could get arrested just for having more than one legal-wedded wife. But Frances scoffed at this. "There was no other woman," she said.

This item would never be settled.

The "Mommy" of the intriguingly mysterious Newark letters, otherwise unidentified, was lost to history at the outset, but she wasn't alone very long. Even while the newsprint was still wet on Haller's peek-a-boo revelations, the New York *Daily News* hit the streets with this tantalizing headline:

DUTCH HAD WIFE 3;
HID RICHES FOR HER

In this account, so blazing hot that the Chicago *Tribune*–New York *News* Syndicate copyrighted it lest it be pilfered by us second-story men on the other gazettes, it turned out that the Dutchman's real love was a party named Ann, nothing more, and that his devotion to this babe was so all-encompassing that he had made "magnificent financial provision" for her in the form of a cool million dollars nestling in a Boston bank vault. Schultz, said this *News* scoop, "was haunted by the notion that Ann would be cut off without a cent when the inevitable gang guns took their toll of him. Associates revealed that he often commented on the comparative poverty at death of Jack Diamond and other mobsters who've passed on. He was determined to be smarter than they were. So he put $1,000,000 in the Boston vault, with the proviso that it was never to be touched except by Ann."

Oh, that lucky Ann.

And oh, that unlucky Frances. No vault and nothing under the rug and one embarrassment piling on another. Even while she was on the hot seat in the prosecutor's stuffy office a hearse from Manhattan, dispatched to pick up Arthur, was delivering a hefty painted doll to the Newark morgue for one last glimpse of the remains.

Francis X. Ginley, then a medical secretary for Dr. Martland and still in the Medical Examiner's office today, recalls that the driver of the hearse parked the vehicle two blocks away to avoid the nosy reporters assigned to the morgue and then approached him. "Have you ever seen a gangster's moll?" death's jockey asked. "They have some pips. I got one in the car. Can I bring her in?" Ginley said he could indeed, so the driver scurried off and returned presently with a flashy peroxide blonde in her mid-thirties, straight out of the *Police Gazette* or the Minsky burlesque line. The woman identified herself as Mrs. Schultz and asked could she have one last look at the deceased? She was ushered inside and Sal Alfone, keeper of the morgue, slid the body out of its chilly wall receptacle and gingerly withdrew the white sheet from the face, whereupon the blonde, in sections, started to sag to the cold white floor. Ginley and the hearse driver caught her just in time. Revived with a glass of water, "Mrs. Schultz" asked if she could have the Dutchman's effects, like that blue sapphire ring and the gold wristwatch the papers had mentioned. Ginley said no, the police had impounded everything and she would have to wait.

"How long?" the blonde asked, picking up strength now.

"I don't know ma'am," the Medical Examiner's young helper replied. "That's up to the cops or the D.A."

The bodies—the Dutchman and the splendidly endowed visitor, that is—were then loaded on the wagon, parked at a side door now, but Ginley had not seen the last of the women in the amorous Flegenheimer's other life.

Six weeks later, on a mission to City Hospital to pick up some papers for Dr. Martland, Ginley overheard a conservatively dressed matron inquiring about the Schultz effects at the reception desk. "Just a minute," he said to the clerk. "You better be sure this is Schultz's widow. There was one at the morgue when we had him over there—and there was another one in the papers." The matron, perhaps ten years older than the frowzy blonde who had made that grim trip with the hearse, turned an icy glare on Ginley, ignoring the clerk at the desk. "That must have been his lady friend," she said. "I happen to be Mrs. Flegenheimer."

"Maybe she has proof," the clerk submitted.

"I most certainly do," the woman said, ruffling in an oversized black pocketbook and producing some legal-looking documents which the interloper Ginley wasn't invited to examine. The clerk glanced at the papers, made an interoffice call, and then told the woman that all of Schultz's effects had been taken out of the hospital by the police. That was the end of it.

Unfortunately, all the heat was off by then and nobody bothered to find out whether this woman was the "Mommy" of those scented hotel room epistles, or the *Daily News*'s filthy-rich Ann—or who. Nobody ever tried to find out who the petitioner at the morgue was either. That one could not have been Frances Flegenheimer, of course; she was in custody then, and Frank Ginley would have known her on sight anyway. He had seen her picture in the papers.

For Frances at that time, there was still no peace.

The police wanted to know more, a helluva lot more, about that fellow "Mike" who had ushered her to Arthur's side in the tavern. You will recall that the amiable bondsman, Max Silverman, had mentioned a party named Mikie at the Palace bar. The cops had an enormous curiosity about all this because they wanted to know about the character who was supposed to have been twirling that key chain outside the door before the enemy patrol made its spectacular entrance. The way the detectives had it, Frances had been brought to the Park Street rendezvous by a man in a pea-green suit and it was a man in that same garish outfit who was on the other end of that key chain. They counted four guys on the death squad—the lead gunner, the shotgun artist, the wheelman, and the fashion plate in green.

Well, it took time but after a while Frances began to remember some things about Mike—and Mike turned out to be none other than Mickey the Mock Marks, previously mentioned in this chronicle as one of the stray inhabitants of the Palace on that bad night. Of course, it wasn't as simple as all that, because the Mock denied Frances' story with some vehemence. Indeed, he denied knowing the girl at all. And if he didn't know her, how could he have delivered her unto Arthur Flegenheimer? So it came down to a question of who the liar was, and on November 6 Frances and Mr. Marks were brought together in a confrontation in Prosecutor Wachenfeld's office.

Q. (to Frances): Do you know this man?

A. Yes. He is the man who met me at the door of the Chop House and led me through the tavern to my husband in the back room.

Q. (to Marks): Now that Mrs. Flegenheimer has recognized you, what have you got to say?

A. She lied. I don't know her. I never saw her before. I never saw her at the Palace that night.

That settled nothing, of course, but then there was no rush. Marks happened to be on ice as a material witness and his memory just needed some thawing out. After a while, still insisting that he didn't know the girl, he remembered that he had seen her in the tavern not once but three times, at 2:00 P.M., 6:00 P.M. and 9:00 P.M., on that ill-starred October 23. Otherwise, his own story never changed. He said he went there to see the Chancellor-of-the-Exchequer-in-exile, Lulu Rosenkrantz, and for no other reason.

There was a faintly damning item in the Mock's dossier just the same. New York detectives prowling around his Bronx apartment came up with a key chain adorned with the figure of a white horse just like the one the suspected finger-man in Newark had been twirling around. Silly, said the Mock, because he happened to be frittering away his time in a nearby night club when everything hit the fan, not to mention his pal Lulu, in the Chop House. Marks evidently was a victim of the inevitable over-reporting on the crime stories of those days, because he did appear to be guilty of nothing more reprehensible than hanging out with the Schultz mob on the wrong night. There was one flurry while he was in custody, however. An anonymous caller asked the Newark cops to tell the Mock, please, that he would be knocked off if he did any talking, but that may have been a prank. After a while Marks, a sometime chauffeur and handyman for the Dutchman in happier days, was turned loose with a mild admonition to the effect that he ought to be more careful about the company he kept.

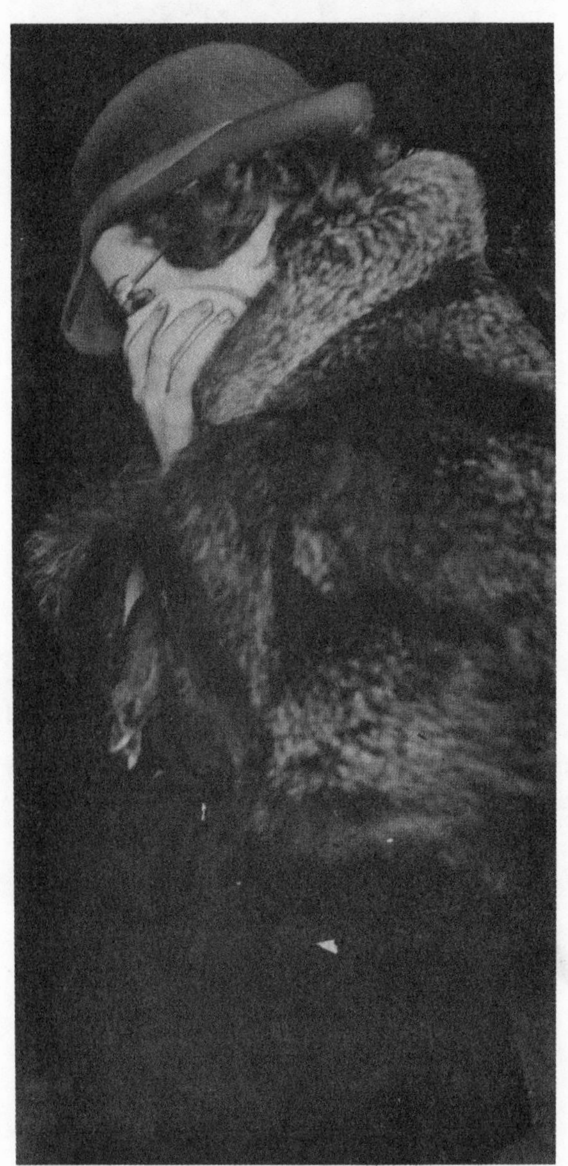

United Press International

Frances Flegenheimer leaving the hospital after her final visit with her husband. When the gangster died, she was under interrogation in the Newark prosecutor's office.

New York *Post,* Barney Stein (top photo)
Wide World Photos (bottom photo)

Frances Flegenheimer during an interview with Maureen McKernan of The New York *Post* in 1938, three years after the massacre in Newark. Bottom, waiting to testify in the 1939 trial of Tammany's James J. Hines, exposed as the protector of her husband's multi-million-dollar policy operation.

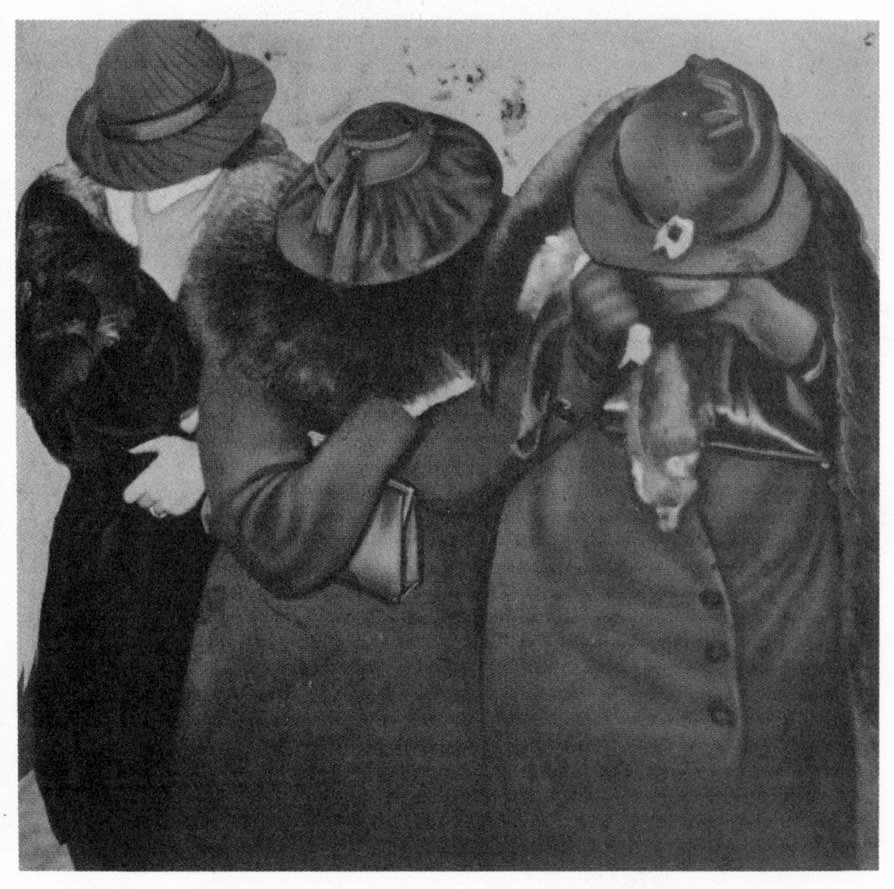

Wide World Photos

Covering up against the photographers, Dutch Schultz's wife, mother and sister leave Newark City Hospital after a deathbed visit. Left to right, Frances Flegenheimer, the aging Mrs. Emma Neu Flegenheimer and her daughter, Mrs. Helen Ursprung.

Apart from that stray character in the assassination drama, Max Silverman also had a problem with the cops about his social itinerary on the fatal evening, but he too came out lily white as far as the fingering bit was concerned. He had not one but five witnesses, including his own favorite hatcheck girl, to attest under oath that he was killing time in another joint, the Blue Mirror, when the assassins reached the Palace. Beyond that, it figured that the bondsman had a more urgent interest in collecting some cash from his friend Schultz than in having him staring helplessly into the business end of a .45 with his yo-yo in his hand.

The Schultz work sheets tended to bear that out, for the records picked up by the cops showed that while $18,000 already had been shoveled along to that expensive New Jersey legal battery another $8,000 was still due. Silverman, you will recall, said that he had gone to the tavern to collect $10,500 for the lawyers and a few bob for himself—and who would quarrel over the trifling difference between the $8,000 on the Dutchman's books and the $10,500 the bondsman said was due?

Speaking of money, it is well to pay an additional tribute here to the impeccable accounting habits of the mobster. Against such moderately impressive figures as that legal bite, one of the incidental items on the sheets showed a few cents owed on a couple of novels (*Anthony Adverse* wasn't enough?) borrowed from a circulating library by Arthur Flegenheimer, a self-confessed bookworm from way back.

The numbers, of course, from that whopping $827,253 income item down to the nickel-and-dime outlays, turned out to have no meaning at all for Frances Flegenheimer. She always insisted that she had been left without means because J. Richard Davis had made off with Arthur's available loose change. "Davis is the only Judas my husband ever knew," she said some time later. "Davis was the only one close enough to him to know how much he actually had. That Arthur died almost a pauper is unbelievable. Davis has lived in luxury while Arthur's family has been struggling to get along."

The barrister, for his part, said he never knew where the Schultz rainy day money, once estimated at $7 million, had gone. He said the Dutchman used to keep his spare bills, always in the larger denominations and frequently in gold banknotes because the guy just adored that kind of paper, in a specially made steel box three feet long and two feet wide. He said he meant to go hunt it up himself some day because his deceased client owed him, oh, $100,000 or so. He didn't say whether he would divvy up anything beyond the 100 large with Frances or any of Arthur's other bereft survivors if he ever happened to stumble on that dandy box.

The fact is, Frances and her small brood could have used some help. Two months after the assassination she had to go to court to establish her claim on two life insurance policies which her ever-loving soulmate had switched from his mother's name to hers in 1933, the year after their odd union was sealed. The policies turned out to be worth $5,000 each, hardly a regal bounty for a man of Arthur Flegenheimer's affluence, even in the Thirties. Hell, the Dutchman once blew that much on a bond for his bail-jumping pal Vincent Coll.

"He was a criminal. . . . But who will close the gates of mercy?"

—MONSIGNOR JOHN L. BELFORD

CHAPTER IX

A FUNERAL— AND SOME POST MORTEMS

WHILE HE LIVED AND DIED SO SPECTACULARLY, THE FUNERAL of Arthur Flegenheimer had to be recorded as one of the more private chapters in his life, conducted in such extraordinary secrecy that it even had cloak-and-dagger touches. The reporters, photographers and newsreel men who massed outside the Coughlin Funeral Home on Manhattan's Tenth Avenue on the bleak Monday following his demise were destined to come away empty-handed.

When the press arrived at 6:00 A.M., one of the brothers Couglin said that the body already had been removed but nobody believed him. In time, a crowd of some 2,000 was on hand and the balconies of Roosevelt Hospital, across the way, were jammed with the curious, but hours passed and nothing happened. There was a flurry of activity finally, at 10:30 A.M., when a mahogany casket was borne out of the funeral home followed by eight mourners. The newsreel cameras started to grind and the crowd edged closer, held back by six badly outnumbered patrolmen, but the Coughlins protested that the casket contained the body of a neighborhood woman, name of Katherine Picket, and why didn't they all go away?

It turned out that Dutch Schultz's coffin—a simple box of chestnut wood, hardly befitting the man's station—had been removed at 5:00 A.M. for a slow 10:30 A.M. rendezvous with the funeral party on Central Avenue in Yonkers and then whisked off to the Gate of Heaven Cemetery in Hawthorne, 25 miles north of the city in Westchester County.

There Father McInerney performed a 15-minute Catholic service, omitting the eulogy, and the bare mourning party departed, but not before Emma Flegenheimer, bent in sorrow, had a Jewish prayer shawl draped over the coffin. Apart from the gangster's mother, as near as could be learned, the graveside witnesses were limited to Frances Flegenheimer, Schultz's sister Helen with her husband, Henry Ursprung, and an elderly, gray-haired man said to be a brother-in-law of the deceased's mother. On a hillside plot overlooking the Bronx River Valley, the Dutchman reposed in a grave just 20 feet from the stage's Anna Held and fairly close to Larry Fay, the flashy but relatively minor racket bum (taxis, booze, milk and night spots) who had been killed in 1932 by a drunken doorman outside his own Casa Blanca club. Schultz's grave cost $350 and the total cost of the very modest funeral was put at $1,200.

In Manhattan, the reporters didn't know any of this until the funeral home invited them in at 1:00 P.M. and gave out the sparse details.

Another item came to light at the same time. It turned out that when the funeral party arrived at Coughlin's in the predawn there were two uninvited guests on hand—Leo I. Keyes, a Treasury agent, and John A. Ross, an attorney on the staff of the State Tax Commission, there to serve writs on Schultz's mother and Frances Flegenheimer calling for the surrender of all of the Dutchman's records for tax purposes. The government had a lien for $115,000 against the Schultz estate, if it could ever find any such thing, and New York

State had a claim in for another $70,279. Ross approached one of the two young women—he did not know whether it was Frances or Helen Ursprung—and handed her the court order. The woman threw the order to the sidewalk and in the same motion whacked the state's emissary with her handbag.

The controversy surrounding Schultz hardly ended with his burial, of course. The funeral was barely over when the great debate began: what right did that man have to be laid to rest with the rites of the Catholic Church? John A. Toomey, S.J., took up the problem in the Catholic weekly, *America*, noting at the outset that there were thousands of people saying that "if a guy like that can go to heaven there won't be anybody in hell." But the article went on:

> To these thousands, glaring contradictions appeared to be involved. Here was the Catholic Church, which always had impressed on her children a horror of even the slightest sin; which had ceaselessly warned them concerning the danger of presuming on the chances of a death-bed conversion, which had ever inculcated high ideals in asceticism, in selflessness, in heroic virtue; here was the Catholic Church beckoning into her fold a man who through his entire life had represented everything which the Church abhorred and condemned.
>
> "Dutch Schultz" with the angels! "Dutch Schultz" whose beer-trucks once rumbled over the Bronx, whose gorillas blustered through the sidewalks! "Dutch Schultz" associating with the holy saints in Heaven!
>
> He to get the same reward as valiant souls who have clung to the Faith through a ceaseless hurricane of trial and temptation. It seemed more than unjust. It seemed ridiculous, preposterous, almost laughable.

But it may not be so laughable after all. There were a number of things not taken into account by the . . . judges. One little thing they missed completely was the fact that there is just One in the entire universe Who is capable of accurately judging the complex skein of a man's life. The influence of bad example, of environment in general: of heredity; the lack of religious training; the exact strength of temptations. . . . That One is God Almighty. No one else can even begin to do the job.

Another element that appeared to be fumbled was the interesting truth that the time of mercy for sinners does not expire until the moment of death; that there is no crime and no series of crime. . . . which God will not forgive, this side of eternity, to the truly contrite of heart.

The dynamic power of Divine Grace to move the most obdurate heart to repentance was also omitted from the consideration. Indeed, the intimate and essential connection of grace with final salvation is widely overlooked. . . .

Other important bits of evidence were neglected as the clamorous verdict was reached: for example, the fact that nothing happens in this world without the permission of God. The reason "Schultz" was not killed instantly was because it was God's will that he be not killed instantly, and so he was conscious the morning after, and able to receive the grace of conversion, a grace that comes from God.

If "Schultz's" conversion was sincere, it means that God gave him a last chance to save his soul, and that "Dutch" took advantage of the offer. It does not mean that God, or His Church, condoned the evil life of

> "Schultz" but that . . .God judged he should be given another opportunity to save his soul. . . .
>
> After all, Heaven belongs to God. If He wants "Dutch Schultz" to be there, it is difficult to see what we can do about it. Perhaps, instead of worrying about "Schultz" a somewhat more profitable occupation for us would be to do a little more worrying about our own salvation—to make sure we get there ourselves. We may not be given the opportunity for a death-bed repentance. Relatively few are given that chance.
>
> And whether we meet "Schultz" in Heaven or not, there is one individual we are certain to encounter there; a gentleman who was in more or less the same line as "Schultz"—the Thief who, as he was dying on Calvary, asked the Man on the next Cross for forgiveness and who heard that Man say: "This day thou shalt be with Me in Paradise."

The penitent thief and the Man on the Cross at Calvary also were called to mind by the Right Reverend Monsignor John L. Belford, pastor of the Roman Catholic Church of the Nativity in Brooklyn, in a defense of Father McInerney's ministrations to Schultz. In an article for *The Monitor*, a church publication, Monsignor Belford decried "the cries of shame . . . from Catholics and non-Catholics . . . who thought it a crime to administer the sacraments of the church to a man who had been all his life not only a stranger to religion but a particularly vile and violent criminal," and he went on:

> Was Dutch Schultz worse than the penitent thief? He was a criminal. He seemed unworthy of the least consideration. Perhaps he was. But who will close the gates of

mercy? The fact that he received the sacraments is no guarantee that he received God's forgiveness.

If he was not really penitent, the priest's absolution had no effect. Yet that priest did right when he baptized or absolved him. The dying man said he was sorry he had offended God; he declared he would do all in his power to avoid sin in the future and to repair the harm he had done. If he meant this, God ratified the action of the minister.

But, remember, the sinner contracts two debts; the debt of guilt and the debt of pain. God can forgive the former and insist on payment of the latter. He could forgive Schultz and yet keep him in purgatory until the end of time to atone, so far as man can atone, for his wickedness.

The religious issue, of course, was overshadowed by much larger earthly matters, such as the endless curiosity of the law enforcement community over the sheet of paper which showed that even in adversity, hounded by society, the Dutchman had been able to rake in $827,253 in the scant six weeks before his demise.

To start with, the "ice" figure—$27,000 in three months is what was recorded on some of the Schultz papers found in the Robert Treat—disturbed everybody. The Newark police hastened to point out that this had to have reference to payoffs made in New York, not in New Jersey, since the man had hardly been in the Garden State long enough to set up any business operations. The New York police brass, in turn, blushing ever so slightly, expressed the most intense and heartfelt desire to ferret out anyone on the force so depraved as to take money from a sinner like Arthur Flegenheimer.

Lewis J. Valentine, up from the ranks himself and Fiorello LaGuardia's Police Commissioner, had said before that he would deal very harshly indeed with any such scoundrels on the force. In December 1934, while Schultz was upstate awaiting trial in the tax case against him and professing great anguish over the fact that his own favorite government had turned down an offer of $100,000 to settle the whole thing and start over, Valentine had made a speech which contained this line:

"Is there any reason why a bum like that (Arthur Flegenheimer, of course) should be protected unless he was paying for protection?"

When the Commissioner was asked whether he meant that the roster of New York's finest included some bounders who may have been dipping their clammy hands into the Dutchman's tainted purse, even at that moment, he said he was convinced that any such naughtiness had ceased back on January 1, 1934 (the day the forces of light took over City Hall).

Now in the chill November following the Dutchman's sudden departure Lewis Valentine could do no better than offer the observation that nothing in the fastidious Schultz accounting—a record that would put a neighborhood bank to shame—indicated that "any money was directly passed to any appointive or elective official." This was probably in response to a passing statement by Newark Police Chief Harris about prominent names turning up in the Schultz papers. Harris never went any further and Valentine's remark evidently was meant to let the citizenry know that none of the men who assumed the seats of power when Fusion's LaGuardia moved in had taken any handouts from Arthur Flegenheimer or that ilk. It did not really mean that the policemen on the beats—and some of the brass-adorned types back in the station houses—weren't on the "pad," or payoff roster, that had made it possible for the policy banks to thrive in New York City year after year after year (into this writing in 1970, by the way).

Valentine did take pains to put down a reporter who inquired whether as much as 40 percent of the Dutchman's take had found its way, somewhere along the line, into police pockets. "No," he said, coining a non sequitur, "this was big business and they weren't paying out any such amount for protection." The Commissioner went on to point out that tracing any payoffs to individual cops was proving most difficult because the Schultz accounts, for all their minute attention to detail, used initials, nicknames and symbols rather than full names.

Mayor LaGuardia, talking about the fraternity of crime, had issued his famous "muss 'em up" directive to the New York police after the Dutchman's death, and now Valentine went perhaps a step further. "I want the gangster to tip his hat to the cop today," he said. "I'll promote the men who kick these gorillas around and bring them in. And I'll demote any policemen who are friendly with gangsters."

But Valentine tried to soften the disclosure of the hefty Schultz payoffs by noting that the records indicated that in the more recent labors preceding his death the Dutchman had been taking more money out of the Coney Island track in Cincinnati, in a gambling operation of some kind, than he had out of policy. The race-track funny business, whatever it was, would never be explained, but it did furnish still another reason for the presence of Abbadabba Berman, at one time the official handicapper at Coney Island, in the Palace Chop

House with Schultz on the fatal night. The Commissioner also noted that the Schultz records showed operations in Westchester County and Connecticut as well but didn't say what they were. He said his men were also going over papers scattered amidst the garish wardrobe and rich items of personal jewelry of the murdered Pretty Louis Amberg, picked up in a midtown hotel after that party's demise, just ahead of Schultz's, to see if by chance the "Jewish gangs" had been working in concert against the "Italian gangs" (Luciano, et al., even with guys like Lepke and Gurrah and Siegel and Lansky spoiling their ethnic purity). Valentine spoke of a "racial war of extermination," citing one impressive item in support of it: each and every victim in the October 23 carnage, in Newark and Manhattan, was Jewish. So were the Ambergs, for that matter, but there was at least a smidgen of reason to believe that their little war could have been with Schultz rather than the Italians.

The Commissioner said, finally, that he had information that four members of Detroit's Purple Gang had been imported to New Jersey for the rubout of the Dutchman and his high command, but this would prove to be way off base.

Before that statement was made, a 21-year-old killer named Albert Stein, alias Stern and nicknamed "The Teacher," had emerged as one of the prime early suspects in the New York end of the mission that wiped out the Dutchman's gang. Stein, a junkie under indictment in the slaying of Patrolman John J. Frazer in Brooklyn in 1934, had been credited with seven gangland murders in a brief but busy span as a triggerman. The slayings of both Joe and Pretty Louis Amberg also seemed to the police to have his brand on them and when Marty Krompier was shot there was a report that three of the witnesses had identified photos of Stein as the barber shop gunman. All this proved academic just three days later when Stein was found dead in a broken-down Newark rooming house, evidently a suicide by gas.

For a while, the scatter-gun speculation also included the notion that Chink Sherman might have been the guy who killed the Dutchman. This proved to be terribly deficient, for when that Catskill grave yielded up the Chinaman on November 4 it was abundantly clear that he had been dead for quite a while, so thoroughly shot up and mutilated that he could never have been identified except for his fingerprints. The discovery of the cadaver, by the way, furnished some good public relations for the Dutchman, however belatedly. It turned out that not long before he met his doom Sherman had come up with a million dollars worth of heroin from Romania only to suffer a summary rejection when he offered Schultz a piece of the profits in return for some help on the distribution end through the policy operation.

The story was that Schultz not only spurned the big score but also proceeded to take away some pieces Sherman had in the restaurant racket. When that happened, the guy began to talk about dipping into the numbers game to repair his fortunes—and that probably explains his sudden exit better than anything else; the Dutchman never could abide the idea of poachers in the Harlem preserve.

As far as any live Schultz suspects were concerned, the police on both sides of the water were rather anxious to talk to Lucky Luciano and Johnny Torrio after the mass slayings in Newark, but Luciano happened to be in Miami, taking the sun, and Torrio was in St. Petersburg looking into a deal for some of his Florida real estate holdings. A report that

Reprinted by permission of the New York *Daily News*

For all its super-secrecy, the sparsely attended Westchester funeral of Dutch Schultz did not escape the attention of at least one press photographer.

Luciano had made a quick trip to Newark the night before that grotesque scene was played out in the Palace was never confirmed. Abner (Longy) Zwillman did show up on November 1 for an audience with the Newark bluecoats, and he managed to satisfy all hands that while there may have been some suspected misdeeds in his speckled past he personally had no involvement in the last supper of Dutch Schultz & Co.

Down in Washington in mid-November, the FBI's J. Edgar Hoover took a dim view of the revelations in the Schultz papers, scratched together not just from the Dutchman's ledger sheets but even from the backs of envelopes, napkins and remnants of paper bags. Hoover was mildly amused by the incidental outlays in the juicy racket operation ("newspapers today, 21 cents." "cigarettes for bondsman, 15 cents," "carfare bondsman to Newark, 25 cents"), but the item of $827,253 taken into the house from September 2 to the week before the assassinations bothered him considerably.

"That means $1 million every two months was being paid to just one racketeer," Hoover said. "From that you can get some idea of the effect of racketeering on the community, and don't forget that all this money was collected when Dutch Schultz was supposed to be laying low, taking things easy, because of Federal prosecutions. His profits may have been much higher while he was 'in the clear.' It's a big business, run by big business methods. Schultz's accounts were obviously kept by an expert accountant. The entries were in perfect order, just like the books of a big corporation. And Schultz, who was notoriously close-fisted, knew where every penny went, even to buying the morning papers."

Hoover also took chilly note of the ice payments. "There are sizeable expenditures too, mostly for protection," he said.

"The identity of the persons to whom this was paid is known, and they are all under sharp scrutiny." Who were those persons? "Due to the fact that the Schultz murder case is under active investigation at the present time, I am reluctant to make the names of these persons public, but the spotlight of publicity will be turned upon them in due time."

Something happened to that spotlight, for the Dutchman's payoff roster never did suffer any wholesale exposure. Only one name would come out—Jimmy Hines—and that was years away.

"Success has ruined many a man."

—BENJAMIN FRANKLIN

CHAPTER X

HOW IT ALL BEGAN

THERE MUST HAVE BEEN A DEEP HURT SOMEWHERE IN Arthur Flegenheimer's earliest days, because while he could be quite garrulous about his young manhood in The Bronx, he never wanted to talk about the Yorkville time. Indeed, it wasn't until he turned up for his tax trial in Syracuse in the spring of 1935, sitting for his first (and last) full-dress press conference, that he conceded that he was really a product of the Manhattan area which around the turn of the century had begun to draw off huge numbers of German-Jewish immigrants from the Lower East Side ghetto. He said he was born at 1690 Second Avenue, off 89th Street, on August 6, 1902. He said his parents were not religious and had never taken him to a synagogue. He said his father was a glazier, then a baker for a while and then ran a livery stable. Where was he now? "He died when I was 14." The story before that was that Herman Flegenheimer had deserted his small brood in 1910, when Arthur was eight. What about that? "He just died, that's all," Schultz said, cutting off the subject.

Whenever it was, Emma Neu Flegenheimer moved out of Yorkville to the lower Bronx. Schultz went to Public School 12, where the principal was Dr. John F. (Jafsie) Condon, the man who in 1932 would toss the $50,000 ransom money for the Lindbergh baby over the wall in St. Raymond's Cemetery. Schultz said he stayed in PS 12 until the sixth grade, and liked it, especially the courses in history and composition, but had to quit at 14 to help support the family. "It was tough bucks them days," he said, and, perhaps mindful of all the money the U.S. was trying to pry from him at the time, like $92,000 and some change, he added, "It's tough bucks now." He said he sold papers and cut-rate two-cent "El"-to-subway transfers around the busy station at 149th Street and Third Avenue in the South Bronx's Hub, ran errands, worked as an office boy. "When I got a little older," he went on, "I worked at printing. I was a feeder and pressman. I worked in quite a few places. I worked at composition roofing, too, when I was 17." Would he go back to roofing if he beat the government's case and wanted to stay out of trouble? "I don't know," he said, smiling faintly over the silly question. Schultz passed over something else that happened in his 17th year—the first of the 13 arrests which would mark the career he ultimately chose over the more pedestrian occupations.

In December 1919, he was convicted of unlawful entry and sentenced to an indeterminate term in the Blackwell's Island Penitentiary. This old gray stone pile, put up over the East River in 1832 because the treacherous tides would make escape almost impossible, proved so uncongenial to young Arthur that he had to be transferred to Westhampton Prison Farms, near Goshen. The boy didn't care too much for that correctional institution either, so he broke out. He was recaptured within 15 hours and two more months were tagged on to the only prison sentence he would ever suffer. He did 15 months all together.

Apart from his arrest in the original tax case and again in Perth Amboy when he turned himself in four weeks before the Palace shoot-'em-up, Schultz's varied record included brief brushes with the law, under a splendid variety of names, for everything from such mundane items as disorderly conduct (1926 and 1928) to grand larceny (1921) to felonious assault (1924, 1930 and 1931) to assault and robbery (1929), robbery with a gun (1929), and Sullivan Law (1931) to homicide with a gun (1928). Asked about all this once, the glib Dutchman had an answer ready.

"That solves itself," he said. "Every time the cops started one of their supposed clean-ups and all, they'd send some cop over to wherever I was located and they'd charge me with anything. Then some A. & P. clerk would come and identify me for some stickup just to get their name in the papers, and next day I'd be turned out. That's how come I got a record."

Was it that simple?

No.

The tousle-haired Arthur, a pool shark and a kid with an eye for the easy dollar, glorying in a never-proven reputation as a tough guy, found kindred souls in one slum neighborhood after another as the struggling Emma Flegenheimer moved around The Bronx. Still a stripling, Arthur began to hang around the Bergen Social Club, home of the Bergen Gang, near the Yankee Stadium of the early Babe Ruth days. Somewhere along the way, Arthur fell in with a local hoodlum named Marcel Poffo whose substantial police record had endowed him with some note. Only a year or so Arthur's senior, Poffo made it all the way from simple exercises in burglary to post-graduate efforts in bank robberies before somebody dumped his bullet-and-knife-riddled body onto a lonely piece of real estate near the Westchester Country Club in Harrison in 1933. In the beginning, he served as Arthur's drill sergeant in basic training: boosting packages off delivery trucks, looting the neighborhood stores, breaking into apartments, sticking up dice games that wouldn't pay for protection. Little things like that. It was in this period that Arthur carelessly got caught cleaning out that Bronx flat. Between Blackwell's Island and Westhampton, he came back into the streets suitably hardened and deemed to be entitled to the new name of Dutch Schultz, supposedly borrowed from a much-feared brawler in the early days of the enemy Frog Hollow Gang.

Now, long out of his knickers, wearing a jaunty cap and chewing tobacco, Arthur also enjoyed an occasional glimpse at the more affluent citizens of the Dry Decade as they trooped into the Hub's Criterion Restaurant, operated by Billy Gibson, onetime manager of Gene Tunney and Benny Leonard, or into Legs Diamond's Bronx Theatrical Club across the way. It is altogether conceivable that these envious peeks into the higher social life of The Bronx suggested to the boy that there was money in beer and liquor even at a moment when the ruling fathers in Washington had declared all spirits null, void, evil, and against the law as well.

There is a famous retired detective in The Bronx, laden with honors, who knew L'il Arthur in those days and never ceased to wonder over his meteoric rise. This is Fred Schaedel, the big, good-natured cop who served as the human target the day the celebrated Francis (Two-Gun) Crowley earned his nickname. It happened in March 1931 when a brother-in-law of Crowley's invited Schaedel to a midtown office building to accept the surrender of the youthful desperado, wanted in a double murder in The Bronx. Crowley did show up, and he let the detective relieve him of his shooting iron. Then he changed his mind, drew a smaller model out of a shirt sleeve, sprayed Schaedel with bullets in the pelvis, bladder and thigh, and escaped. Even while the detective was still recuperating, Crowley was trapped in a West Side rooming house on May 7 in a Hollywood-style shootout with 150 cops, finally taken by Detective Johnny Broderick, and put to death in the electric chair at Sing Sing eight months later. So much for that. The Dutch Schultz that Schaedel knew had his moments of bad temper but could never be equated with a gun-crazed animal like Francis Crowley.

Schaedel remembers Schultz in the old Morrisania district as one of the street-corner toughs in a gang which also included the handsome Vincent Coll and a boy named Thomas (Fatty) Walsh, who also would go on to worse things. Schaedel lived in the same neighborhood and occasionally had to fight his way past those guys, especially when he was escorting his kid sister home from her piano lessons. Schultz's later descriptions of all his earnest labors as a boy always amused the cop, although he did recall that a roofer in the neighborhood had at times succeeded in getting Arthur and some of his playmates to work for him. The Flegenheimers were in such dire straits then that Arthur's mother was functioning as the janitor of a tenement; in her time she had also taken in washing to feed the children. and while Arthur always said his family was not religious, people in that building recalled a familiar sight: little Emma Flegenheimer buying kosher chickens for the traditional Friday family dinner.

Somewhere in this period our hero, a bare 19 and already in police hands three times, on his burglary conviction and in a larceny case under the name of Charles Harmon and an assault case in his own name, figured in an episode so remarkable that it would be aired in the United States Senate 18 years later.

Arthur Flegenheimer, of all people, became a Deputy Sheriff in The Bronx, appointed by Edward J. Flynn, then Sheriff of that borough but destined for much larger things. Schultz was appointed in July 1925 and held his brass potsy until he made the mistake of getting picked up in a raid on Jack Diamond's Bronx club after a shooting there in the winter of 1926. That arrest made Schultz an ex-Deputy Sheriff, but it did not inconvenience him in any other way.

Flynn, in time Boss of The Bronx and the single most influential Democratic machine leader in the nation, helped Franklin Delano Roosevelt along the path to the White House and in 1943 Mr. Roosevelt returned the favor by naming him his Ambassador to Australia. It was then that the matter of Deputy Sheriff Arthur Flegenheimer came up again, figuring rather prominently in the Senate Foreign Relations Committee's hearings on the nomination.

Flynn, in his defense, said that when he named that Flegenheimer fellow, among "several hundred" simultaneous appointments, he did not know the man was something less than an adornment in the Borough of Universities. In his rebuttal when the thing was initially raised by Tom Dewey in his 1938 race for District Attorney, Flynn had made the additional point that law enforcement in The Bronx was so stern and relentless that once a police ax squad demolished his headquarters early in the bootlegging game "Schultz never operated in our county." This was grievously in error, of course, since the Dutchman continued to run his beer business from The Bronx until the very day that Repeal knocked him out. In any case, with his qualifications under challenge on issues beyond the matter of that badge for the budding gangster in his bailiwick, Ed Flynn withdrew his name rather than let the nomination face the test of a floor fight and a certain close vote.

Why would Arthur Flegenheimer want to be an unpaid Deputy Sheriff, among his other aspirations? For the same reason that Lulu Rosenkrantz took the trouble to pick up a badge in New Jersey years later when the now grown-up mobsters had to spend some time over there. The badge gave a man the right to carry a gun without getting arrested for it.

Somewhere in the period in his life when, with Ed Flynn's help, he enlisted on the side of the law, Arthur did engage in an occupation which while only faintly illegal never was included in the employment dossier he furnished for the press. He was a sometime helper on the wagons of the brothers Otto and Jake Gass, who had a small trucking business until Prohibition taught them that there was more money in carrying beer than almost anything else. Similarly, a friend of Arthur's named Joey Noe (pronounced Noy), whose father was a beer pipe cleaner, was finding out that there was more money in the barrel than in the cleaning of the pipes. The brew cost $3 or $4 a keg to make then, went to the illicit distributors for $8 or $9 and brought $18 or $19 in the speakeasies. For both Joey and Arthur, these simple economics had considerable appeal. Joey made the first move: he set up a hole-in-the-wall speakeasy of his own in a Brook Avenue tenement, christened it the Hub Social Club, and eventually took Arthur in with him. This was in 1928, and it was the beginning of a business partnership that would be sundered only by enemy guns.

Joey and Arthur, both in their mid-twenties, set up a series of other watering places with their Brook Avenue profits and it took them no time at all to decide that they might as well furnish the beer for their rivals as well. All this required was three old trucks and a connection with a brewer named Frankie Dunn in Union City, New Jersey—and some muscle.

It was just like the movies of the time. Somebody came in, tilted his fedora back on his head, ordered a beer, licked his lips, made a face, said something about the brew being unfit for human consumption, asked where the slop was coming from, and then said, "Well, from now on ya gonna buy it from us." After that, you bought it from "us" or "us" came back with some helpers and wrecked your joint, never failing to open up all the taps in the process.

Joey and Arthur, enormously persuasive, had to do nothing more than dispose of some competing beer-runners to set up what amounted to a monopoly in the central portion of the borough, fanning out from their own flagship operations in the Mott Haven section.

As in any enterprise nourished by the profit motive, of course, the two chums did run into some spoilsports, notably a pair of brothers named John and Joe Rock who had established a foothold in The Bronx while Joey and Arthur were still standing around on street corners and bothering the nicer people, like Fred Schaedel. John Rock stepped aside with a decent show of early resistance but Joe, made of sterner Irish stuff, refused to withdraw from the beer business. He paid a very high price: he was kidnapped one night, beaten, hung by the thumbs on a meat hook and then blindfolded with a strip of gauze which, so the story goes, had been dipped into a mixture containing the drippings from a gonorrhea infection. Whatever the potion was, Joe Rock came out of it a blind man—and even at that there was a story that the family had to ante up a $35,000 ransom to get back what was left of him.

This lesson was not lost on the remnants of the bootlegging fraternity. It hardly could have been, for by this time Joey and Arthur had some imposing helpmates around them. Bo Weinberg was one of their persuaders. Vincent Coll and his kid brother, Peter, were in the organization. Larry Carney, a very tough customer and an early Schultz loyalist, was on hand, along with Fatty Walsh, who later became an Arnold Rothstein bodyguard and died under a hail of bullets in a Coral Gables card game. Joey Rao, just coming up in the rackets and due to stake out East Harlem for himself, handled occasional strong-arm assignments. So did Edward (Fats) McCarthy, also known as Edward Popke and John the Polack, the much-vaunted trigger man who in time would split away to the rebel Coll force and later still pick up such extraordinary credits—unconfirmed, of course—as the assassinations both of Legs Diamond and of Mr. Coll himself. Troops of the McCarthy caliber made the Bronx combination a force to be reckoned with at the outset. You could take over a South American government with a band like that.

The operation grew so fast, dealing the hard stuff as well as beer, that the ferried spirits from Jersey, too slow, had to be supplemented by deals with Frenchy Dillon and Jay Culhane, who had brewery operations on both sides of the river. Now an expanded fleet began to rumble up the West Side and over the bridges into The Bronx or ride the cobblestones of upper Broadway down from Yonkers, generally traveling at night to some 17 drops and hardly ever disturbed by the federal liquor snoops, which tells you something about that piece of hypocritical frippery called Prohibition.

One of the Noe-Schultz drops, an underground affair called "The Tins," was so elaborate it was practically a showplace. Near the Mott Haven railroad yards, it had disappearing elevators which took empty beer trucks down into a huge loading area and sent them up fully packed and on their way not only to Bronx outlets but eventually moving as well into Manhattan's upper West Side and Washington Heights and down into Yorkville and Harlem. The modest little wholesale operation was now a big business. As it grew, the young entrepreneurs also found themselves buying beer from such gentlemen as Owney Madden and William V. (Big Bill) Dwyer; they were on the big time.

By this time, having outgrown the Brook Avenue GHQ, Noe and Schultz moved into an office building on East 149th Street and set themselves up a command post befitting both their broadened stature and its attendant dangers. The inner walls of their office were lined with steel and the front door was similarly bullet-proofed. To visit with the owners, you had to get past a character called Blind Sam who wasn't blind at all. He sat behind a ten-inch peephole and looked you over, and if you got past him you encountered two other guys with rifles at the ready.

So nobody was foolish enough to bother the Bronx playmates while they worked out of that imitation Fort Knox—nobody, that is, but the police. Fred Schaedel, who went way back with Joey Noe and had been confirmed with him in the same Catholic church, recalls that the ax raid which chased that operation off 149th Street, the bust that Boss Flynn had mentioned, turned up some rather interesting furnishings: a 12-gauge shotgun, a loaded magazine for a Thompson submachine gun, two brand new .38s, two loaded and well-used .45s equipped to carry silencers, and perhaps 2,000 rounds of ammo, like enough to start a small war. The owners, of course, were not on the premises when the law dropped in, wrecked the joint, and went away shaking its collective head. Joey and Arthur had come a long way from the original two-bit gin mill where to see the proprietors you just went up to the rough oak bar and stated your business and a gentleman with a bulge under his left shoulder came out and delivered you into a creepy back room office.

This period was not without its humor, by the way. Former General Sessions Judge Edward J. Breslin, who was an Assistant District Attorney in The Bronx at the time, recalled an arrest of the Dutchman that might have been open to question. It seems that our hero sampled too much of his own bootleg brand in a Third Avenue speakeasy one day and, feeling the need of some fresh air, staggered out to his Packard touring sedan, curled up in the back seat and went to sleep after taking the precaution of wrapping a fist securely around a heavy wad of bills reposing in his left pants pocket. A short time later, Schultz was in the Morrisania station house when Breslin, who knew him, came in on some business.

"What are you in for this time, Dutch?" Breslin asked.

"Me?" came the reply. "Disorderly conduct or something, but they should have booked the bum who brought me in instead."

Breslin asked why.

"I was sleepin' in my car when I felt some guy yankin' on my pocket, tryin' to get my roll, and it was this cop and when I wake up and grab his hand he arrests me."

The Dutchman beat that pinch, but it was one of the last of the lighter moments for him. Things were about to take a grim turn.

On the night of October 15, 1928, Arthur and Joey Noe, all but inseparable, dropped into the Swanee Club under the famous Apollo Theater on West 125th Street, Harlem's main drag. Not too many years back, Schultz was just a penny-ante thief and Noe was a kid helping his father clean beer pipes.

Now they were a pair of very prosperous dealers in the product that the Reverend Billy Sunday liked to call "Hell's best friend" and they were taking time out to sample some of the opposition's stuff. They had some business downtown, but they had hours to spare and there weren't many places in New York more congenial than the Swanee.

The Harlem watering spot, also known as Joe Ward's Uptown Club, played to the more affluent blacks as well as the white swells from downtown, 400 at a time. Its adornments included long-stemmed hostesses and twelve (12) chorus girls who didn't wear too much and stood out nicely under a rotating bank of colored lights. The decor featured a soft, pleasant Southern motif, with cardboard riverboats moving along a track on the wall and cotton fields for a backdrop. And the club had the best in bands and headline acts like the beautiful Evelyn Nesbit, the girl whose love had prompted millionaire Harry K. Thaw to go and kill the architect Stanford White (Evelyn, you remember, said Mr. White violated her when she was very young) back in 1906. Miss Nesbit had all kinds of songs, including novelty numbers. On a given night, you might walk in and hear her singing something like *When the banana skins are falling, I'll come sliding back to you.*

And that wasn't all. The Swanee had an even more important lure for men who lived dangerously. It was neutral ground, where no man would dream of firing a gun in anger. The rule was that if you came in and encountered a rival mobster you had one drink and got the hell out of there—unless the other guy elected to leave first. In a word, a safe haven—so safe, indeed, that it was also a watering spot for off-duty cops. It was one of the Dutchman's favorite joints and on this night he tarried until the hours after dawn, leaving only when Noe insisted, rather firmly, that they had to go downtown. Noe, only an inch taller but much tougher, was possibly the only man Schultz ever took an order from, the one guy who could say "That's enough" when he took one too many, and the one guy who could shut him up when he started blabbing in the late hours. There were two *Daily Mirror* reporters in the Swanee and when he was leaving, in high spirits, Schultz offered them a lift downtown in a Ford sedan he had outside. The reporters were dropped on Fifth Avenue where the Plaza looks out on the Pulitzer Fountain, the one in which F. Scott Fitzgerald had taken his much-headlined dip in that same live-it-up decade of the Twenties. "Okay, fellas, you can walk to your creepy office," Schultz said; "Joey and I got some business to attend to."

A short time later, toward 7:00 A.M., a fusillade of gunshots sounded in West 54th Street, off Sixth Avenue, and brought tenants of the Hotel Harding and other residential buildings on the street rushing to their windows to see a blue Cadillac speeding erratically away, going East. They saw the Caddy hit a parked car and keep going and when they leaned out they spotted a man stretched on the sidewalk in front of the Chateau Madrid. The man was Joey Noe. He was wearing a bullet-proof vest but he had been shot in the right breast, lower spine and left hand and still managed to return the fire, shooting with both hands. On his person, the arriving police found a spanking new brass badge denoting that like his friend Arthur Flegenheimer before him he had recently been made a Deputy Sheriff of The Bronx (not by Ed Flynn, no longer Sheriff then).

Within the hour, a blue Cadillac with a missing door was found on the Lower East Side with the shot-up body of Louis Weinberg, alias Jacob Kaufman, alias Benjamin Greenberg, reposing in the back seat. The police quickly established that this was the gentleman who had traded all that gunfire with Dutch Schultz's partner. Noe himself didn't help, naturally. In Roosevelt Hospital, desperately wounded but facing a homicide charge if he lived, he would only say that he was parking his car when the Caddy drove up and two guys started shooting at him, so he had to get out his irons. Did he know his assailant? "I'll take care of it myself," he said. But that wasn't in the cards either. Removed to the Bellevue Hospital prison ward after a while, Noe wasted away to 90 pounds and died on November 21.

There is no question that Schultz was crushed. Noe was the closest intimate of all his days. He might have drawn some inspiration from a hoodlum like Marcel Poffo, but Noe, who always called him Arthur, as when they were kids on the street corner without a care in the world, put him on the golden highway. When Noe was with him, he could give the armed guard a night off, and Noe, for that matter, was the only one he ever took along when he went to see his mother.

So much for that. Where was the Dutchman when the lead started to fly? He never said anything about having been with his partner a few minutes earlier. He told Acting Police Inspector Joseph A. Donovan that Joey was going to Jersey to handle a beer transaction and that when he heard of the shooting he went right over there himself "because the business had to go on." Schultz was a little more candid with a detective friend. He told him that Noe had gone to the Chateau Madrid with thousands of dollars to pay off on a big beer deal. Another version was that Noe actually was on an errand to collect some money Legs Diamond owed the Bronx boys.

Dixie Davis lent some support to the latter theory years later, adding some characteristic Davis flourishes. He said

New York *Post,* Samuel Mellor

In this tenement at 543 Brook Avenue, Schultz launched himself on the road to his early eminence as Beer Baron of The Bronx. The Dutchman's first speakeasy, with Joey Noe as the senior partner, was in the store on the left, reduced to selling candy and cigars by the time this photo was made in 1938, five years after Repeal.

that Noe had indeed gone downtown to straighten out some problem with Diamond and that Schultz was in Big Bill Dwyer's office on the street when the cannons went off. Davis said the Dutchman leaped to a balcony, spotted two men shooting at Noe, drew his .38 and killed one while the other, wounded, leaped into the Caddy and got away. The trouble with that story—and there was trouble with so many of the counselor's stories—was that no other cadaver ever turned up on the street.

The Diamond angle may have had some validity, however. The police believed that the freewheeling Legs, who employed Arthur Flegenheimer in his own mob once, briefly, and then found himself pushed out of The Bronx by the Noe-Schultz combination, set up the ambush outside the Chateau Madrid in the hopes of disposing of both of his old buddies in one night. And when Diamond met his own doom three years later, ending a tightwire career in which he had absorbed no less than 14 bullets and at least one dose of birdshot in four other attempts on his life dating back to 1924, the murder was charged to the Dutchman's open account in the matter of Joey Noe.

Fresh off an acquittal that afternoon in a kidnapping-torture case, Diamond was trailed to a cheap Albany rooming house and killed after a long night of celebration first with his ever-loyal wife, Alice and then with his real love, Kiki Roberts of The Follies, the former Marion Strasmick. The general consensus was that the hand that held the gun and poured three bullets into the gangster's whisky-soaked brain belonged to Fats McCarthy but Davis chalked it up for Bo Weinberg when he got around to talking in 1939. Maybe it was Weinberg but the Davis version had to be taken with a pinch of salt because in his more talkative years the counselor developed a habit of crediting the lovable Bo with almost any murder you might ask about, or even if you didn't ask.

The departure of Joey Noe, in any case, held out some splendid consolation for the bereaved Dutch Schultz.

He inherited the business and went on to bigger and better things.

"Prohibition was the greatest curse the country ever saw. For the first time it changed the saying that crime doesn't pay."

—CHARLES B. MCLAUGHLIN, District Attorney of The Bronx, 1933.

CHAPTER XI

THE HIGH LIFE

ARTHUR FLEGENHEIMER REALLY BEGAN TO FLY ONCE THE restraining hand of Joey Noe was lifted from his shoulders. The bootleg operation flourished handsomely, knowing no bounds as the government all but gave up on any pretext of enforcing the Prohibition law, and the Dutchman appeared to be content to confine himself to the drinking needs of the populace and to stay away from the more tawdry rackets. In the Swanee Club one night, so expansive on $10 champagne that he was fumbling with some familiar quotes from Willie Shakespeare, a reporter dared to ask him whether he had ever done any business with such notables as Waxey Gordon and Chink Sherman, who were patrons of the same Harlem establishment.

Schultz turned on his most serious expression.

"I may do a lot of lousy things," he said, "but I'll never make a living off women or narcotics."

He was telling the truth. In his time he did a lot of business with Polly Adler, the most conspicuous of the New York madams, but it was strictly as a paying customer. It had never occurred to him to declare himself in as a partner of Polly's, and he was evidently always content to let others feed off the organized traffic in flesh. This was true of the drug traffic as well. He never had a piece of that.

For all his affluence, Schultz did not move beyond his comparatively minor celebrity as Beer Baron of The Bronx until 1931. It was then that he went on the front pages to stay. The date was January 24. The place was the Club Abbey, on the first floor of the Hotel Harding on West 54th Street, and the party of the other part was Chink Sherman. Whatever bad feelings may have existed between the warring factions, it appeared that this particular pre-dawn engagement on an idle night out was fought over nothing more consequential than a girl or two.

Schultz came in first, with Marty Krompier and Larry Carney and two women, and took a table in the corner reserved for special guests, where Rene Bonnie, an entertainer in the place, joined the party. Little Marty was waltzing Miss Bonnie around the dance floor, his head nestled comfortably against her bosom, when Mr. Sherman arrived with a small party. In some manner, no clearer than in any other night club brawl, then or now, an unpleasantness arose between Mr. Krompier's dancing partner and a mysterious Lorraine in the Sherman entourage and presently there was a confrontation at the Schultz table. With the attention of no less than 80 customers drawn to the undignified display of loud and abusive language, all reason departed in very short order.

Somebody thoughtfully doused the lights, of course, before the big action started. When they came on again over the demolished special corner, Messrs. Schultz, Krompier and Carney were gone and the unfortunate Sherman was on the floor being ministered to by Mavis King, immediately identified by the tabloids as the prettiest cigarette girl in New York. The racketeer's opening line to her was "Girlie, they got me. I'm dying." This was an understandable over-statement.

When Miss King delivered the fallen gladiator to Polyclinic Hospital, the inventory drawn up by a hastily summoned army of medical sleuths showed only that he had been shot three times (nose, chest and shooting arm), slashed on the face ten times or so with the jagged end of a beer bottle, banged over the head with a table leg and also touched up here and there with a heavy ornamental ash tray.

While the 80 Abbey witnesses, to the last guy and the last doll, could not furnish any precise information on the identity of the combatants, the police were able to piece together the story of the action. The emerging consensus was that the broken-nosed guy in the cheap suit, Mr. Schultz, had been taken out rather early by a bullet or two and that the short one, Mr. Krompier, assisted by one of the girl troopers in the company, had inflicted most of the damage on the enemy commander, Mr. Sherman. The communiqué from the thickly carpeted battlefield did concede, however, that the wafer-thin character on the Schultz side, Mr. Carney, had contributed a decent share of the defensive blows himself for all his evident frailty, and this figured. Larry Carney had been a faithful servitor of the Dutchman since the day, long ago, when he fell a victim of tuberculosis—mind you, TB itself was a killer then—and found himself shipped off to the clean air of Saranac in the Adirondacks, all expenses paid, while the scourge was contained.

In the matter of apprehending the ne'er-do-wells who would resort to so much violence over a little misunderstanding, the primary sufferer in the Abbey encounter proved no more helpful than all those nearsighted witnesses. When Sherman was asked who-dun-it, he delivered himself of a statement which had long since become a standard around such underworld capitals as New York and Chicago. "If I knew them," said the Chink, "I could deal with them myself."

This battered cliché proved doubly frustrating to the police brass when it turned out that one of their very own sleuths, James J. Walsh, a figure of some note around Broadway because the unsportsmanlike Arnold Rothstein once creased him with a bullet for intruding on a sociable dice game in the Rothstein residence, happened to have been in the Abbey with the anti-Sherman force and had neglected to mention it to his superiors.

In his departmental trial later, Detective Walsh explained that he had encountered the Dutchman in the after-hours club by pure chance. "When Schultz saw me in there," Walsh testified, "he said, 'Hello, boss.' I asked Schultz if he had ever heard why his partner Joe Noe was shot, and why Noe and Louis Weinberg were shooting at each other three years ago. Schultz said he had never heard." Beyond this, the detective satisfied everybody that he himself had left the Abbey before the blood began to flow.

When the usual call went out for a roundup of all known hoodlums to get to the bottom of the unseemly display, a measure of the times came in a little exchange between reporters and the police involving the oft-arrested Larry Fay, whose name came up as an ex-partner in the fallen Sherman's Club Rendezvous. Fay also was in the Abbey on the lively night in question but when Lieutenant Walter Hourigan was asked whether he was going to submit a question or two to him, his answer was the very model of candor: "No. Talking to that guy is like talking to a wall."

And how about Arthur Flegenheimer? Well, that fellow

would have to be taxed with an assault charge, or even something worse if Mr. Sherman, a mere 32 but a gambler of sorts and a dealer in junk and murder as well, then under indictment for a 1928 gang killing way off the Broadway beat in Boston, fooled the doctors and succumbed to his multiple wounds. So the Lieutenant sure did want to talk to Arthur Flegenheimer.

Schultz, alas, did not respond to the open police solicitation. There was a little flurry on February 8 when the gendarmes swooped down on a modest Bronx apartment where he was supposed to be holed up. He was not there but a birdlike blonde of 22, Jean McCarthy, was flushed out of bed while a search of the premises turned up a bloodstained jacket, two loaded sawed-off shotguns, and a .38-caliber pistol. Could that jacket belong to Arthur Flegenheimer? Well, it had no labels with his name on it and the sleepy Mrs. McCarthy said she did not know anybody by that name. The detectives on the mission, William Cassidy and James Kissane, insisted that she did so know Flegenheimer, or Schultz, or what have you, because she happened to be the legally wedded wife of Fats McCarthy, still on the Dutchman's payroll then.

Apart from this episode, the usual search of the usual haunts also failed to turn up the wounded Beer Baron, although the man was yet to demonstrate the full extent of his remarkable talent for staying outside the law's long arm when he did not wish to have any traffic with the law.

It turned out that the Dutchman, dented by one Sherman slug while his bullet-proof vest deflected two others which might well have killed him, had undergone a leisurely period of tender care and recuperation and then, on April 4, presented himself at the West 47th Street Precinct. The barrister with him put the question to the desk lieutenant: "Did somebody want to talk to Mr. Flegenheimer?" Of course, and in no time at all a whole array of witnesses—including Chink Sherman, patched together like new—were summoned to the venerable old Broadway station house to confront the suspect. You can guess what happened if you have ever sampled the offerings of the silver screen, then or now: nobody recognized the Beer Baron, even with that distinctively twisted nose of his, as having been among those present in the Abbey on that unfortunate night in January. Why, Chink Sherman himself didn't recognize the guy. Needless to say, nobody was ever going to recognize Marty Krompier or Larry Carney either.

That was the end of it, except that nine more days elapsed before the police told anybody about it. This was most disturbing to the great horde of newspapers (only eight) then reporting the never-dull New York scene, but Lieutenant Hourigan, backed by by Assistant Chief Inspector John J. Sullivan, head of the detective force, had an explanation all ready. The Lieutenant said he had told Schultz on April 4 that "we don't expect to build you up into a hero by giving you a lot of publicity." The Inspector added that the Dutchman, even though he forswore any knowledge of any fight in the Abbey, ever, had been advised to watch his step in the future because the police were going to keep a sharper eye, or perhaps even eyes, on him from that moment on.

In fairness to Mr. Sherman a footnote is imperative here for those who would think ill of him for carrying anything so dangerous as the gun he had pinked Dutch Schultz with: Chink Sherman was a Deputy Sheriff in far-off Saratoga County, upstate. He had a right to arm himself against the naughtier elements in the society of his time.

For Mr. Flegenheimer, l'affaire Abbey, however perilous,

would pale by comparison with a traumatic experience he was to suffer on the splendidly moonlit night of June 18 in that same fun-filled year. This one began when two of the then more earnest sleuths on the rolls of New York's finest, Detectives Stephen DiRosa and Julius Salke, stationed themselves on a bench across the street from the plush building at 1212 Fifth Avenue in Manhattan in response to a call from a mysterious woman tipster. The woman had said that a new tenant bearing the name of Russell Jones, occupying a ninth-floor apartment ($2,500 a year, sort of high then) with a picture-postcard view of Central Park, really was Arthur Flegenheimer.

There seemed to be inordinately heavy traffic into the building that night, male and female, and judicious inquiry established that practically everybody was going to the apartment of Mr. Jones. Sensing an underworld summit of some kind, the detectives trained a pair of field glasses on the living room window of the four-room flat and settled back. Unbeknownst to them, somebody up there had binoculars pointed their way, possibly because the Dutchman was so squeamish at the time about being the Number One man on Vincent Coll's current drop-dead list.

In time, like 6:10 A.M., four men emerged from the building, crossed the avenue, and approached the bench.

"Who are you guys and whaddya doin' here?" one of them said, advancing to within ten feet.

"We are the law," Steve DiRosa replied, drawing his police special, "put up your hands."

The first man thereupon came up with a popgun of his own and the second reached for his belt, so DiRosa, one of the better marksmen in the department, let three shots go. One caught the pistol-wielder in the abdomen and one in the left wrist, the third going wild. As the wounded man fell to the pavement, the stocky one alongside him started running toward 101st Street and the other two vaulted the low stone wall into the park and disappeared into the balmy night.

The man who ran down the avenue, discarding a .38 Colt as Julius Salke pursued him, was Mr. Jones—or Arthur Flegenheimer. He came to an abrupt stop and put his hands up after the detective squeezed off one shot that whistled by him. Salke said that when he caught up, Schultz said to him, "Listen I've got a large sum of money. Take it and let me run. I'm having a lot of trouble. I'm on the edge. I'm being followed by mobsters. They want to give me the works. I don't fight cops." Salke brought the Dutchman back to DiRosa and asked him to identify the party who was on the ground, screaming in agony. Schultz refused.

"You're not going to leave your friend in this predicament," the detective said. "He's gonna die. Tell us who he is."

"It's Danny," Schultz replied, choking up. "Poor Danny Iamascia."

Poor Danny Iamascia was a long-time buddy and occasional bodyguard of the Dutchman's and a hoodlum of more than passing notice in the community. The detectives knew the name if not the face.

DiRosa stopped a cab for the hop-skip-and-jump to Mt. Sinai Hospital, three blocks up the avenue, and hauled the blood-drenched Iamascia into it, stretching him out on the floor, while Salke got in with his captive.

Somewhere along the brief way, Schultz tried to buy off both cops, according to DiRosa. "He said he was a rich man," the detective reported, "and if we would give him a break he would give us fifty grand and a house in Westchester apiece."

Once Iamascia was deposited in the hospital, the Beer

Baron was taken a little further east, to the 104th Street station house. There, facing twin charges of felonious assault and violation of Mr. Sullivan's law, he asked for a sedative to calm his frayed nerves and then, according to DiRosa again, some further conversation about the coin of the realm took place in the back room. "Why don't you fellows give me a break?" the detective quoted the prisoner. "I've got plenty of money you fellows could use, and a good home for each of you. After all, fifty grand is a lot of money. Why don't you take it and give me a break?"

The Dutchman wasn't just boasting, it turned out. The necessary search of his person turned up an even $18,645, mostly in $500 and $100 notes, and a little black book recording collections of $52,000 in the preceding eleven days. The detectives were somehow not stirred by all that evidence of prosperity.

Later in the police lineup, an educational entertainment that had to be discarded once the Supreme Court ordained in the Sixties that you just couldn't go throwing nasty questions at people who didn't happen to have their legal counsel right at hand, Schultz proved much less talkative.

"What was the name of the man shot with you this morning?" asked Assistant Chief Inspector Sullivan, an acquaintance from the Abbey frolic.

"No man was with me," the Dutchman replied. "I wasn't with anybody."

Wouldn't he admit that he knew Danny Iamascia?

No.

Wouldn't he admit that he threw a revolver (held aloft by the Inspector) into the gutter when Detective Salke was pursuing him?

No.

Did he know anything about the two loaded automatics found afterwards in the Fifth Avenue apartment?

No.

This sort of thing left the Inspector positively distraught. "It is a sad commentary on the detectives of the upper part of this city," he said for the benefit of the press and the assembled sleuths in the Lineup Room, "that this bum was allowed to roam around for so long with this gun."

The next stop was Magistrates' Court in Harlem and there the Dutchman, a mere 25 but now driven to the barricades again to stand off the state's ninth challenge to his personal honor in 12 years, heard himself described in somewhat conflicting ways. Attorney Gilbert S. Rosenthal respectfully submitted (it's the only way in the courts) that his client was "a much-persecuted man and a victim of a police pickup." Detective Salke disagreed. He insisted that the accused was "a notorious criminal and one of the worst young men in the city."

Bail was set at $15,000 on each count and furnished with blinding speed, but the prisoner was carted off to "The Flats," a sanctuary reserved for first offenders and very special guests on the fifth floor of the ancient Tombs Prison, when the District Attorney insisted that he was entitled to some time to investigate the source of those fast bonds. Once that was out of the way and Schultz emerged into the daylight again, he spoke as follows: "I wouldn't stay in that jail another night if they gave me the place. Who do they think I am? Some poor punk? Well, I'm not. I'm a big shot. I've got some mighty important business that needs my attention."

An immediate order of business, whatever else happened to be pressing upon him, was the matter of ordering a suitable wreath for Danny Iamascia, who had succumbed to his wounds the day after the shootout and was destined for one of the more classic underworld farewells. The Dutchman, a man of conservative tastes in dress and everything else, selected a diamond-shaped bouquet of white roses and a white stuffed pigeon nestled in the middle of a cross bearing the word "Sympathy" across the bottom. Ciro Terranova, the Artichoke King, so called because he had thought to corner the market in that particular vegetable some years earlier, made the Dutchman look like a struggling beer salesman by comparison. His floral offering came in the form of a gate 15 feet high and fashioned of lilies, roses and carnations. The great variety of other scented tributes, bearing such legends as "Dear Pal," "From the Boys," "From Your Best Pal," and "Why Did It Have to be You, Danny?" filled 35 cars in the cortege to St. Raymond's Cemetery, where Iamascia, strangely, had bought himself a whole stack of plots on the very day preceding his death. One wreath, incidentally, simply said, "6:10 A.M."—the very moment that Steve DiRosa's quick trigger went off. The services at Our Lady of Carmel Church in The Bronx drew thousands and it took 125 cars to carry the mourners accompanying the body to St. Raymond's, where a low mass was performed because the Roman Catholic Archdiocese had ruled against a high requiem.

Young Danny was laid out in a coffin listed at $10,000 and stored away in a mausoleum advertised as a $25,000 item. Those numbers, coupled with the high incidentals, put his leave-taking in a rather heady class. Joe (The Baker) Catania, consigned to the spot on the preceding February 3 in some Mafia unpleasantness, had enjoyed a $40,000 funeral. And that wasn't embarrassingly far behind the $52,000 splash for Frankie Yale (Uale), a 1928 rubout victim who would be remembered less for his assorted misdeeds than for the fact that two card-carrying widows, not one, showed up at the graveside. Iamascia had the more conventional one wife.

If you wonder why the 30-year-old Danny merited such an outpouring of grief and money (oh, they just don't have funerals like that in that broken-down town any more), his varied career had included services for both Terranova and Schultz, among other gangland luminaries, and had earned him a generously mixed bag of ten arrests between 1918 and 1924. Thus Danny was not without honor in his set. And beyond his more pedestrian adventures in crime Danny had earned considerable renown as one of the trio of professionals who had carried out a most delicate mission in 1929 when seven bandits invaded the Roman Gardens Restaurant in The Bronx and stuck up a jam-packed testimonial for Magistrate Albert H. Vitale, who had friends in all walks of life. The invaders came away with $2,000 in cash, $3,000 in jewelry, and the service revolver of Detective Arthur C. Johnson, another guest. Iamascia and, yes, the aforementioned Catania and another handy fellow named John Savino, alias Zacci, all in soup and fish themselves to honor the Honorable Vitale, were delegated to go downtown and get back what those brash bandits had carried off—and they did, quick like anything.

The intriguing matter of the Fifth Avenue gun duel would occupy much space in the press for a couple of months after the interment of the only casualty. Dutch Schultz, giving his occupation as "roofer" for his court pedigree in this case, was indicted on assorted counts carrying a possible 20 years behind bars. When he was arraigned, the state said it would prove that the accused had admitted to the police that he left the regal comfort of his apartment that morning in June and headed for the park bench with his trio of helpers because "he thought the two detectives were 'mobsters' and he had come down to 'give 'em the works.' "

There seemed to be some substance in that notion. No less than five murders had been chalked up in a flurry of the Schultz-Coll war (the next chapter in this serial of Old New York) in the week before the shootout, so it figured that the Dutchman might well have felt somewhat nervous at the time. Perhaps, but it didn't serve to button up the case in the ensuing trial, held in a General Sessions courtroom ringed by 40 extra detectives because there were rumors abroad that somebody, maybe somebody like Vincent Coll, would rather see the defendant dead than stashed away in anything so secure as a prison.

Schultz beat the assault charges rather handily, his peers deciding in 5 hours and 15 minutes that there was no evidence that he had actually waved his own pea shooter at the two detectives. The state thereupon conceded that there wouldn't be any point in going before another jury with the remaining Sullivan Law count. Why? The man on trial was able to produce a license for the very kind of automatic that had clattered to the pavement the morning Julius Salke chased him down Manhattan's most antiseptic street. It seems that the former Deputy Sheriff of The Bronx had picked up the permit through the simple device of persuading a Suffolk County judge, George W. Furman, that he was an honest toiler in the employ of an emporium called the Belle Terrace Club in Port Jefferson, Long Island, and that his assorted responsibilities included such a perilous chore as transporting large sums of money for the establishment's owners.

The Dutchman did have to suffer a small embarrassment while he was on trial, however. Leaving the steamy, unsanitary old Criminal Courts Building after one session, he ran into trouble just because a couple of snoops on the outside detail, Detectives John J. Quinn and John J. Duffy, thought they spotted a shotgun nestling under some wrapping paper on the floor of the shiny Lincoln sedan Schultz and constant companion Marty Krompier were about to board for the short journey uptown. Well, it was a shotgun, a single-barreled affair, and it had five shells in it, and it was in splendid working order, so the cops hustled the much-harassed Beer Baron over to the nearest station house.

Much more resplendent than usual in a soft blue summer suit and shirt to match, topped off by the inevitable gray fedora, the Dutchman protested with some vehemence. "What the hell is this? Another frameup? I never saw that gun before." Sure enough, the State of New York came up short versus Arthur Flegenheimer once again.

In the first place, Schultz insisted that the big Lincoln, conveniently armored with shatterproof windows half an inch thick, was a borrowed vehicle and so the blowgun must have belonged to two other guys. In the second and third places, learned counsel, named David Goldstein, cited an 1897 statute which held that it was not unlawful to possess a shotgun on the streets of New York unless felonious intent could be shown and an 1898 statute which held that a man had to have a blunderbuss in his actual possession—in his hot little hands, say, or somewhere on his person—to be incarcerated for same. So the charge was dropped just as the Dutchman was recording his triumph in the larger case. This gave him two fresh wins over the law in but three days and pushed his string to ten in a row over The People in the twelve eventful years since some overzealous cop had caught him pilfering that apartment in The Bronx. It was a Won and

New York *Post*

Jack (Legs) Diamond could not be counted among the Dutchman's warmer friends and may have had a hand in the slaying of Schultz's bootlegging partner, Joey Noe.

New York *Post*

Dutch Schultz (seated) is questioned by Assistant District Attorney Saul Price after the Fifth Avenue shootout with Detectives Stephen DiRosa and Julius Salke (standing, left and right) which cost the life of one of the hoodlum prince's favorite lieutenants, Danny Iamascia. The Dutchman fled the scene after DiRosa shot Iamascia but gave up meekly when Salke outran him.

Lost record one had to admire in any time or place—a tribute at once both to the great and hoary innocent-until-proven-guilty concept imported from the Mother Country and to the high skills engendered in the law schools here in the ever-progressive Colonies.

Now there remained the trifling matter of the $18,600 (let us forgo the small change) that constituted the Dutchman's other bulge on the morning of the shootout. Never mind what that depression-time roll was for; the question was, who gets it?

Tom Dewey, then in the United States Attorney's office in Manhattan, went into Federal Court and filed a lien against the money even as the bloodstains were being washed off Fifth Avenue. The Treasury had Mr. Flegenheimer on its delinquency rolls as a chap who still owed $79,236.72 on his 1930 tax returns and Dewey thought it would be just dandy if the $18,600 could be applied against that debt. The court agreed quite readily but the Police Property Clerk demurred. He submitted that the green constituted evidence seized during the commission of a crime and accordingly would have to remain in his custody until the defendant Flegenheimer's trial. When that was over, the pesky Dewey trotted around for the money once more but—oh, dastardly fate—even swifter feet had beaten him to the window.

Big feet, too. Long before Dewey made his dash, the Property Clerk and the office of the Corporation Counsel had enjoyed visits on behalf of the Schultz roll from the persuasive J. Richard Davis and an acquaintance of his named James J. Hines, a townsman not without friends both in the constabulary and in the municipality's legal department. This formidable duet, just helping out, had submitted that the disputed roll really wasn't Arthur Flegenheimer's at all but belonged to Larry Carney. Larry Carney? Of course. The old con said he was too feeble to look after his own poke at the age of 50 and that Arthur, his long-time benefactor, had graciously consented to hold it for him in the dark night. Carney even put it in an affidavit and this moving affirmation of the greater-love-hath-no-man bit stood up when Dewey's superior, United States Attorney George Z. Medalie, went back into court and sued to recover the money.

In the long battle that followed, Arthur J. W. Hilly, Corporation Counsel in the administration of the fun-loving Night Mayor of New York, James J. Walker, argued successfully that his office had observed all the legal proprieties when it authorized the Property Clerk to honor the Carney affidavit. Hilly submitted that one of his very own aides, George O. Arkin, had personally studied the document before giving the signal for the transfer of all those big bills. "It was just an ordinary replevin action such as we handle every day in the week," said the city's highest legal officer, reminding the court that since the police had not established that the $18,600 represented the proceeds of a crime then "it was not theirs to hold." Jimmy Walker's Police Commissioner, gruff old Edward P. Mulrooney, found himself constrained to join in that view. It had not only not been established that the roll had come from any illicit source but the eminently fair men in blue had never so much as made any such claim. So indeed it "was not theirs to hold."

It was Larry Carney's to hold.

And by now another year had turned on the calendar and it was time for Arthur and Larry and all the merry men of Arthur's court to turn their full attention to the very pressing problem represented by that nasty, ill-tempered Coll boy.

"What man was ever content with one crime?"

—JUVENAL

CHAPTER XII

THE WAR THAT ENDED IN A TELEPHONE BOOTH

JOHNNY BRODERICK, THE HAM-FISTED DETECTIVE WHO retired in 1947 with a string of one-punch KOs over underworld hard guys dating back to the mid-Twenties, wasn't much for handing out compliments to the natural enemy in the Broadway jungle, but he did say this once:

"Vincent Coll and Fats McCarthy, his partner, are the two toughest guys I ever met."

On the first end of that twin endorsement, Broderick never would have gotten an argument from Dutch Schultz. A chum dating back to the street corners of his teens and then, too briefly, an officer candidate in his hoodlum army, the baby-faced Coll brought more travail on the Dutchman than the entire New York Police Department. Indeed, the brash Mick, born into a decent family from County Kildare in Ireland in 1908, four years after Arthur Flegenheimer's debut, caused his old buddy more damn trouble than anybody but the paid assassin who put that last slug into his side. There was just no way to deal with Vincent Coll except by force; you could not set up a peace conference with him no matter how soft you made the terms.

Coll drove Arthur to such distraction that the Dutchman went around to the 42nd Police Precinct in The Bronx one day in 1931 and offered to put a bounty on his head, the way they used to do it in the Old West. Of course it strains the imagination, but it happened. Schultz simply walked into the detective's squad room and said, "Look, I want the Mick killed. He's driving me out of my mind. I'll give a house in Westchester to any of you guys who knocks him off." There were three detectives on hand and the one who knew the beer merchant best, Fred Schaedel, from his old neighborhood, answered him.

"Arthur," the big cop said, "do you know what the hell you're saying? You know you're in the Morrisania station?"

"I know where I am," Schultz snapped. "I've been here before. I just came in to tell ya I'll pay good to any cop that kills the Mick."

Schaedel gathered by now that this wasn't one of those days when L'il Arthur might have been sampling his own bottled goods. Now he addressed him a bit more seriously.

"If you tell us you know what you're saying, Arthur," he said, "then you must be out of your head."

"I know what I'm saying," Schultz replied. "The guy that kills the Mick gets the Honor Medal anyway—I'm just makin' it more interesting."

"Okay," Schaedel said, getting up out of his chair. "Then get your ass out of here before we pinch you. You hafta be out of your head."

Can you imagine a time so carefree and happy that a known gangster could walk into his friendly neighborhood station house and offer the police a contract like that? Talking to Fred Schaedel in 1969, the author, who counted Morrisania among the way stations of his own youth, asked why Schultz had not indeed been pinched if he was seriously trying to exchange Vincent Coll's life for one of those medium-priced Westchester houses Steve DiRosa and Julius Salke had turned down that night outside Central Park.

"We never could have made it stick," Schaedel said. "The Dutchman would have walked out five minutes after his lawyer arrived. He'd just say he was kiddin' with us. Besides, it was a good bet by then that Schultz and the Mick were going to take care of each other, one or the other, without our help. We had our hands full just picking up the bodies they were scattering around the borough in those days."

And there was no shortage of bodies, for that matter.

The precise origin of the Schultz-Coll war is difficult to trace because none of the principals kept diaries and there was nobody in that set blessed with the total recall of a Joe Valachi and the same compulsion to share it with his fellow citizens. What is known is that no one in the Dutchman's band grew more restive than Vincent Coll as the rapid successes of the fading Twenties blossomed into the even more limitless prosperity of the early Thirties. The sky seemed to be the limit—and Vincent and Peter Coll were still nothing more than a pair of hired hands. This was not calculated to sit well with a man of Vincent's tastes and temperament.

From information in the files of the Manhattan District Attorney's office, it would appear that the war broke out when the high-spirited, dimple-chinned Coll, an athletic five-ten with curly blond hair and a face that might have made the movies if he had not chosen the gun instead, announced that he wanted his own piece of the beer business in The Bronx and Harlem. Schultz's one and only partner, of course, had been Joey Noe, and he had managed quite well on his own since Noe's death.

So the answer was no and Coll went on a rampage. Schultz trucks suddenly began to fall to hijackers—remember when beer trucks were being hijacked, not jet planes?—and, inevitably, Schultz men began to die. The toll, unfortunately for the historian, would never be known because the Dutchman, a more private man then, didn't put out any casualty lists. Nor did Coll when the bullets started coming the other way. You can imagine the result. Denied official communiqués, the newspapers competed strenuously to come up with some kind of count of the dead and injured. It started conservatively, like *SEVEN DEAD IN SCHULTZ–COLL WAR*, then it was 12, then 15, then 20 and by 1932 outlandishly round numbers like 50 were being kicked around. It was really idle, all of it, because there was no way to count; the victims in the main were faceless gunmen, unknown to fame, or simple toilers in the beer drops and garages Coll put under siege when he made his move.

If there ever was any lingering question about the Mick's private renown as a modern-day gunslinger, Joe Valachi would sweep it away more than three decades later by spilling the details of a murder contract of staggering proportions. The pint-sized underworld turncoat told his new-found buddies in the United States Senate that in 1931 Coll hired out to Cosa Nostra chieftain Salvatore Maranzano to kill nobody less than Lucky Luciano and his equally-terrifying first lieutenant, Vito Genovese.

There, indeed, is the measure of the man—a summons from a *Capo di tutti Capi* ("Boss of all Bosses") to knock over two of his contemporaries in an enemy Family. The Mick had to be most flattered. Don Salvatore had selected him, every inch the outsider, over all the soldiers in his own army.

The mission did not come off, as Valachi recounted it from the storehouse of his bottomless memory, only because the contract was cancelled—with guns and knives—by its intended victims. To get to the heart of it, a little background is in order.

Salvatore Maranzano was the leader of the Castellammarese forces, mostly imports from the area around the Gulf of Castellammare in Sicily, who in 1929 challenged the New York rule of Giuseppe (Joe the Boss) Masseria. This was the war in which Joe (The Baker) Catania eventually fell in the Masseria cause, dispatched by a Maranzano execution team which included Mr. Valachi himself, before some of the Boss's own partisans, led by Luciano and Genovese, decided that he himself would have to go—in the interests of peace, of course. This item was attended to in a Coney Island restaurant on April 15, 1931, with Charley Lucky himself on the premises but responding to a hurry call in the washroom when the usual "person or persons unknown" deposited some slugs in the Masseria brain.

This happenstance removed the worst of his irritations from Don Salvatore's world, or underworld, but the Luciano-Genovese ascension to power on the enemy side found the Castellammarese forces still beleaguered, and this is where the Mick comes in.

Don Salvatore, according to Valachi, set up a peace session for September 10 in his well-fortified office in the New York Central Building on Park Avenue and arranged for Vincent Coll to drop in and blow some holes into his high-level guests, Charley and Vito. Well, you know about the best laid plans. The Maranzano peace formula fell short because Messrs. Luciano and Genovese failed to show up.

Instead, the host had a visit from four kosher delegates on loan from Murder Inc., dressed as policemen for his special occasion. When they left, Don Salvatore's life was leaking away from a combination of four gunshots, a slashed throat and six stab wounds. It turned out, moreover, that September 10 had been set aside as a kind of Moscow purge day, Italian-style, and that perhaps 30 to 40 other Sicilian notables had fallen around the American countryside in the bloodiest of the Italian family quarrels; once again, there would never be an exact count suitable for engraving on any memorial scroll.

Where was Mr. Coll when Maranzano fell? He was on his way into the scheduled hearts-and-flowers (and bullets) session, right on time, just as the early-bird assassins were coming out. Valachi said he heard this at the time from Bobby Doyle (a very free translation of Girolamo Santucci), a fellow Costa Nostra soldier who happened to be on the premises that day, and that six years later a self-certified member of the murder band, Sam (Red) Levine, confirmed the story in a moment of high confidence. Here is some of the reformed badman's testimony from that point on under the questioning of general counsel Jerome S. Adlerman and Senator John L. McClellan, the Arkansas Democrat who is chairman of the Senate's Permanent Subcommittee on Investigations:

MR. ADLERMAN: As I understand it, then, Red Levine and two or three others, Jewish gangsters, had gone in there to kill Maranzano. They killed him. As they were leaving the scene of the killing they met Vincent Coll coming in?

MR. VALACHI: Coming in as they were going out and they waved him away.

MR. ADLERMAN: What did they say to Vincent Coll?

MR. VALACHI: Just like that, "Beat it."

MR. ADLERMAN: Did they tell him the cops were on the way?

MR. VALACHI: Yes. "Beat it, the cops are on the way."

THE CHAIRMAN: What was Coll doing there?

MR. VALACHI: It came out that Maranzano had hired or got Vincent Coll—I never knew he was contacting Coll—the purpose was that they were going to kill Vito and Charley which Vito and Charley never showed up.

The Valachi revelations conflicted in one key respect—who done it—with a version put forth years before by Dixie Davis. In his memoir, the Schultz barrister listed Bo Weinberg as Don Salvatore's killer, but the point already has been made in this chronicle of death and taxes that Davis had a habit of putting notches on the trusty Weinberg .45 with utter abandon. The way he told it, poor Bo barely would have had a chance to switch his gabardines and matching shoulder holster from one murder errand to the next.

The failure of the Coll mission, it is worth noting here, was a tough break both for Joe Valachi and Dutch Schultz. It was bad for Valachi because Genovese lived and went onward and upward and years later, when they were cellmates in Atlanta on narcotics raps, put the "kiss of death" on him as a suspected turncoat, causing the old soldier to turn government informer because that seemed so much better than getting knocked off in prison. It was bad for Schultz because Lucky Luciano lived and he was going to have trouble with that droopy-eyed charmer after a while.

As far as the Mick himself goes, bear in mind that in the time under discussion he wasn't relying solely on his outside shooting contracts to keep body and soul (and his combat platoon) together during his profitless war with the Dutchman. He had to have money to finance the expedition against Fortress Flegenheimer. One way to raise it was in the popular kidnapping trade.

Thus in 1931 Coll staged the exploit that made the rest of his career up to that time—marked by 14 arrests for everything from juvenile delinquency in 1920 to homicide in 1930—pale by comparison. On the balmy night of June 15, he piled some helpers into a sedan and drove over to the Club Argonaut on Seventh Avenue and there, on the street, picked up the establishment's large and prosperous owner, George Jean (Big Frenchy) DeMange. Now DeMange happened to be Owney Madden's partner in a string of Manhattan rackets ranging all the way from booze to extortion to protection to the sport of boxing. It was a power almost akin to the kind-hearted police force itself, but there was the Mick, on Owney the Killer's turf, taking Big Frenchy into temporary custody.

"Why, men, this is silly," DeMange protested while his midsection was being tickled with the barrel of a .38 concealed in Coll's right-hand jacket pocket. "If it's money you want you can have it, but don't try this gun stuff."

You can imagine how much impression that made.

"Get inna car," Coll said, "I ain't here to argue."

The prisoner was driven up Riverside Drive, the scenic route, into Westchester County. It was a springtime outing fraught with distress for Big Frenchy, since he knew as much about the quick Coll trigger finger as anybody in town, but it was kept fairly diverting with a low-key man-to-man discussion: how many American dollars would Mr. DeMange's life be worth in the current market?

The Mick had an absolutely outlandish sum in mind, in six figures or close enough, while his harried but practical guest thought that something like $10,000 might be more equitable in the current market (the economic upturn, one must note here, was still awaiting the arrival of Mr. Roosevelt in the

White House). Some of the stories later had it that the wily Frenchman had managed to buy his body back for the paltry ten grand. Other estimates ran way beyond that.

What was paid, once the necessary phone call was made to midtown and Owney Madden could scratch the cash ransom together toward midnight, was a round $35,000, C.O.D. This is the figure reposing in the confidential files of the Manhattan District Attorney. Of course, the Madden-DeMange cartel, with its heavy beer and liquor interests, if nothing else, could have shelled out the low number or the high one with equal ease, if not downright nonchalance. What had to hurt was the principle of the thing. Vincent Coll had committed an act of the worst possible form—not that kidnapping wasn't so rife in the land at this time as to drive even the vaunted FBI to distraction. And not that this was just an instance of the boys stealing bodies from each other. This one was at once unthinkable and unforgivable because a trigger-happy punk from The Bronx, without a full-blown mob beyond a handful of other mindless guns, had challenged the power and muscle of Mr. Madden. It's worth some reflection.

Owney Madden came out of the slums of Liverpool to settle in the slums of Hell's Kitchen. He made his mark in no time. He was only 17 when they started calling him Owney the Killer, 18 when he took over the West Side's Gopher Gang, 19 when at least two murders were credited to him, 20 when a small army of rival Hudson Dusters put five slugs into him, and 22 when he went up the river in the barroom murder of Little Patsy Doyle. That was in 1914, but Owney was out of Sing Sing by 1923 and moving pretty well (look, he piled up 57 arrests altogether). He was a very big man on Broadway, known as the Duke of the West Side in his own court, when Coll decided to put the snatch on his partner. Madden had to have the dimmest possible view of any such breach of underworld etiquette.

Did it bother the Mick? It wouldn't seem so, because after a while the word was around that Coll, far from being alarmed by the reports of the irascible Madden's displeasure, was talking about kidnapping the racket boss's brother-in-law, Jack Marron, the very next time he had the shorts. For a while after that, Marron was almost as scarce around the midtown haunts as Dutch Schultz, who had become almost entirely invisible once the shooting war with Coll began.

Beyond the successful DeMange adventure, the Mick's other exploits in his sideline remained vague because of the universal reticence of kidnapping victims to talk about such mundane matters as money. Coll was believed to be the cad who made off one day with George Immerman, brother of Connie, the Harlem night club impresario, in a case of mistaken identity which reportedly produced some $45,000 in spending money for him nonetheless. It is hard to imagine what kind of price tag the zestful hoodlum might have pinned on the body of the well-heeled Connie Immerman himself.

The Mick also drew the credit in the supposed kidnapping of Rudy Vallee, a saga of the Broadway badlands which came down in popular history in two versions. In one, the ever-thrifty crooner bargained his ferocious captor down to such a low figure—say, $10,000—as to make the whole venture a questionable risk at best. In the other, originally put forth by the *Daily Mirror*, Vallee came up with a round $100,000 after the soles of his feet had been toasted to a crisp. The singer-turned-actor, a smash hit on Broadway in the Sixties in *How to Succeed in Business Without Really Trying*, told the author that none of it was true. "Larry Fay used to come into my club, the Villa Vallee," he said. "He took a liking to me and sometimes gave me a lift downtown in his armored car. One of my friends spotted me in the car with Larry one day and nearly fainted at the thought that I was being taken for a ride.That's how the kidnapping thing got around but I can't imagine how Coll got mixed up in it."

Coll did have a legitimate credit line in the kidnapping of an affluent bookmaker named Billy Warren but no ransom figure ever emerged. This is understandable, since an honest turf accountant who talked openly about showering large sums of cash on virtual strangers might have some explaining to do to the Internal Revenue Bureau. Whether the highly placed Owney Madden ever had to tell the tax men how he scratched together that $35,000 for Mr. Coll is something else; if the government was at all curious about the sources of the Madden-DeMange income the secret was rather well kept.

While Coll's kidnapping proclivities made him an extremely poor risk in the lower levels of the town's society even beyond his little problem with Dutch Schultz, he was about to suffer a rash of publicity that would put him on the very bottom of all the popularity charts in every walk of the city's life. It happened on July 28, 1931, even before the full story of the DeMange caper had dribbled out through the underworld's paper curtain. On that steaming summer day, a touring car carrying five gunmen drove into crowded East 107th Street in Spanish Harlem, slowed down in front of Joey Rao's Helmar Social Club and laid down a stream of fire, presumably aiming at some lucky bum who had been marked for the spot but wasn't on it. While the mission failed,it had a far more tragic effect, for in the hail of some 60 bullets a five-year-old boy, Michael Vengalli, was killed, and four other children playing on the slum street were wounded.

The headline writers labelled the deed the "Baby Killing" and the police lost no time in naming Coll as the maestro of the assassination band in the car. Now he wasn't just the Mick but the Mad Mick and the Mad Dog and a nationwide alarm went out for his arrest. The cops leaned to the theory that the real victim was supposed to be Mr. Rao himself. That gentleman was a long-time ally of Dutch Schultz's but the story was that the senseless shooting spree had nothing to do with the Dutchman but rather marked a battle for control of the East Harlem rackets, including narcotics and policy.

Coll grew a mustache and dyed his sandy locks black and managed to stay out of the dragnet for three months, probably without leaving town at all. When he was picked up, finally, two of his principal lieutenants, Frank Giordano and Pasquale Del Greco, alias Patsy Dugan, were charged with him but the murder trial that December ended in a disaster for the state. Coll had the services of one of the nation's leading criminal lawyers, Samuel Leibowitz, later a County Judge in Brooklyn and very hard on malefactors of any stripe, while the District Attorney, with a thin case at best, had to depend on a rather fragile star witness. That character, George Brecht, turned out to be a felon from St. Louis who had made something of a specialty as an eyewitness in murder trials. Leibowitz left him in so many shreds that the state itself had to ask for a directed verdict of acquittal.

Coll, a blond again and with 23-year-old Lottie Kriesberger, his best girl, beaming at his side, emerged from the Criminal Courts Building with a prepared statement to mark the biggest of his courtroom victories.

"I have been charged with all kinds of crimes but baby killing was the limit," the statement said. "I'd like nothing better than to lay my hands on the man who did this. I'd tear his throat out. There is nothing more despicable than a man who would harm an innocent child."

The Mick celebrated his triumph by marrying the lanky Lottie, culminating a courtship which began when she was 16 and had suffered nothing more serious than the minor interruptions occasioned by Coll's difficulties with the law. Lottie was a German import who had arrived on these shores at the age of two with the name of Van Denninger or Denerlein. The Kriesberger handle came from an unsuccessful robber to whom she had been married almost too briefly to remember.

In October 1931, even while Coll presumably was rather taken up with his defense preparations in the Vengalli case, one of the more consequential events of the war with Schultz took place.

Joe Mullins, a 50-year-old $50-a-week odd-job man for the Dutchman, was cut down in front of a beer drop on the poorer part of Park Avenue, in the Lower Bronx, by two trained torpedomen who had made the switch from the Schultz legions to the hotheaded Coll band. It proved to be a poorly conceived killing—or poorly executed at best—because a couple of Edison Company repairmen, working right there in a manhole, happened to be close enough to form a perfectly splendid image of the distinctively hard faces of the Coll handymen, Dominic (Toughy) Odierno, 23, and the aforementioned Frank Giordano, 32, so they might as well have left their calling cards at the scene.

Both hoodlums paid for the spot killing in the electric chair but the Dutchman himself, to the day he died, insisted that the cops had the wrong men in that case. He was wrong, but it would have been a nice piece of irony if true. Odierno and Giordano were the only two mercenaries ever brought before the bar in the widespread and seemingly endless warfare touched off by the Mick.

The Mullins murder capped a period in the strife which had been stepped up quite a bit since the preceding Decoration Day, a memorable date because it marked the killing of Peter Coll. He was cut down on a Harlem street corner and the word was that the Dutchman had decided that Peter, the older brother, would have to go because the Mick had violated one of the underworld's more treasured codes. Schultz had come up with the $10,000 bail Coll needed on a Sullivan Law rap some time back, in happier days, but the Mick, due for trial in the spring of 1931, failed to show up. Since he was always so elusive, Schultz evidently sent his messengers after the next of kin to square the account.

Vincent took Peter's passing very hard. Four Schultz men fell before blazing guns in the next few weeks as the war reached its peak. It was from that moment on that the Dutchman became rather scarce around town. He confided to someone once that this period, however extended, had not been a total loss. He said he had caught up with a lot of reading, from Dickens to a spate of American history as well as some biography and a peek into a few medical tomes. He did not say what had prompted his interest in the human anatomy; his own physique, neither seriously neglected nor challenged with too much of the stuff Schultz was selling, was generally in tip-top condition.

By then, there was so much artillery going off that the police found themselves doing free guard duty at the Schultz beer drops. Thus Fred Schaedel and a sidekick were assigned at one time to station themselves in an unmarked sedan outside of one of the Dutchman's larger plants, on Randall Avenue in the Hunts Point section of The Bronx. A Schultz marksman, Big Sid Goldstein, manned the roof of the drop with a rifle and Henny Ahearn, one of the insiders whose name could be detected later in the Dutchman's deathbed ravings, was the man in charge. Schaedel said the Schultz men spotted the police detail right off the bat and couldn't have been more charming, since it was a time when a little police protection was as good as an ounce of prevention. If you wonder why the drop wasn't busted, well, that was the job of the federal Prohibition snoops, and they couldn't dam up that whole river of amber, could they? Who would watch the 50,000 speakeasies? Who would watch the door-to-door deliverers of the bathtub gin? Who would knock over the economy-size stills in the private homes?

And who could measure the corruption of that moment in history?

Fred Schaedel recalls that one day a heedless young foot cop, seething with ambition, pulled into the 42nd Precinct with a brand new Lincoln truck loaded with 55 barrels of beer, parked it in the station house yard—and watched it driven off by its rightful owners a couple of hours later. Illegal search and seizure, you know. The officer had no right to go take that truck away from Mr. Flegenheimer without a warrant, and the feds weren't going to follow it to the drop and snatch it back either. The wonder is that the Dutchman didn't demand either a letter of apology or some reparations for the time lost in the delivery of the golden brew.

Be that as it may, the intensified watch on the drops was credited with cutting down some of the bloodletting even if it didn't interfere with the flow of the Dutchman's high quality needle beer. Nonetheless, any count in the two-year Schultz-Coll showdown had to show that it ranked with, or even surpassed, any other gang war going back to the turn of the century in a metropolis so rich in spoils that it would always have its share of self-purges in its underworld society. (In New York, as in Chicago or Detroit or Cleveland or Philadelphia, name it, the hoodlum community in its higher echelons often will do more than the law itself about thinning out its own ranks. Perhaps it isn't that the law is so grossly inefficient; maybe it is just that the underworld, unencumbered by due process and the other restraints of the Bill of Rights, has so much less difficulty keeping the house clean. Hell, maybe because it's sometimes easier to buy off a cop than a rival gangster with mayhem on his mind.)

A single incident will perhaps illustrate best the no-limits nature of the Schultz-Coll blood purge.

On February 1, 1932, a quartet of gunmen dropped in on a card game in a four-family frame dwelling on Commonwealth Avenue in the North Bronx and sprayed the room with gunshots. There was no return fire; nobody had a chance. When the police arrived, Patsy Del Greco, Coll's man and the possessor of a decently long police record, was dead on the floor along with Fiorio Basile, another Coll triggerman, and a woman, Mrs. Emily Torrizello. Louis Basile, a brother of Fiorio, was wounded, along with another woman guest. Two children playing in the apartment, and two babies in cribs, were unhurt.

The inevitable comparisons with the St. Valentine's Day massacre made the early tabloids but that was too much of a stretch. It was a major atrocity just the same, surely one of the worst mass shootings in the city's history, and it had to be charged up to the going war because those two Coll men were among the dead. The police said the executioners actually were on the hunt for Coll himself on information that the apartment was one of his hideouts and that he was due there that night with his tough-talking bride, Lottie.

Fairly strong confirmation would be forthcoming exactly seven nights later—over the riddled body of the Mick himself, in fact.

On the evening of February 8, not long after the darkness threw its veil over the towers of Manhattan, the *Daily Mirror's* "bulldog" edition for the next morning hit the street with a Walter Winchell column which contained this sizzling paragraph:

"Five planes brought dozens of machine gats from Chicago Friday to combat the Town's Capone. Local banditti have made one hotel a virtual arsenal and several hot-spots are ditto because Master Coll is giving them the headache."

It was the sort of thing that made the early Winchell—before he began to see himself on a more global canvas—such an incomparable peek-a-boo columnist. He had good information, bobbing above the engulfing waves of his bad information, much of the time. This time, while it was patently silly to imagine that anyone would have to import guns into the armed camp that was New York, Winchell, who was going to need a bodyguard after a while, surely was on to something sizzling hot.

The word had been around for months now that there was a $50,000 price on Master Coll's head, and he was holed up with Lottie either in the Cornish Arms Hotel on 23rd Street or in a furnished room in that block. Whether he troubled to pick up an early *Mirror* to see whether Master Winchell had any tidbits about Vincent Coll, or what the often-shrill news columns might be saying about him, is not known. In any event, he left his room around 12:30 A.M. and went to the

London Chemists drugstore across the street either to take a pre-arranged phone call or to make some calls without running the risk of a police bug. He had $101.48 in his pockets and no artillery on him. He went directly to one of the three phone booths in the back and he was in it about 10 minutes when a limousine drew to the curb and three men got out. Two of them stayed outside the drugstore. The third went in, observed that there were five people there—two clerks and a woman and two men customers—and said, calmly, "All right, everybody, keep cool now and you won't get hurt." Then he drew a Tommy gun from under his coat, lined up in a firm stance a few feet away from the Mick's booth, and opened fire.

There never was an accurate count of all the lead poured in the next minute or so, but the body of Vincent Coll pitched forward out of the booth even as the executioner turned to leave. One slug had smashed into the right side of the Mick's face, broken his nose and lodged in the brain. Two others entered his forehead, one came to rest above his heart, and he had seven wounds in the right arm and four in the left arm, so there was just no doubt that the man with the machine gun had the glass trim of the booth in his sights, not the heavy wood frame, from the time he squeezed off the first burst. The autopsy would show 15 steel-jacketed slugs in what was left of Coll's body but it would not necessarily show how many others had passed through him.

The assassin and his outside helpers had to be forever thankful that they had brought along a real good car, because Patrolman James Sherlock, on the beat, heard the shattering noise of the automatic fire and ran up just as they were pulling out of 23rd Street into Eighth Avenue. Sherlock stopped a cab and rode the running board all the way to 50th Street before giving up the uneven chase. It is possible that the getaway car happened to be in the hands of a cool and competent driver. Dixie Davis said the man at the wheel was none other than Bo Weinberg, apparently having stepped aside, uncommonly, for an even surer marksman. Davis also said that the man who had Coll engaged in that long dialog on the phone was Owney Madden, calling from Harlem's Cotton Club and talking overtime because somebody with a heater had suddenly materialized at his side and told him to keep the Mick occupied for a while.

Even while the chase up Eighth Avenue was still in progress, Lottie Coll rushed into the drugstore, screaming and weeping hysterically over the horrifying scene she encountered. She did not wish to have any traffic with the arriving police. Was she with her husband before he was shot? No, she was in the hotel across the street. When did she see her husband last? The afternoon before. Did he say where he was going? No. How did she know about the shooting so quickly? "Well, a telephone call was made and I heard about it." Who called? "I don't want to be stubborn but I'm not going to say anymore about Vincent and me." That was all, except that the young widow, 24 then, did say to someone who approached her that she was madly in love with Coll and that even at that moment she was wearing the same red dress she had on the day they were married.

Vincent's messy departure, by the way, failed to turn the ex-Mrs. Kriesberger onto the straight and narrow. She would do time on a Sullivan Law rap after a while and then draw 6 to 12 years in the Bedford Reformatory for Women because she happened to be along when two new-found friends unwittingly killed a girl bystander during a stickup in The Bronx.

The morning after the drugstore party, Police Commissioner Mulrooney, calling the execution "a positive defiance of law and order," which was a fairly conservative way to put it, contributed an interesting footnote to the story. He said that another man had come into the store with the victim, seated himself at the soda fountain while Coll entered the booth, and then got up and strolled out when the fellow with the Tommy gun went to work. "He was double-crossed and put on the spot by his own bodyguard," the Commissioner said. Who did it? Had Owney Madden finally caught up with the Mick for the kidnapping of Frenchy DeMange the year before? No. Then was it the Dutchman's crowd? The Commissioner wouldn't answer that one way or the other. He did say that the two getaway cars used in the Commonwealth Avenue shooting party bore plates stolen from a shipment out of Auburn Prison and so did the souped-up limo used by the Coll assassin. Moreover, a Tommy gun like the one employed so effectively in the London Chemists had been found in one of The Bronx cars. And what was Commissioner Valentine's parting estimate of Vincent Coll? It was just like Johnny Broderick's: "He was a real tough fellow."

Apart from its "positive defiance of law and order," hardly an unusual phenomenon in the Big Town, then or now, the Coll murder turned some Police Department faces red for another reason. There was supposed to be an around-the-clock tail on the Mick in the hopes that he might lead the cops to the thick-lipped, quick-on-the-trigger Fats McCarthy. The paunchy killer, freely named as one of the mechanics in the East Harlem shooting spree, was rather badly wanted in the slaying of Detective Guido Passagno in a gun battle in Manhattan back on October 19. On the side, the police had some questions for McCarthy about the

United Press International (top)
Wide World Photos (bottom)

Vincent Coll shakes hands with his lawyer, Samuel Leibowitz, after winning an acquittal in the celebrated "Baby Killing" in which a five-year-old boy died when a carload of gunmen raked an East Harlem street on a spot killing that went wrong. At bottom, less than two months later, in February 1932, Coll's widow, Lottie, is comforted by Leibowitz after the gangster was assassinated. Coll was Dutch Schultz's worst enemy but the police couldn't pin the murder on the Dutchman.

United Press International

Cut down by a machine-gunner while making a phone call in a Manhattan drugstore, Vincent Coll is carried off to the morgue.

Wide World Photos

Family portrait: Vincent Coll (far right, wearing the mustache he grew when he was a fugitive) in custody in the Harlem baby killing with four members of his gang. From left, Dominic Odierno, Pasquale Del Greco, Mike Basile and Frank Giordano. Odierno and Giordano died in the electric chair for the spot killing of a Schultz helper in a Bronx beer drop.

thoroughly professional job that had rid the community of Legs Diamond in that same month. The question now, of course, was where was the tail on Coll when that sub-machine gun went off? Like so many other questions of that kind, it would never be answered.

It wouldn't matter either, for the fat guy ceased to be a problem for the harried men in blue come summer. Trailed to a hideaway outside Albany with his bride and two helpers that July, he perished shooting it out with State Police Sergeant Walter Riley, State Trooper W. A. Chesterfield and Detective Harold Moore, who was hit three times himself before he put a bullet into McCarthy's head. In a moment of loosely credited murders, the obituaries suggested that Fats may have taken the Coll contract from his ex-employer, Dutch Schultz, because of some momentary unpleasantness in the insurgent band.

The Coll funeral on February 11, in a steady drizzle, reminded no one of that spare-no-expense affair for Danny Iamascia, who had never turned his back on the Dutchman. The underworld, still busily breathing sighs of relief, skipped the obsequies, and a church service announced by Coll's sister, Mrs. Florence Redden, was interdicted by the Archdiocese. There was no priest at the Walter B. Cooke Funeral Home on Willis Avenue in The Bronx, where less than 100 persons came to pay their last respects. and none at St. Raymond's Cemetery. The undertaker simply read the Lord's Prayer at the graveside and Coll was laid to rest in an imitation metal coffin over which there was a simple wreath of red and white flowers bearing that age-old legend of the ever-anonymous underworld, "From The Boys."

On the headstone over the grave alongside this mortal

enemy of the Dutchman's, the mourners could read this:

"In loving memory of my beloved brother, Peter. Died May 30, 1931. Age 24. Rest in peace. Coll."

Now all the Coll men were out of the way, but this did not mean that the streets of New York would forever be safe for Arthur Flegenheimer. Indeed, that cautious citizen waited only three days after Vincent's messy passing—he missed the funeral, but then he had passed up Danny Iamascia's too, and Danny was his friend—to slip up into Hamilton County in the foothills of the Adirondacks and get himself a brand new appointment as a Deputy Sheriff so he could always keep his waistband filled with his trusted .45 without having to worry about the more finicky cops.

Sheriff Peter Wilson had made that appointment even after the state troopers counseled him that the applicant was a person of somewhat questionable background. "I never saw this Flegenheimer," the Sheriff said when the heat caused him to drop his new deputy on February 19. "A friend of mine, who didn't know the man either, asked me to make the appointment because he had been informed the man intended to become a resident of the county. Naturally, we thought he might be opening a camp and wanted to protect it."

Open a camp up there in the tall grass?

Ridiculous.

The Dutchman by now, way beyond his modest role as The Beer Baron of The Bronx, was sitting astride one of New York's richest industries. Without a Deputy Sheriff's badge, and without any registered guns, he had taken the policy game away from the colored bankers of Harlem. He was a very busy man.

TOM DEWEY: Have you ever told the truth prior to your appearance here?
DIXIE DAVIS: I may have on some occasions.

—FROM THE RECORD OF THE HINES TRIAL

CHAPTER XIII
THE ONE-PENNY GOLD RUSH

IT MIGHT BE SAID, IN ONE OF HISTORY'S MORE MARVELOUS ironies, that the man who put Dutch Schultz in the policy business was the same man who drove Jimmy Walker out of New York's City Hall into exile in Europe and set the stage for reform—Samuel Seabury. This is not as fanciful as it sounds, for one of the by-products of the Judge's three muck-raking investigation's into official corruption, starting early in 1930, was a disruption of the numbers game that opened the door for the Dutchman's takeover.

What happened was this:

Poking around the Magistrates Courts because everybody knew that the lower bench was a resort where you could fix everything from a traffic ticket to a felony and there was a swinging door for gambling and vice arrests, the white-haired Seabury called in one of his top aides, Irving Ben Cooper, and said he would like to have a look at the policy racket. How big was it?

Well, the Harlem game simply reeked with prosperity—an oasis of plenty in the city's most depressed area. Everybody played it, even the masses on home relief, because you could bet a single penny and win $6. That had a sweet sound but in truth it was the worst bet in the world. You put up your penny—or nickel or dime or quarter or half-dollar—on any three-digit number up to 999. That made the odds 999 to 1 but the game paid off at the rate of 600 to 1, as prohibitive a house percentage as the greediest gamblers in all the ages of the wheel ever coveted. So the profits had to be staggering. The gross play in the major Harlem banks in 1931 was estimated at $35,000 a day and the rule-of-thumb figure for what the lucky players were getting back was $7,700, or about 25 percent. Hell, that other outlandish gyp of the time, the slot machine, or one-armed bandit, paid out closer to 66 percent.

Did anybody give a damn about a game like policy emptying the pockets of the poor? No. The numbers banks had run virtually unmolested, except for regular shakedowns by the police, much of the time since a white man named Al Adams introduced it to New York back in 1832. In Dutch Schultz's time just a century later, when the occasional honest cop hauled the small-fry runners and controllers into court some Magistrate invariably turned them loose for lack of evidence.

Irving Ben Cooper dropped a line into this rich stream and then decided to have a talk with two of the most prosperous Harlem bankers—Wilfred Adolphus Brunder and Jose Enrique Miro, known to his intimates as just plain Henry. This was quite a pair.

Brunder was a West Indian who had abandoned a humdrum career as a shirt-waist maker to go into policy in 1923. He started with a day's play of $7.13—he liked to remember that figure—and ran it all the way up to $11,000 a day by 1930. Once, in 1927, he was busted and sent off to prison for four months, a sentence hardly calculated to disrupt his operation. When Cooper had him in, early in 1931, he happened to be burdened with bank books showing deposits of $1,753,342.33 between January 1, 1925, and December 31, 1930. Rather than see this vulgar display of wealth hashed over in public hearings before Judge Seabury and face a pending income tax rap as well, Brunder elected to withdraw to the sun-splashed beaches of Bermuda. On the way out, he turned his policy bank over to his top man, Joseph Matthias Ison, also known as Big Joe and Spasm (because his face did all kinds of tricks in Harlem's high-stakes poker games).

Miro, a Puerto Rican who was a common laborer before he discovered policy in 1926, suffered an embarrassment almost equivalent to Brunder's. The six bank books he admitted owning showed deposits of $1,111,730.08 between July 7, 1927, and December 12, 1930, with some pocket money turned up by the nosy Cooper pushing the total up to a tidier $1,215,556.29. Miro did testify before the relentless Seabury but there were so many contradictions in his recital that he found himself taxed with a charge of perjury. Fight or run? Miro decided to follow the example set by Wilfred Brunder, his biggest competitor. He selected the soothing climate of his native San Juan but first, like Brunder, he asked the same Big Joe Ison to mind his policy store while he was away.

This is where Dutch Schultz comes in, courtesy of Mr. Ison.

Big Joe, a West Indian, had toiled as an elevator operator and shipyard worker before breaking into policy as a collector in 1923. Now, eight years later, he had the best of all possible policy worlds—Brunder's and Miro's, that is—in his hands, but he ran into trouble in no time at all and found himself in business with the Dutchman.

There are, of course, two versions of what happened.

One came from Dixie Davis, who was the Babe Ruth of the

policy lawyers at the time and numbered Big Joe among his clients. Davis said that Big Joe called on him one day, sort of upset, and complained that some gangsters, jealous of his unbounded prosperity, were trying to shake him down. Davis said he thereupon arranged for the distraught numbers banker to meet George and Bo Weinberg so that some orderly system of protection might be set up, say for $500 a week or so, and keep the creepier elements away from his door.

The other version, more graphic and a good deal more revealing, issued from Big Joe himself. He said he was standing on a Harlem corner one day when a car pulled up and an impressive-looking white man got out and said, rather firmly, "We're cops, get inna car." In the course of a ten-block ride up toward the Polo Grounds, home of John McGraw's Giants, Big Joe learned that his captor was a Mr. Bo Weinberg, built like a football linebacker but without the college-bred manner, and that his chauffeur was a Mr. Abe Landau, also a paleface. One of the things that impressed Big Joe about the earnestness of this pair was that Mr. Weinberg held a gun against his side all during the brief ride along St. Nicholas Avenue.

"There were threats made, telling me they were a couple of the boys, they knew I took over Brunder's business, and they are in it for their cuts out of the business," Big Joe said. "I told them I just started the business, I had no money and I couldn't consider what they were talking about. After the conversation they threw me out of the car and said, 'You go ahead and don't let us hear any more of this shit. We will give you a week to decide on this matter, and you will meet us on 145th Street and St. Nicholas Avenue at the Golden Grill.' " Big Joe said that was the incident which had sent him scurrying to his silver-tongued counselor. He said that Davis confided to him that Dutch Schultz was about to bring his vast organizational talents to the policy industry and "it would be wise if you would do the things I will suggest to you." He said that Davis then, quick like a fox, introduced him to George Weinberg, Bo's infinitely gentler brother, and that George proved to be just the man to see. George, bless him, could arrange all the protection Big Joe needed, and without any of that rough stuff—for $600 a week.

Mark it paid.

It was only a down payment, of course.

Abe Landau and the Weinbergs were Schultz men and Big Joe Ison, without quite understanding the enormity of it, was about to see his game converted into the pilot bank for the biggest operation of the Dutchman's career.

Within just a few months, the 40-year-old West Indian, coal-black and brawny, would be privileged to meet the new Caucasian master himself.

It seems that Henry Miro, refreshed by his self-exile in the Caribbean and no longer fretting over that Seabury thing, had come back and settled his tax problems with some ready cash and the kind of soft prison term the underworld calls a "meat-ball rap," or something so short a man can do it standing on his head. Out in the chill gray streets of Harlem again and a subscriber to the John D. Rockefeller Sr. maxim that the Devil makes work for idle hands, Miro called Big Joe and said he would like to have his bank back, please. Big Joe conveyed this dismaying intelligence to his attorney, Mr. Davis, who wasn't too thrilled by it himself.

The counselor said he would ask the brothers Weinberg to arrange a speedy powwow where all the principals could sit down with Mr. Schultz, whom he himself had never had the pleasure of meeting, and so it happened. The summit was convened in the East 98th Street apartment of Davis's plump brunette fiancée, Martha Delaney, later his wife until the arrival of the staggeringly beautiful Hope Dare, who was the former Rosie Lutzinger, out of the Ziegfeld Follies via a broken home somewhere in Iowa. Davis described the session this way when he elected,years later, to treat the readers of *Collier's* to his real true-life story:

> His murderous reputation had led me to expect a ruffian, but he was not at all that way. He was a small but well-set man, with good features. The girls used to say he looked like Bing Crosby with his nose bashed in. With his mob, I was to learn, Schultz could be boisterous and noisy, and talk a rough thieves' argot, but this night he was polite, well-spoken, amiable.
>
> There was something incongruous about his appearance and not until later did I realize what it was: he was wearing splendid silk haberdashery with a nondescript, ill-fitting gray suit. Sycophants used to give him presents of $25 shirts and $10 neckties, but he bought his own suits, ready-made, and never paid more than $35 for them. There was a bulge at his waistline, where he had his pistol under his vest.
>
> Joe Ison came quickly to the point. He told Schultz that if Miro was coming back he wanted to supervise Miro's bank.
>
> It was the old story—the way a racket usually starts. The businessman calls in the gangster to take care of labor trouble or competition, and then pretty soon he finds himself taking orders from the gangster.
>
> Schultz told Miro that Ison's idea was reasonable, and

he should go along with it. But Miro, who had known Schultz for a long time, put up an argument, started protesting about percentages and one thing and another.

The Dutchman spoke quietly and pretty soon he went out in the kitchen with Miro and George Weinberg. They were gone only a minute or two and then Miro came back into the room ahead of them, all smiles.

"Okay, Joe," said Miro to Ison in a cheerful tone. "When do we start?"

Gosh, I thought to myself, what a personality this man Schultz has! Miro had calmed down in an instant. Two years later Henry and George told me what the Dutchman said there in the kitchen. It had been very simple.

"Henry, you do what I say," said the Dutchman, "or I will kill you."

"Why, Arthur," said Henry, "you know I always do what you say."

It needs to be noted here that Arthur had taken no chances on any foolhardly show of resistance from his new business associates on that fateful night. Bo Weinberg, who did not have to lug his artillery very far because he had a penthouse in that same building, was on hand, taking up an awful lot of room, when the Harlem principals arrived. And when the Dutchman came in he was flanked by two other gunbearers, Lulu Rosenkrantz and the devoted Larry Carney.

Big Joe's own account of the session, recited from the witness stand in the trial of Jimmy Hines for "licensing" the policy racket and perhaps more instructive than Davis's ghosted effort in *Collier's,* included this quote from the Dutchman: "I am eventually going to take control of all the business." This is useful to the historian because it was happening during Schultz's shooting war with Vincent Coll. The Beer Baron had been quoted as saying, in the summer of 1931, that "as soon as he gets the Mick off his back and gets rid of him, he wants to step into the numbers business and look to take it over," but here he was taking it over while the Mick was very much in evidence, big as life, armed to the teeth, and gunning for his old pal Arthur Flegenheimer. Thus it is apparent that when the Dutchman said he was "eventually" going to take over policy he was already satisfied that his own search-and-destroy parties in the Manhattan jungle would catch up with the Mick in due course and dispose of that particular nuisance.

This is the way Big Joe described the financial arrangements arrived at on that big night in Martha Delaney's place, after noting that the presiding officer had deposited a revolver on the kitchen table before calling the meeting to order:

"The Dutchman said that the business that Ison has from Henry Miro he will return it back to Henry Miro and that Henry Miro will establish his independent bank or his own bank, and that Ison should finance the bank for Henry Miro and he would draw a salary from that bank, and the end of a period of time, if there was any money made, he will get back a certain percentage from that bank."

Q. (by Sol Gelb, one of Dewey's assistants) What was your interest in the bank?
A. I was supposed to get a third out of it.
Q. What did Miro say?
A. He agreed to that.
Q. And you did too?
A. I did.

So now Big Joe had one-third of the Miro bank instead of all of it—and he was about to find out what it might be like to have one-third of his very own bank instead of a magnificent three-thirds, shrunken only by that trivial $600-a-week bite for protection. He was about to find it out because the worst Thanksgiving in all the festive seasons of the policy bankers of Harlem was just around the crooked corner.

Number 527 (five + two equals Lucky Seven, get it?), a long-time superstition play traditionally bet very heavily in the month of November (the eleventh month, so make it Seven-Eleven and a new pair of shoes for Baby), came in on Thanksgiving Eve. The Ison bank was hit for every cent bet into it on that day—and $18,000 on top of that. Ison happened to have that much on hand but thought it might be a good time to get the Dutchman to ante up some cash for a change. So he called J. Richard Davis and told him about that horrid 527 coming in and said he couldn't raise more than $7,000 toward the $18,000 shy, what with the high cost of overhead nowadays, and who would play in his game if he welched?

Well, J. Richard had told him to call anytime he had the shorts and, presto, in no time at all Big Joe found himself once again in Miss Delaney's manse down Central Park way, and Bo and George were there and after a while Mr. Schultz, in person, came through the portal.

Q. (by Sol Gelb, again in the Hines trial) What did Schultz do when he came in?

A. When he came in he took off his coat and sat down.

Q. Did he do anything else?

A. Rested his gun on the table.

Q. Yes?

A. And sat down. Then Davis said to him that "Ison has been heavily hit and he is negotiating a loan." And Schultz answered and said "Has he any securities?" and I replied and said "No, I had no securities." He says, "Well, I will loan the money that he requires on one condition, that I will take charge of the business and become a partner with him in the business and he will get one-third from the business in the future."

Q. What did you say to that proposition?

A. I told him I didn't think it was a fair proposition. That I thought fifty-fifty was about the best proposition of business, and he says, "That is all it is going to be," and I can't do any better with him.

The merger was concluded without further quibbling. The Chairman of the Board, Davis and the Weinbergs withdrew to another room and came back in a few minutes and advised Big Joe, now beginning to look more like Small Joe, that Mr. Schultz was prepared to advance him $11,000 toward that claimed $18,000 deficit of his, to be delivered by George Weinberg on a Harlem corner the very next morning. And that wasn't all. Counselor Davis found his voice and spoke as follows: "Well, Ison has been heavily hit. Now he is broke, and naturally we will have to see to it that he gets a salary from the business." And the Dutchman, the very model of the openhanded partner and employer in a moment when labor and management were at each other's throats all over the deeply troubled American landscape, readily agreed.

From now on, Harlem's biggest policy banker was not only going to get one-third of the profits of his own policy bank (when the directorate deemed it to be making a profit, that is) but also a $200-a-week paycheck on the side. Big Joe was learning about class. Mr. Schultz had never even waved that heater at him.

Alas, a hitch quickly developed. While George Weinberg was on hand to supervise things with the help of another dependable Schultz hand, the beefy Big Harry (Harry the Horse) Schoenhaus, the Ison bank somehow failed to show any surplus available for profit-sharing. Weinberg and Schoenhaus were handling the cash, of course, and the emerging policy conglomerate had something of a bulging payroll in its other corporate ventures.

Now that might explain the streamlined bookkeeping to an outsider, but it left Big Joe somewhat bewildered when his entire share of the operation added up to the $200-a-week stipend his attorney had so thoughtfully suggested. Big Joe couldn't understand all this for a pretty good reason: his own trained eyes showed a profit of no less than $75,000 on hand (or somewhere in any event) for the first year in which he was in business with Mr. Schultz. His third should have added up to around $25,000. Where was it? He never saw anything like that.

In due course, Wilfred Brunder ran into this same depressing problem.

Quickly tiring of Bermuda (what do you do after you ride the bike down there, anyway?), this retired policy mogul slipped back into town late in 1931, staked the government to $44,784 in back taxes and penalties compounded by a mere 90 days behind bars, and then called up his old pal Joe Ison. Just like Henry Miro, he said he would like to have his bank back—and *he* heard some most disquieting news. "The game is controlled by one man now," Ison told him, "and that is a Combination headed by the Dutchman."

The dapper Brunder, an intelligent sort in his mid-thirties, still suave and nicely plump despite his brief ordeal with jailhouse food, didn't need too much elaboration. His next question was, well, couldn't he get something, any little something, out of the operation? Big Joe asked what he needed for walking-around money and the price agreed upon proved to be $100 a week, which is what Ison himself had been reduced to by then. Even this minimal arrangement collapsed within the month. Big Joe stopped paying and said he was sorry but henceforth Wilfred would have to do some work for his money. Wilfred wanted to know what kind of friendship that was and Joe said he ought to go and meet some of the new faces in the bank and see for himself.

The proud Brunder spurned that suggestion and shortly had a visit at his home from J. Richard Davis, whom he knew from the old days, along with Ison and one of the new faces—George Weinberg. Davis laid it right on the line. He told Brunder that if he wanted to get any loot out of policy he was going to get it only if he opened his own bank—under the Combination's auspices, of course. And if he opened it he would get a nifty one-third of the profits, just like Big Joe and Henry Miro. And he would get that fat $100 a week on the side. So Brunder, the man who had the know-how to salt away an admitted million and three-quarters in policy profits before Arthur Flegenheimer got interested in that business, joined the Combination in October 1932 and he was still waiting for his first touch of profit-sharing a year later. In this extremity, Brunder called Big Joe again and Big Joe took him down to Dixie Davis's plush law office at 1450 Broadway.

"Brunder is here in regards to his third, his money," said Big Joe.

"What money?" said the now-fleshy counselor.

Brunder made the long journey from Harlem down to that

full-floor legal factory no less than nine times after that and the answer, with variations, continued to be, "What money?" Davis, however, did seek to reassure him. "All you have to have is a little patience," he said, always adding that he would see Dutch Schultz and find out what could be done. After a while, Brunder caught on and walked away from policy. The game simply wasn't what it used to be—for the bankers, that is.

It was no great loss. The Combination by this time had picked up a few other recruits in its branch operations, among them the Cuban delegate in policy, Alexander Pompez. A lawyer's son, Pompez came to New York as a stripling of 20 in 1910 and went to work as a cigar maker for $20 a week. In no time at all, he had his own business in stogies—and his own numbers bank. He got off the ground with a play of $600 a day, out of his cigar store, and ran it all the way up to a respectable $8,000 or $9,000. On the side, the handsome quadroon operated the Cuban Stars semi-professional baseball team, dabbled in restaurants, night clubs and bars, and enjoyed a reputation as an elegant, suave and stylish member of the Harlem community. He was called El Cubano and he had everything going for him—until that Black Wednesday of 1931, the day in Harlem infamy which cost the assembled bankers something in the neighborhood of a quarter of a million dollars.

The Thanksgiving Eve play on the magic Number 527 in the Pompez bank was so extraordinary that he got hit for no less than $68,000. Burdened with his high standing in the community, Pompez undertook to meet his obligations down to the last dime. Short of some $8,000 or $9,000, he had it all paid and he wasn't looking for any co-makers when he found himself summoned one night to a basement rendezvous in the Cayuga Democratic Club in Harlem. Big Joe Ison was there but the hombre who did the talking was Solly Girsch, a thug of some note and a spokesman on this occasion for Arthur Flegenheimer.

Girsch, who had been known to carry a gun in certain delicate situations, suggested that for the future health of his operation Mr. Pompez really should buy himself some insurance, just like Ison. The Cuban was given two weeks to think it over. Even with all that time, he failed to think it over adequately, and so he had a visit from Solly Girsch and another rather intent Americano, and when nothing happened Bo Weinberg and Lulu Rosenkrantz dropped into his cigar store.

"The Dutchman wants to see you," the visitors said, suggesting that Mr. Pompez should sit down with Mr. Schultz at the earliest, like the following Sabbath, and just so there wouldn't be any mistake they dropped in on him that Saturday and drove him down to the home of J. Richard Davis's very own mother on West End Avenue. Presently, the Chairman of the Board arrived, with Lulu Rosenkrantz and Larry Carney to give some weight to his side of the table.

"What's the matter you don't want to come in with me?" Schultz inquired in his soft-spoken, gracious way. "You think you are going to find a man with horns in his head?"

The answer proved unsatisfactory, so the Dutchman took off his coat, exposing the dependable old bargaining weapon in his waistband (.45 caliber), and got down to business.

"I hate a liar," he said, "and you are going to be the first nigger that I am going to make an example in Harlem, because I don't like nobody telling me lies. You promised to turn in your business and you has not done it [this is Pompez quoting Schultz], and we have been waiting for your business regardless. I don't care if you make a statement from here to the Battery to the Police Department. It ain't do you no good."

While Pompez could not quite remember the dishonored promise that had made him the first Negro candidate for the spot marked X, he was impressed nonetheless. Beyond that, he knew that he couldn't go squealing to the law. He too had employed J. Richard Davis as his barrister in happier days, so he knew that the law wasn't much of a factor in the town. And now Davis was in that very room and there was nothing coming from that quarter about the legal rights of Alexander Pompez in his present dilemma.

There was some further discussion nevertheless, and finally a dispute arose over something Pompez was supposed to have said to Henry Miro about fighting off the Combination and going back to the way things used to be in the good old days. El Cubano denied that he had ever said such a bad thing and a mobile unit was dispatched forthwith to bring in the Puerto Rican. Routed out of the sheets in the middle of the night and delivered to the scene with nothing under his Chesterfield but his rumpled silk pajamas, Miro had to stand for a dressing down in front of the whole company. The Dutchman, who didn't like him from an earlier script and often referred to him as "nothing but a smart Spick," called Miro some very bad names for reporting Mr. Pompez's position so carelessly.

And so in due course, like 5:00 A.M., everything was settled happily. That is, when Alexander Pompez headed back to Harlem he was a 40 percent shareholder in the new policy bank of Alexander Pompez with a salary of $250 a week on the side. And that wasn't all, no, sir; his new 60 percent partner henceforth would stand any and all losses in the business as they might, perish the thought, occur. The old class again, escalating.

Of course, there will always be people you can't do enough for, and the cigar-and-numbers impresario proved to be one of them. He simply neglected to turn in any of the proceeds of the new Schultz-Pompez bank and had to have a visit from Bo and Lulu, followed by a second meeting with his senior partner. It is even possible that somewhere along the way El Cubano was the beneficiary of some corrective treatment, like any wayward son, although he always denied that anybody had ever laid a glove on him in anger. In any case, Pompez found once again that he was dealing with some very high-type people. When he said that he had no receipts to pass along to the Combination because he was still scratching together the $8,000 or $9,000 shy from that bad Thanksgiving, the Dutchman arranged for George Weinberg to cover the shortage the very next morning so that everybody could start out clean.

George did that, of course, and while he was there he picked up the keys to the Pompez bank. There would now be a full-time resident manager on the premises from the front office, watching the small change roll in, and there would be no further trouble. Schultz was pleased the way things flourished off such a rocky start. "I wore Pompez out," he said.

There were a few strays left to be worn out at the time.

With the help of the "smart Spick" Henry Miro and a little side-of-the-mouth talk, another substantial operator named Marcial Flores, a West Indian, was brought into the fold, and then there was some prolonged bargaining with the only two Irishmen in policy. Edwin and Elmer Maloney had built up a snug little $5,000-a-day bank, snow-white down to the runners, and they weren't interested in protection or partners or anything. Stubborn types, they shook off the Schultz emissaries and when the tough talk started they put in a call to another Irishman, Jimmy Hines, who knew the people to deal with to get them a little breathing time. The Maloneys had to come into the Combination anyway, towards April 1932, although they did manage to extract a better deal from the Dutchman than any of the other bankers. The split was fifty-fifty and Elmer Maloney, the boss, always known thereafter as "Lucky Elmer" because he had held the Schultz legions at arm's length for more than a year and never even had to have his nose fixed, drew a salary of $300 a week (so did equal partner Schultz, naturally).

There weren't many worlds left to conquer after that, because the Combination now began to encounter Negro bankers who would rather fight than switch. Stephanie St. Clair, the one who sent that drop-dead wire to Schultz when he was expiring in Newark, furnished the most outstanding example of the resistance. In policy since 1923, Madam Queen happened to be anything but a shrinking violet. Back in 1930, she had protested bitterly to Samuel Seabury that she had paid out $7,100 in ice to the Sixth Division and kept on getting busted just the same; a lieutenant and 13 plainclothesmen were suspended over that breach of police etiquette. Now in 1932 the enemy for Madam Queen was no longer the dishonorable cops but the interloper from The Bronx, and she wasn't about to hold still for that kind of shake. Once she went before a Magistrate and demanded a bench warrant for the Dutchman and some of his helpers.

"It's Schultz's life or mine," said the lady from Marseilles. "Dutch's men know I am the only one in Harlem who can take back from their boss the racket he stole from my colored friends and they know I'm going into action. That's why he wants me knifed."

Nothing came of that, of course, and presently Madam Queen took her fight right down to City Hall itself. The interim Mayor, Joseph V. McKee, sitting in pending the election of a successor to the self-exiled Jimmy Walker, a victim of Judge Seabury's probings, had his police aide, Lieutenant James Harten, entertain the fiery visitor. Madam Queen submitted that the Dutchman planned to put her on the spot and what did the city of New York propose to do about it? Lieutenant Harten said he would alert the police of Harlem to see that no harm befell her at the hands of Mr. Schultz or any other ne'er-do-well.

Around the same period, the New York *Age*, a Harlem weekly, addressed itself to the white takeover of policy with something less than a violent show of anger. While deploring the loss of Negro control of the game and observing that not enough of the take was staying in Harlem, the *Age* paid a left-handed compliment to the new, centralized policy operation:

"This arrangement is said to have one good feature, however, and that is that it insures the players of getting paid off when they hit. Formerly, when the bankers were too hard hit on any one day or succeeding days they either had to welch on payment of the hits or else go out of business. Now, it is said, with Schultz money behind the game the players are assured of payment."

One had to wonder less about this mild endorsement from a Harlem newspaper than about the New York Police Department. Did anything happen after the *Age* openly discussed the Dutchman's move into the policy racket? No.

nited Press International (above)
ew York *Post,* Anthony Calvacca (top ght)
nited Press International (bottom right)

ere are three of the Harlem policy rons who found themselves reduced to orking stiffs when Schultz moved in as artner" in the lush numbers game in the rly Thirties. Above, Wilfred Brunder. Top ght, Alexander Pompez. Bottom right, g Joe Ison.

Wide World Photos

Schultz and his counselor, J. Richard Davis. The dapper mouthpiece had a corner on the policy cases in Manhattan before the Beer Baron cast an eye toward the Negro community. Davis was a prime mover in the takeover of the $20-million-a-year racket.

Now let's see how well the business was doing.

The one who kept track of the incoming pennies of the Combination for Dutch Schultz was Big Harry Schoenhaus, no strong-arm type but perhaps the most educated man in the mob and therefore qualified for the post of Dutch Schultz's Secretary of the Treasury. A product of the Lower East Side, Schoenhaus had a whole year at Stuyvesant High School under his belt and some square employment after that. He put in 13½ years as a Post Office clerk before his retirement in 1927 (he was a mere 33 then but there was $50 in his locker that belonged in one of the cash trays). Then he started dealing poker in cigar store games and playing the horses for a living, an item a probation report would deal with in years to come, as follows: "It provided an emotional release from the stifling and confining influence of the drab and impoverished existence of his childhood and held forth the possibility of quickly and easily acquired funds which might enable him to escape from that existence." Got it? Then we shall go on with this adventure in delinquency.

After a while, Harry the Horse evidently despaired of "the possibility of quickly and easily acquired funds" in the sport of kings and went into a little policy operation with a friend —George Weinberg, of all people—before the man from The Bronx turned his acute talents to the field. Big Harry was put in charge of the Combination's books because he had demonstrated a good head for figures in the Schoenhaus-Weinberg operation, even though he hadn't been able to make it come out ahead.

What follows is his daily rundown on the One-Penny Gold Rush in the assorted banks come the winter of 1932 when the Vincent Coll trouble was just a memory (London Chemists, phone booth, lead poisoning, DOA, February 9, 1932) and the business had the Dutchman's virtually undivided attention:

ISON	$12,000
POMPEZ	11,000
MALONEY	11,000
MIRO	6,000
FLORES	3,000
BRUNDER	2,000
total	$45,000

Now take the Sundays off the calendar, since the banks paid off on the pari-mutuel numbers at the race tracks and thoroughbred horses always rest on the seventh day. Then multiply $45,000 by the remaining 313 days and you reach an annual gross of $14,085,000. Then take off the 25 percent comeback that is generally conceded to the players and that $14,085,000 is reduced by $3,520,000 to a round $10,560,000, minus the overhead, of course. A fair number, but try to remember that Big Harry was a generally conservative fellow and that this after all was Arthur Flegenheimer's sophomore semester in the industry. Growing all the time under its forceful (.38s and .45s, generally) new leadership, spreading out into The Bronx and Westchester and below the borders of Harlem into white Manhattan's slums and Brooklyn, the Combination was on its way to that peachy $20 million a year. Indeed, it was George Weinberg's estimate that the $20 million plateau was achieved before 1932 ended. Dixie Davis once put the play at $300,000 a day—or something periously close to 100 million a year, but when the overexuberant mouthpiece said that, he was referring to the policy racket as a whole. Beyond the big new conglomerate, he had to be talking about the Negro banks outside the Schultz umbrella, like Joey Rao's operation in East Harlem and all the scattered independents; even then he was way too high.

Tom Dewey told the author that the $20 million figure for the Dutchman's operation alone was the correct one. Twenty million to the company, that is. An awful lot, as noted, came off the top in addition to the winnings and whatever amounts the captive bankers could get their mitts on ("if there are profits") and what a whole Broadway law firm cost (J. Richard Davis, prop.) and what the best shooters drew (Rosenkrantz and Landau, $1,875 per week, Krompier $1,500) and the shares of the army of runners and controllers and the high cost of the occasional bust—and the even higher cost of the cops who didn't make any busts.

Finally, bear in mind that Dutch Schultz, the man come to protect the Harlem policy racket, had to have a man to protect Dutch Schultz and his racket. He had to have Jimmy Hines, and this item would run into some cash too. Oodles of cash.

"Once in a while the police and the courts and the prosecutors stand helpless, or at least seem to, before a robber gang that is bloated with wealth filched from the meager funds of the hungry and the cold. Such a time is now."

—THE REVEREND GEORGE DREW EGBERT, president of the Society for the Prevention of Crime, to Mayor Fiorello H. LaGuardia on January 21, 1935.

CHAPTER XIV
THE BIG FIX

FOR J. RICHARD DAVIS, SON OF A TAILOR FROM ROMANIA and just plain Julius Davis when he was playing the violin in the village orchestra in upstate Tannersville to earn his tuition for the University of Syracuse, nothing came easy in the early days. He had to work as a bank clerk to pay for his night classes at the New York Law School and then scratch out a bare living as a law clerk when he got his degree in 1927. When he put together enough money to hang out his own shingle, no great clamor developed for his services. It was so bad, in fact, that he finally had to open an office opposite the Washington Heights Magistrates' Court in what was perilously close to an ambulance-chasing operation, except that he went after policy defendants, not accident cases. He started with a grand total of 10 to 15 cases a week, springing the hired hands of the racket for a cut-rate $15 fee. Small potatoes, but it turned out to be an excellent investment. Pretty soon the word got around Harlem that there was a kid around the courthouse who could get you the hell out of there about as fast as the cops dragged you in. This guy knew the legal ropes. He could get a runner off even if he had been bagged with armful of policy slips. He made the great oaken portals of the smelly old house of justice look like the revolving doors of the automat; it was a rare day when a Davis client had to lose any time behind bars.

And so by 1930 J. Richard Davis, still only 26, had a virtual lock on all the Harlem policy cases. By 1931, he was handling all the business of Big Joe Ison, then the biggest of the bankers because he had inherited the operations of both Wilfred Brunder and Henry Miro. And when the arm was put on Big Joe early in that year he was able to put his client in touch with the right people so he wouldn't get pushed around too much, or maybe even hurt. The right people, of course, turned out to be the same musclemen who set out to shake Big Joe in the first place. Coincidence? Let's be charitable here. It all worked out splendidly in any case, and pretty soon Mr. Davis, the smartly efficient intermediary, had the pleasure of meeting Mr. Dutch Schultz, who was the employer of all those roughnecks and seemed so much gentler. By 1932, J. Richard was wearing $165 suits and $190 overcoats and he wasn't hustling policy clients in the corridors of the courthouse anymore. He had a platoon of hired helpers handling the minions of the racket out of a lavish office on Broadway and he was working full time for his impressive new client, who liked him so much that he called him "Sonny Boy," presumably from the smash-hit Al Jolson ballad of that name.

The real break, the one to kick the door wide open for the ugly new white faces in policy, came in that same year—with Davis again the middleman. So simple, too. All the lawyer had to do was to find a way to bring the Dutchman together with Jimmy Hines, Democratic boss of the 11th Assembly

District and the effective ruler not only of Harlem but of the whole upper West Side and a mover and shaker inside the councils of Tammany Hall. And, it followed, the man to see about almost anything. The initial "meet" took place well below the borders of Hines' uptown barony and a long way from Harlem. The district leader waited on a street corner on Sixth Avenue in Greenwich Village and the gangster drove up in his bulletproof Caddy with Davis and Leo Rosenthal, a restaurant owner and contact man for the political leader, and Hines got in and pretty soon it was just like they had all been buddies for years.

There will be conflicts in any chronicle of this kind, because different men tell the same story differently, but what follows is nonetheless the most vividly detailed account of any alliance between politics and the underworld up to that time in the endlessly corrupt and colorful annals of the world's richest city.

It began with what you might call some social warmups, or orientation sessions, perhaps, to see if both principals talked the same language. No more than a few days elapsed before the Dutchman and the bright new Attorney General in his government-within-the-government were visiting Jimmy Hines in his home and getting together three or four times a week, going to the fights, meeting in Mr. Hines' Monongahela Club or sitting around in the more exclusive speakeasies. And very shortly, around March of 1932, there was a critical business session in Bo Weinberg's penthouse just below the southern tip of Harlem, sometimes shared by Mr. Schultz himself. Everybody was there, even Lulu Rosenkrantz, the taciturn No. 3 gunbearer behind Bo and Abe Landau, and there were introductions all around and then policy's Chairman of the Board spoke.

"I can arm these different bankers but I can't protect them

in the courts, or protect them from police making arrests," the Dutchman said in his opening. The guest of honor did not ask for a definition of the word "arm." He knew it meant force, or muscle. He knew that kind of terminology as well as anyone in the room. He knew other people who talked that way. He had been exposed once as the absentee overlord of the Welfare Island Penitentiary, the man to reach if you needed a favor on the inside, or maybe even to turn the key to the outside. The Chairman, in any event, did not have much more to say. He turned the floor over to the sharp-faced six-footer who was his $200-a-week vice president for field operations—George Weinberg.

Let's pause for a moment with the wayward 30-year-old operative delegated by the Dutchman to set forth policy's inner travail for Jimmy Hines. George Weinberg, one of a brood of five left in penury when their father died young, made it through grammar school in Manhattan, worked as a parcel wrapper for Macy's and Gimbels, drove a cab at 18, did a year behind bars when he got caught carrying a gun and some burglar tools, beat three other burglary arrests, ran some slot machines in upstate Fleischmanns, set up a policy bank in Harlem in 1929 with a small-timer named Moe Levy and went broke in it, dipped into policy again with Harry Schoenhaus and blew that too, and finally turned up in the Schultz legions with an introduction from his brother Bo.

Jimmy Hines had to find George a considerably more appealing—or let's say less repugnant—figure than the gun-toting Bo. The political boss listened intently as the earnest George explained that the worst trouble with the policy business was the damned honest cop who wouldn't take the ice and kept coming around and making the same pinches over and over again. George said it was awfully hard to keep a bank operating efficiently when the little people who are its life blood—the runners and controllers—were being hauled off the streets and locked up. He told the ruddy, white-haired Hines that sometimes the honest cops, generally from outside the division, came in and busted a whole bank and threw everyone into paddy wagons even while the office help was still toting up the day's play and sorting out the winners. How'ya gonna pay off and keep your bank clean when things like that are happening? Hell, how'ya gonna get the bets in the house if your people are getting rousted on the streets before they can bring in the slips?

"I explained," George Weinberg recalled later when Jimmy Hines was on the first of his two trials and facing a possible sentence of 25 years in prison, "that in order to be able to run our business and bring it up the right way we would have to protect the controllers that are working for us. We would have to protect them from going to jail and if we got any big arrests that would hurt our business. We would want them dismissed in Magistrates' Court so that they wouldn't have to go downtown (that meant the sometimes tougher three-judge Court of Special Sessions). I explained to him that we did not mind the small arrests but if we got any large arrests we would want them dismissed in Magistrates' Court to show the people in Harlem that are working for us that we had the right kind of protection up there, and that we would want to protect them from going to jail."

Could Mr. Hines do anything about this problem?

The ex-blacksmith, brimming over with compassion for the struggling masses and happily endowed with lots of wallop both around the Police Department and the Magistrates' Courts, said sure, he could try to help.

You can imagine how much this pleased Dutch Schultz—

not that he didn't have the word before this session. He was so pleased that he told the assembled executives, the way George Weinberg recalled it, "I will give him a thousand dollars down and you pay him $500 a week from now on and any extra amounts he asks for—any reasonable amounts he might ask for." George, a meticulous sort, asked what "reasonable" meant and the Chairman said, "anything up to a thousand."

The history books will never agree on the exact amount that flowed from this loose arrangement. George Weinberg, the guy Tom Dewey initially broke in order to nail Hines but a mute witness in the district leader's second trial because he pinched a gun from one of his keepers and killed himself on January 29, 1939, in the White Plains mansion where Dewey had stashed away his witnesses, was perhaps the most reliable source. He said the $500-a-week payoff went to $750 in no time at all. Dixie Davis, in the confessional that ran in *Collier's* while he was finishing the one-year term he got off with on his own policy rap (also a round 25 years) in exchange for his testimony against Hines, said the policy banks anted up $500 but that he tossed in another $500 himself "without even telling Schultz." And that wasn't all. The way the big spender told it, he also put up the loot for the Friday night fights and all that when Mr. Hines did the necessary entertaining—judges, officeholders, big businessmen—that kept his political power mower oiled.

"I cultivated Jimmy Hines right from the beginning," said the modest barrister, who later retired to California and prospered in assorted selling ventures until he was 65, only to die of a heart attack on the last day of 1969 when he returned to his Bel Air home with his adopted son, Barkley, and found that two masked gunmen had terrorized Hope Dare in a holdup. "I soon learned that to run an organized mob you've got to have a politician. You have heard about the suspected link between organized crime and politics. Well, I became the missing link."

This was hardly an idle boast. New York's Appellate Division lifted the missing link's license in 1937 because of his wheeling and dealing for the criminal end of the chain in the good old days. The disbarment ruling established a precedent by holding that when an attorney knowingly lends advice and counsel to "a combination of persons engaged in a crime, he becomes, in effect, a member of the criminal organization and forfeits his right to membership in an honorable profession."

What it all came to for Hines, over the years, is a substantial amount, perhaps in excess of $100,000, whether you take Weinberg's $500-a-week figure or Davis's $1,000 or split it down the middle and then deduct the little pay cut the busy political boss had to suffer when the Dutchman was indicted for tax evasion and ran into heavy legal costs. The arrangement evidently lasted the better part of four years, if Weinberg and Davis are to be believed, because Hines was still supposed to be on the policy payroll a year after Schultz was assassinated. That was the year Davis remained the nominal head of the policy operation, the item Tom Dewey had him indicted for, although by then Lucky Luciano had moved in some Italian huskies, like Trigger Mike Coppola, to keep an eye on the take.

The time the payoffs started is easier to nail down with certainty because there was confirmation for it from the policy bankers, a band of rogues who for all their frailties did not possess the track record of a J. Richard Davis in the liars' sweepstakes, under oath or otherwise. Big Joe Ison traced it to the spring of 1932 because it was then that he found a fresh bite of $125 a week on his books. Struggling to make ends meet at the time so that a few dollars might show on the profit side of his bank to supplement that $200 paycheck, he asked Harry Schoenhaus about the new grunt. The bookkeeping wizard said he didn't know but he would try to find out from George and Dixie. "They said the $125 was going to Jimmy Hines' club," he reported back presently. And sure enough it turned out that the four banks then in the Combination—Ison, Pompez, Miro and Flores—were being touched for $125 apiece toward the little bundle George Weinberg was supposed to be parceling out to the district leader every Friday night (including holidays).

Once again, the bankers, now nothing more than hired hands, would discover that anything as trifling as $125 (just "a dollar and a quarter" in underworld terminology) could only be for openers. The inflationary pressures on the Combination never seemed to slacken no matter what the general economic condition in the community was, so the tab had to go higher and higher as time wore on, especially with an election year around the corner. You could only measure it against the good it might be doing you, and there was plenty of testing room for that in the policy laboratories.

The fact is that the fruits of the new arrangement blossomed like hothouse flowers. The new man in the Combination, initially listed on the Schultz books as J. H., perish the thought, but then switched to "Jimmy" or "Pop" or "the Old Man," needed very little time to show what he could deliver for his money.

Right off the bat, the Sixth Division's token policy arrests, say 20 a day or so, dropped down to eight, and then to four. And anytime a little heat came on and the arrests started going back the other way George Weinberg just had to give the Old Man a tinkle and the cops would start to show some better manners again.

The larger problem with the police was "downtown"—and it turned out that Mr. Hines could do a thing or two about the outlanders as well. This is where the real muscle evidenced itself, where the man who in effect was licensing the policy racket earned his keep and more. Now the Dutchman's real craft showed; he had bought himself the bargain of the ages.

Let's see how it paid off:

Around Thanksgiving, the pesky young men of Chief Inspector John J. O'Brien's Confidential Squad, a 16-man force working out of Police Headquarters, a safe distance away from the Hines preserve, went in and busted the big $11,000-a-day Pompez bank. It was an eminently successful trip uptown for the shooflies. They picked up 200,000 policy slips and ten men and four women employees, among them George Weinberg himself, using the name of Klein for purposes of this particular pinch. Sergeant Thomas W. Gray led the raiding force and when he thought he heard too much lip from Weinberg he whacked him so hard on the left ear that the guy had trouble with it forever after. The blow did not take too much out of the Schultz executive, however. In the paddy wagon on the way downtown, he addressed himself rather severely to another one of the arresting officers, James Canavan.

"This pinch is a lot of horseshit," said Weinberg-Klein, dabbing the damaged ear with a silk handkerchief. "If you think you're going to get any medals for this, you better get it out of your head. We will have it thrown out and you might get yourself in a bit of trouble and find yourself back in uniform."

The formerly gentle George wasn't just angry at the plainclothesmen, by the way. He was even angrier at himself for not barring the bank's portal, in a Harlem tenement, when the strangers came calling. "I wish you would have broken that door down," he said to young Canavan. "I am going to get the shit bawled out of me for opening it up."

Canavan, needless to say, felt badly about that but not so badly as to find himself adequately stirred later in the clerk's room of the court when Weinberg-Klein asked could he please have those 200,000 slips back so he could sort out the winners and pay them, like any honest policy bank should. Canavan's "no" left no room for further discourse.

Still seething, the resident manager of the Pompez branch hauled J. Richard Davis out of a sick bed as soon as the Combination's handy bondsman got him out of the toils. The barrister, drawing from his vast experience in policy cases when he was poor, offered a rather glum curbstone view of the case. He said it was a sticky one because the cops had swept up so much evidence, like those 200,000 separate items which suggested that some people were playing the numbers and some other people were covering their bets. Withal, he said he would do the best he could once his health returned. And, lo, a few days later Weinberg-Klein found himself in an audience with Jimmy Hines in the political heavyweight's apartment at 444 Central Park West.

Mr. Hines listened to the first-person account of the unfortunate raid and, ill-trained in Blackstone, did not show any undue concern about that mountain of policy slips. He did observe that those fellows from the Confidential Squad could be damned tough to handle, and the way it registered in the good ear of Weinberg-Klein, he suggested that it might be well to get the case postponed. He said it would be better if it could come before Magistrate Hulon Capshaw.

And so the case came before His Honor Mr. Capshaw, who

by great good chance had been a card-carrying member of Jimmy Hines' Monongahela Club way back in the days when he was taking his law degree at Columbia University. More than that, the Magistrate turned out to be a transplanted son of the Old South whose heart simply bled for the downtrodden blacks of the North, especially the ones slaving away in the Harlem policy banks. He tossed out the case that worried J. Richard Davis so much. How come? Well, the Magistrate found the evidence insufficient even though each and everyone of the prisoners before the bar had to admit that they were indeed toiling in the Pompez factory when the interlopers from the Confidential Squad dropped in. And all those slips vacuumed up off the table by the cops? The Magistrate found that there was no evidence of any physical possession —"constructive possession" is the legal term—of any of the slips. It was sort of like all those hapless defendants just happened to be in the same room where all those pieces of paper happened to be. The Magistrate said—this was later, under cross-examination in the Hines trial—that it would have violated his oath of office to convict anyone on the evidence before him in that case. He said that the oath required him to protect the innocent as well as the guilty.

Later on another interesting policy case came before the same jurist. Plainclothesmen Edward J. McCarthy and Robert L. Jones spotted Lulu Rosenkrantz picking up a large paper bag from a Negro outside a Harlem tenement and then driving off. Since the office work of the numbers banks had been removed to Mount Vernon in May 1933 because of the Confidential Squad's exertions, the cops had to assume that the bag contained policy slips and that Lulu was speeding them north to Westchester. So they gave chase. Lulu threw the bag out of the car before the shooflies caught up with him, still inside the jurisdiction, but the cops recovered it and found their worst suspicions confirmed. The treasure trove did indeed contain policy slips, causing them to detain Mr. Rosenkrantz.

George Weinberg turned up in due course, as an unofficial counsel for the defense, and McCarthy and Jones were assured that some suitable punishment would have to be devised for their impetuous behavior, like both of them would be back in harness in no time at all. Then Weinberg scurried around to Jimmy Hines' manse on Central Park West. In fairness, let it be noted here that this Schultz functionary also described some excursions to that sanctuary *before* Hines moved into the building, but that testimony involved some earlier history. In the visit at hand, in any case, Weinberg said the kindly district leader received him cordially and then took him to a beefsteak dinner at the Andrew B. Keating Democratic Club where, as luck would have it, they ran into Magistrate Hulon Capshaw on the very steps. The way Weinberg told it, Hines said, "I have a policy case, a very important one, coming up before you that I'd like you to take care of for me," and the Judge replied, "I haven't failed you yet. I'll take care of it."

While that hasty dialog rested on the bad ear of George Weinberg, Dixie Davis, who had all good ears, said that he also talked to Jimmy Hines about the case of Lulu Rosenkrantz—Louis Silverstein in this instance—and that the word he got was, "It will be OK." And that's the way it came out.

Hulon Capshaw found the plainclothesmen's story entirely deficient from a legal point of view—how could they show any connection between that paper bag full of policy slips and that fellow they were chasing in that car?—and Rosenkrantz-Silverstein walked out.

The Magistrate, eventually thrown off the bench by the Appellate Division over his handling of the two cases described here, compounded by the nature of his testimony in the second Hines trial before Judge Charles C. Nott Jr., always denied the stories told by Weinberg and Davis. He denied ever having seen Weinberg—the "Klein" of the Pompez raid—at the Andrew Keating club with the district leader. He denied any improper influence in the Pompez case itself. He would spend the rest of his life in a tireless losing battle to clear his name, supporting himself by doing legal chores—but not practicing law, of course—in his brother's law firm.

Be that as it may, Tom Dewey insisted in his bill of particulars in the case against Hines that Hulon Capshaw and at least one other Magistrate, Francis J. Erwin (deceased before the dirty linen was hung out), as well as the Honorable District Attorney, Bill Dodge, had been either "influenced, intimidated or bribed" by the district leader in the interests of Dutch Schultz. And the Hines trials were simply chock full of evidence that a policy defendant with any kind of know-how invariably made every effort to come before the bar when either Capshaw or Erwin happened to be wearing the black robes. Moreover, there was no shortage of testimony to suggest that the Dutchman's more highly placed toilers exhibited a king-sized contempt for the honest cops once the alliance between the Combination and Hines was sealed.

Take the time the Confidential Squad went back and busted the Pompez bank again after the big raid failed to pass Judge Capshaw's strict scrutiny. George Weinberg escaped the net on the second sweep but as he stood outside watching the fresh band of prisoners being led away he spotted Jim Canavan and said, sourly, "I see you're still at it."

"Yes," said Canavan, "and I'm not in uniform yet."

"You will be," said Weinberg, and it will be seen that he knew what he was talking about.

While nobody was going to jail in the continuing raids, with the plainclothesmen hitting all the banks impartially, even Big Joe Ison's $12,000-a-day operation, Schultz did have to switch the office operation to Westchester for a while to get the enemy cops off his back. Canavan ran into Abbadabba Berman outside of Dave's Blue Room on Broadway during this period—

ABBADABBA: I see you guys made the mob move to Mount Vernon.

CANAVAN: Yes. Now we've got nothing to worry about.

ABBADABBA: You have so got something to worry about. They're working on you to get you transferred. You know they can do it.

Similarly, when the raiders knocked over the numbers drops of the Maloney brothers sometime earlier and Plainclothesman Raymond R. Stilley encountered George Weinberg outside of court, this dialog ensued—

WEINBERG: Is there anything we can do in this case?

STILLEY: There's nothing you can do.

WEINBERG: Oh, you're one of those tough cops from downtown. We're going to have you transferred.

This must have sounded like so much blather, but the hoodlums' threats, as suggested, were hardly idle. The raids had proved awfully expensive. The two Pompez busts cost that bank $100,000 worth of action; the rule-of-thumb was that any numbers operation needed no less than two weeks to get its normal play back after being knocked out, however briefly, by the cops. On top of that, in long-range terms, the mob had to worry about the fractured morale of the bettors. How long would they stay with it after any of the banks stopped paying because the cops had made off with all them cherished dream book numbers?

Well, that was the sort of problem which had prompted the alliance between Dutch Schultz and Jimmy Hines in the first place, wasn't it? It was indeed—and come winter the bright young men of the Confidential Squad began to disappear from Harlem like so many policy slips blowing away in the wind. Sergeant Gray found himself pounding a beat. Canavan had to go dig his old blues out of the closet and take a $240-a-year pay cut in the process until Tom Dewey brought him over to his special staff so that he could help make the case against Hines. The captain of the squad, William P. Bennett, was transferred. And Stilley. And Jacob Katz, another one of Gray's troops. And Joe Terminello, who made some policy busts and found himself back in harness just 48 hours after running into George Weinberg one day and hearing this quiet lecture: "You cannot do this sort of thing to us. It will just harm you, Terminello." Julius Salke, the detective who had captured Dutch Schultz in the shootout on Fifth Avenue in 1931, had the very same experience with Bo Weinberg when he picked him up in 1933. "You will be wearing a bag [uniform] in Staten Island," said the prisoner. "It won't be long." Salke scoffed. "You are a lot of noise," he told the big gunman. "A lot of bull." Oh, yeah? Salke was busted in no time—on the orders of the Police Commissioner himself.

It turned out in the Hines trial that all the transfers stemmed from calls Jimmy Hines made to the man he had helped install as leader of Tammany Hall, John F. Curry. It was a simple triple play after that kind of call: Curry to his hand-picked Commissioner, James S. Bolan, to the head of the Confidential Squad, Inspector John O'Brien, and, presto, the heads rolled. This was very good for the Combination. Nobody ever had any occasion to squawk about Jimmy Hines or question his wallop with the high brass or the judges (hell, out of 278 gambling arrests in one of his own political clubs over a four-year period a total of three convictions had been racked up in the courts) or the D. A's. office. The fellow knew his way around. Dutch Schultz would always be indebted to Dixie Davis for that street-corner introduction.

The man who had one of the most trying experiences on the stand in the Hines trial was Commissioner Bolan. Small, gaunt and drawn, out of office by then, he appeared as the opening defense witness—and he would always regret that encounter with Tom Dewey. His first mistake was to insist that no politician ever would have had the unspeakable gall to call upon him for a favor of any kind, an item any alert juror might have questioned even if Dewey had elected to let it go unchallenged. Bolan, after all, succeeded Edward P. Mulrooney in that exalted office in 1933 in the wake of the celebrated press conference in which incoming Mayor John Patrick O'Brien, the ultimate in Tammany hacks, performed the greatest single act of candor in the city's political history when he was asked who was going to be his Police Commissioner. "I haven't had any word on that yet," said the rotund O'Brien.

Now here was Jim Bolan waxing wroth over a suggestion by the prosecutor that men like John Curry or Jimmy Hines, wired into the municipal government, had pulled some strings in his office. The witness conceded that he knew the gentlemen but swore that he had never busted a single cop for either of them. Under Dewey's probing, this didn't hold. Bolan had to admit that, well, yes, come to think of it, he had passed some "requests" for transfers along to some cops' commanding officers on occasion. It took some squirming but the ex-Commissioner didn't have much choice.

The aging John Curry, long since fallen out with his pal Hines in some internecine warfare in the Tammany Wigwam, had testified that it was his practice to pass along 50 to 75 requests for police transfers every year. He said the requests generally came from district leaders—including James J. Hines—and he always transmitted them to the Police Commissioners (including Mr. Bolan) through Bert W. Stand, secretary of Tammany Hall. Lloyd Paul Stryker, the tall and distinguished defense attorney, fought the Curry testimony bitterly but Dewey had strong confirmation on the transfers from Inspector O'Brien himself. He swore that he had tossed Gray, Canavan and Stilley off the Confidential Squad on the orders—not request, orders—of Bolan.

Once this aspect of the policy story was all in the record, Dewey took the ex-Commissioner through a blistering intelligence test on the underworld of his time.

DEWEY: Did you ever hear of Dutch Schultz?

BOLAN: Yes.

DEWEY: When was the last time you heard of him?

BOLAN: Oh, I don't know.

DEWEY: Don't you know that Dutch Schultz rose to fame and power in the county over which you had command and in which you were personally responsible?

Wide World Photos

Head high, Jimmy Hines takes a last look at the outside world as he enters Sing Sing Prison.

New York *Post,* Calvacca

Four years later, in the fall of 1944, Jimmy Hines waves a farewell to the prison on the Hudson.

New York *Post,* Anthony Calvacca

District Attorney Thomas E. Dewey on his way into Manhattan Supreme Court during the first trial of Jimmy Hines, in September 1938.

New York *Post, Calvacca* (above)
New York *Post* (top right)
Wide World Photos (bottom right)

The three songbirds, all ex-Schultz helpmates, who helped Tom Dewey put the powerful Jimmy Hines behind bars: George Weinberg (above), office manager for the Schultz policy "business." Top right, Dixie Davis, who brought the gangster and the political boss together. Bottom right, Big Harry Schoenhaus, bookkeeper for the ring. Weinberg killed himself between the two Hines trials but his testimony stood up.

Wide World Photos

Trailed to a Philadelphia hideout after skipping town when Tom Dewey had them indicted in the policy racket, Dixie Davis (with a new mustache) and George Weinberg are booked in court. The woman is Davis's sweetheart, ex-Follies girl Hope Dare, held on a fugitive charge which was later dropped. The man on the left is Charles P. Grimes, a Dewey assistant.

Wide World Photos

With the Hines trial and a short jail term behind him, Dixie Davis married Hope Dare in the summer of 1939.

(Bolan was Deputy Chief Inspector, commanding the uniformed force, while the Dutchman was on the rise.)

BOLAN: I didn't know that. It has been said.

DEWEY: Have you any doubt about it?

BOLAN: I have.

DEWEY: What doubt?

BOLAN: Well, I get some information from the press.

DEWEY: Don't you know he was the biggest gangster in the city?

BOLAN: There was some newspaper talk about it.

DEWEY: Who did you think was the biggest gangster in the city?

BOLAN: I didn't think there was any.

The prosecutor then reeled off the names of some of the Schultz troops—Marty Krompier, the Weinbergs, Abe Landau, Lulu Rosenkrantz.

DEWEY: Did you know any of these?

BOLAN: I read of them in the newspapers.

DEWEY: What did you do about them when you read of them in the newspapers?

BOLAN: Why, nothing.

DEWEY: You thought they were just a lot of fiction the newspapers were printing to amuse their readers?

BOLAN: I don't know why they did it.

"Don't you know about the biggest mob of gangsters this country has ever seen?" Dewey demanded at another point, elevating Dutch Schultz to an eminence he never really quite enjoyed.

"Only what I read in the newspapers," said old Jim Bolan, a cop for 38 years.

Well, if the police themselves—even the Commissioner—had to find it out from the newspapers in the time of Arthur Flegenheimer . . .

"The Tax Collector's letters are invariably mimeographed and all they say is that you still haven't paid him."

—WILLIAM SAROYAN

CHAPTER XV

ON THE LAM?

ON JANUARY 25, 1933, A FEDERAL GRAND JURY IN NEW York wound up a wearying 20-month marathon and indicted Arthur Flegenheimer on the same charge that had brought down Al Capone: income tax evasion. The jurors had examined carloads of evidence and taken testimony from 300 witnesses paraded before them by that 31-year-old prodigy in the United States Attorney's office—Thomas E. Dewey.

The indictment cited the reformed Beer Baron for neglecting to file returns during 1929, 1930 and 1931 on $481,637.35 in taxable income from his multimillion-dollar bootlegging operations. The figures for 1931, showing a gross of $728,000 and a net of $237,000, made no reference to any odd nickels and dimes which may have come into the Dutchman's coffers from the policy racket in his maiden year in that Harlem vineyard. The government may not have known about the new Flegenheimer sideline, since the police of that happy time weren't taking any pains to broadcast the guy's connection with anything so odious as a game that preyed on the poor.

Schultz, charged with cheating Uncle out of $92,103.34 in the three-year period, did not need to be reminded that a tax rap had reduced Al Capone from his baronial underworld eminence to the overall shop in the federal pen in Atlanta before consigning him to an even drearier existence on that dreadful rock in the Pacific called Alcatraz. The Capone conviction only went back to October 1931.

But even beyond any painful reflections about how nasty the courts could be with racket bums who failed to cut the government in on a decent share of the proceeds, the Dutchman had to think twice about standing trial at that moment in a case in which he faced a possible 43 years in prison and something like $110,000 in fines.

In the first place, he was too busy.

While Repeal was about to remove him from the beer and whisky trade, he had his hands full with the infinitely more complex and troublesome policy operation. and he was going to need to wring more and more money out of the numbers, not just for the inevitable showdown over taxes but for a much more immediate necessity. There was an election coming and the mob had to put its holstered shoulder to the wheel to help Jimmy Hines see that the right kind of guy occupied the office of District Attorney of Manhattan. To raise the loot for this worthy cause, Schultz would have to tap the policy banks harder and harder—an item that could not well be left entirely to the Combination's subordinates.

So the Dutchman, hardly caught by surprise when the indictment was handed down, elected to become a fugitive rather than tangle with Tom Dewey. Now lest there be any undue concern about the man's plight, it is well to note that he did not become a fugitive in the pure Webster sense ("resorting to flight, running away, fleeing as from pursuit, danger, or restraint"). No. None of those conditions could be applied to Arthur Flegenheimer. While he would be identified for the next 22 months as the "fugitive mobster" he wasn't going to have to do much running. He wasn't even going to have to spoil that plain raw map of his with a mustache or dye his hair the way Vincent Coll had to do when he was on the lam.

Thus we come to one of the more intriguing periods in the Schultz saga, because it says something about his brash ways and, more important, it says something about the police of New York in the Year of Our Lord 1933—and 1934, too.

Manhattan Headquarters launched the search for Arthur Flegenheimer by putting out 50,000 wanted cards on him for worldwide distribution—and the face on the card supposedly was the object of a manhunt by the city's 18,000 men in blue as well as that little band of never-say-die federal men on the Eastern Seaboard. The same face adorned post office bulletin boards everywhere and might as well have been up in lights on Broadway along with such other familiar faces of the time as George M. Cohan, Fred Astaire or Bert Lahr. Beyond this, we were told that there was a round-the-clock vigil on all airports, piers and depots. Get it? The Big Town was locked up tight. The hunted man could never get away.

He never had to.

He was home, tending to his business. Oh, he kept some spare haberdashery in Connecticut, outside the Dewey jurisdiction, but George Weinberg never had to take any time away from the on-the-scene policy operation to go all the way up there to see the Chairman of the Board. George could always see the boss in a flat he had on East 44th Street or in a hideaway apartment at 89th Street and Riverside Drive, where Dixie Davis talked about seeing him too, or in a spare place he kept way up at Broadway and 207th Street. For that matter there were moments of crisis when one could see the

Dutchman in the wide-open storefront GHQ of the policy racket at 351 Lenox Avenue in the very heart of Harlem.

But wait. The portrait of the mobster in flight gets more interesting as it goes along.

Frances Flegenheimer said she had gone to Pennsylvania Station with Arthur several times in 1933—did you note above how the depots were being watched?—to see Jimmy Hines or Dixie Davis off for Washington. This was in the period when efforts were being made to straighten out Schultz's tax problems; presumably some eleventh-hour strategy sessions at the station were indicated. Frances furnished some other interesting tidbits on the fugitive as well. She said that one night in 1934 she had a late dinner with Arthur and Mr. Hines at Luchow's after the three of them had killed some time in a night club. She didn't name the club; it might have been one of the more secluded oases. As for Luchow's, that celebrated downtown haven of the sauerbraten crowd was about as private as Penn Station itself, although it is conceivable that the manhunters could have missed their quarry in such roomy quarters. It's a shame the sleuths never tried the Embassy Club on East 57th Street, a carriage trade joint the Dutchman himself owned at one time or another. Edward Severi, bartender at the Embassy, something of a Manhattan shrine because that's where Helen Morgan used to sit on the old upright and tear everybody's heart out with her rendition of *Bill,* said that he served Mr. Schultz somewhere between 20 to 25 times while he was on the lam —and on four or five of those occasions he thought the party drinking with the underworld potentate looked an awful lot like James J. Hines.

None of this, of course, is meant to suggest that the fugitive made it a universal practice to flaunt himself in public places.

In the more idle hours, he managed to keep up his customary attendance in the play-for-pay boudoirs operated by that outstanding saleswoman of the time, Miss Polly Adler. In her book, *A House Is Not a Home*, the mini-sized Madam recalled that while the Dutchman treated her girls to a welcome respite when he had to go underground after the murder of Vincent Coll "he reappeared upon the scene in the late summer of 1933" and was very much in evidence from that point on, escorting "important political figures" to all-night soirees with the hired help.

Night? The hunted man also was available in the daytime. Miss Adler said he turned up on a moment's notice one time after a band of neighborhood hoodlums made unscheduled visits to her playpen on successive nights and wrecked the joint. All she had to do, she said, was to tell Bo Weinberg what had happened and there was her friend Schultz—moving through midtown Manhattan in broad daylight without a care in the world. Now this may not have been as daring a feat as it sounded, because the Dutchman generally didn't have to go very far to get to Polly's place. They were neighbors. The Adler love-for-sale emporium in those days was on West 54th Street and the amorous gangster by then had a night club of his own on that same thoroughfare. This was the Chateau Madrid, always a favorite resort of Schultz's even though the sidewalk outside ran with the blood of Joey Noe on that fateful night back in 1928. On a dummy floor below the club, Schultz maintained a lavish office spread, complete with living quarters as well as all the accoutrements of a small fortress.

While George Weinberg never mentioned it, the fact is that the fugitive was also available to insiders in that snug haven in the heart of the little village Peter Minuit had picked up from the Indians for $24 some 300 years before the modern-time Dutchman decided to make Manhattan *his* preserve. And without wishing to be nasty the author invites the reader to bear in mind that the Chateau Madrid not only was conveniently close to Polly Adler's place but also was just a hop-skip-and-jump away from the West 54th Street police station, like three blocks. It is also well to remember that when the new year turned there was a new broom in the City Hall, wielded by Fiorello LaGuardia, and a tough new Commissioner, Lewis J. Valentine, at Police Headquarters. This is not necessarily to infer either a lack of concern or any corruption on such lofty 1934 levels but just to underline the extraordinary immunity enjoyed by Arthur Flegenheimer when whole armies were supposed to be beating the bushes for him. Obviously, Lewis Valentine could not get the top brass under him to get the gold badges under them to get a couple of plain ordinary detectives to go bring in the most celebrated tax dodger of the time and, incidentally, the boss of the policy racket which the new Mayor was talking about stamping out.

Now if Schultz was so much as playing the part of the hunted man during his cash-and-carry idylls with the inmates of Polly Adler's house of all nations, he surely never betrayed it. Thus one day, Polly, returning from a visit to her parents in Brooklyn, found her Number One customer "in the kitchen, sitting with his feet propped on the window sill, reading *The Life of Al Capone.*" Doing some research, no doubt, but there's a larger point here. The Dutchman evidently felt as safe in Polly Adler's midtown sin den—at the window, indeed—as he would have felt on the Island of Elba (mentioned in this connection only because Dixie Davis once listed Emil Ludwig's *Life of Napoleon* as one of his client's favorite tomes).

Perhaps one should be charitable and concede that the fugitive really ran no risk of detection in Polly Adler's window because all the town's Javerts had their eyes peeled squarely to the ground looking for footprints in the relentless search for him. But this brings up still another item: only two years had elapsed since Judge Seabury had plastered the peppery Madam all over the front pages in his investigation into the prostitution industry and its alliances with officialdom. What is noteworthy is that the Dutchman could loll around Miss Adler's new pleasure palace secure in the knowledge that no nosy cops were ever coming around perchance to see if that woman of scarlet had fallen upon her errant ways again. You might say that Mr. Schultz was just as safe from apprehension there as he was at Penn Station, Luchow's or the Embassy Club.

Lest any impression get abroad here that the eternal weakness of the flesh is what kept the fugitive around Manhattan so much with all that cold heat on him, let us consider here not just his policy and tax headaches but his 1933 debut in Democratic machine politics. Schultz had a fair amount of muscle and money—and a pretty good piece of his future—wrapped up in the municipal campaign that winter. Maybe he couldn't keep those stiff-necked federal tax snoops off his back, but he could do himself a great deal of good in his "business" if he had the right kind of guys in high office in the town. This is not to say that the Dutchman had set his sights on any impossible dream. Being so close to a district leader whose father and grandfather before him had served as Tammany captains under such monumental boodle boys as Richard Croker and William Marcy Tweed, Schultz knew better.

"We have to concentrate on the D.A. more than anything

else," he told George Weinberg in one of his Manhattan hideaways that September. "It looks like the D.A. has a chance where the Mayor might not have a chance."

Did it pay to know Jimmy Hines or not? Of course. Jimmy Hines knew that LaGuardia, bobbing downstream with the sweet wind of reform at his back, was unbeatable. The Little Flower was running against Tammany's bumbling John P. O'Brien with Joe McKee of The Bronx on the ballot as an independent Democrat, a cinch to draw off O'Brien votes. So the mob's mission, as Arthur told George, was to elect itself a District Attorney—and Mr. Hines happened to have the man for the job. Tom Dewey said that Jimmy Hines wanted William Copeland Dodge because William Copeland Dodge was "stupid, respectable and my man." In the first Hines trial, before Judge Ferdinand Pecora, Dewey would introduce evidence to show that those quotes belonged to the district leader.

Dixie Davis, for example, swore that when Hines told him he was going to back Dodge, then a Magistrate, for the nomination, this dialog ensued—

> DAVIS: I don't see why you should be for Dodge because I think he is very stupid and he doesn't know what it is all about, and he would be harmful to us because of his stupidity.
>
> HINES: I wouldn't worry about it. I can handle him.
>
> DAVIS: If he's Okay with you he'll be all right with me —but I still think he's stupid.

When Davis in another reference testified that he told Hines that he did not think that Dodge "would make a good man" as District Attorney, Judge Pecora broke in:

"A good man for whom or what?"

"I meant by that that he might make a good man for the people of New York City but I didn't have any faith in what he might do for us."

"Us?" asked Pecora.

"I meant Schultz and those people who afterwards financed his campaign," Davis said.

Pecora ordered that answer stricken as too vague.

"I meant the underworld," Davis then said.

"Who, name them," said the Judge, and now he got this answer from the busted barrister:

"I meant Schultz. I meant Bo. I meant Ison. I meant Pompez. I meant Hines and I meant myself. I meant everybody that was in any way connected with us."

Getting the nomination for Dodge proved to be no problem, naturally. Jimmy Hines simply passed the word along to John Curry in the Tammany wigwam and, lo, the Judge turned up on the O'Brien ticket. Henry Sobel, one of the party faithful, was named campaign manager for the austere-looking candidate and when he asked Mr. Curry about the wherewithal, like money to hustle up the votes, he was referred to Hines. There were 70 district leaders in the Hall at the time, mind you, but only Mr. Hines was to be tapped for the drive to install Bill Dodge in that big, musty office in the Criminal Courts Building.

Sobel, an insurance man, said that Hines came up with $11,000—and there's a small embarrassment there too. George Weinberg testified that the policy banks were tapped for $32,000 for the Dodge campaign, and Dixie Davis swore that he personally had $12,000 to $15,000 of that amount shoveled along to Hines. Beyond that, there was a smattering of testimony from some of the policy bankers on the amounts the mob had slugged them for during the campaign. Big Joe Ison, for one, said he had to hold still for successive bites of $2,500 each that fall and when he asked George Weinberg about the fresh assessments on the banks he was told, "They're campaign funds for the Democratic Party. We want a Democratic Mayor and a Democratic District Attorney."

Indeed, the Combination's enthusiasm for the party of progress and social enlightenment was so boundless that year that Big Spender Davis threw in two or three grand of his very own—or so he said—as shortages afflicted the campaign kitty. It adds up then not just to $32,000 but perhaps to 34 or 35 Big Ones against the $11,000 Sobel reported collecting for the Dodge drive. One can only wonder which portions of the missing currency stuck to whose hands while Bill Dodge labored valorously on the stump to bring a new kind of crime-fighting to the racket-infested metropolis. It is a fair assumption that Henry Sobel didn't get away with any of it, because the mob must have had all kinds of eyes trained on him while he made his journeys back and forth from Harlem to replenish that anemic campaign chest. If you can believe men like Weinberg and Davis, the sticky fingers had to belong to nobody other than James J. Hines, but then you would have to allow for the fact that the district leader might have done some direct spending in that campaign without using Henry Sobel as a middleman. Hines, having protested his innocence all the way in the matter of Dutch Schultz, never had occasion to try to set any portion of the record straight. Found guilty and sent to Sing Sing on a four-to-eight-year sentence, he did three years and ten months behind the gray walls and, burdened with garlands for his labors in the prison greenhouse, came out at the age of 67 just as grimly tight-lipped as ever.

George Weinberg told of one instance a month before the election when Davis called him and said the "Old Man" (Hines) needed some instant cash for the Dodge campaign and to scoop up $3,000 in small bills and rush them right down to the law office of Joseph Shalleck, a Hines pal. "I greeted Hines and told him, 'I have that money for you,' " whereupon—this is Weinberg's testimony—the "Old Man" turned to a bespectacled gentleman in the room and said, "Do you know George? This is one of Dutch Schultz's boys. This is where I am getting my money for your campaign." The way Weinberg remembered it, the man with the glasses was William Copeland Dodge. And he remembered that the candidate was so grateful that he staked him to a handshake. Dodge, for his part, had no memory of such a meeting in the Shalleck office or anywhere else. "I never saw that man in my entire life," he said on the witness stand. "I was never introduced to him. I never shook hands with him. And no money was ever passed by him to Mr. Hines in my presence."

Beyond that, the beleaguered Dodge denied that Hines ever told him that the mob was picking up all the grunts for his campaign. He said that Henry Sobel, an honorable sort, never would have taken that kind of tainted money.

The former District Attorney had a bad time on the stand when it was brought out that a Grand Jury he impaneled in 1935 to look into policy and other naughty things had heard testimony to the effect that the underworld had bankrolled his election. Dodge had trouble remembering whether the assistant who presented that evidence, Maurice G. Wahl, had told him precisely what had come out.

"Is it your testimony here in this courtroom," Dewey asked him, "that Wahl did not tell you that the underworld or Dutch Schultz or gangsters, or something like that, had contributed money to your campaign?"

"Now he may have mentioned Dutch Schultz, I have forgotten about that," Dodge replied. Then he said no, Wahl had not mentioned Schultz. Then he said well, maybe Wahl did say the money had come from the Schultz crowd. Then, worse, Dodge had to admit under Dewey's insistent prodding that while Wahl had indeed told him something about that interesting testimony on May 13 he didn't bother to look into it until August 16 when the Grand Jury transcript reached his desk. And what did he do then? Whatever it was, it had to be minimal at best, according to Dodge's own admissions. He said he did not question Hines, or Sobel, or his campaign treasurer, William R. McIntosh or, for that matter, anybody else. It added up to a highly damaging portrait of a District Attorney maintaining either an extraordinary calm or an inexplicable indifference after a Grand Jury—in this case his *own* Grand Jury—had heard a qualified witness testify that known criminals had put him in office.

The questioning of Dodge, unfortunately, did not touch upon his skintight victory in the election. While the Republican-Fusion forces of LaGuardia were marching triumphantly into City Hall with a plurality of 259,469, the Hines-Schultz candidate for District Attorney of Manhattan managed to squeeze in with a bare 15,015 votes to spare over Jacob Gould Schurman Jr., the GOP standard bearer, and Ferdinand Pecora, the same Pecora who would turn up on the bench five years later to preside over Jimmy Hines' first ordeal before the bar (Pecora declared a mistrial when Tom Dewey made the mistake of throwing in a question about the poultry racket).

How much did the mob help with the votes Dodge needed? Dixie Davis said that on Election Night the more muscular luminaries of the Dutchman were assembled in force in Hines' Monongahela Club to direct an army of floaters recruited to go to the polls and cast their votes—four or five times each, that is—for William Copeland Dodge. Davis said the floaters were handed a variety of registration cards—the traditional "graveyard vote" of the big-city machines—and some assorted dollar bills to compensate them for their labors. Davis listed Abe Landau, Marty Krompier, Lulu Rosenkrantz, Larry Carney, George Weinberg, Big Harry Schoenhaus and Jules Martin, the Schultz restaurant racket associate who later came to a rather bad end (the Dutchman, as will be seen, blew his head off to settle an argument). When Dewey reeled off all those names, throwing in Abbadabba Berman for good measure, Dodge submitted that it was a gallery of scoundrels utterly unbeknownst to him. He denied that Hines had ever mentioned that guy Dixie Davis to him, for that matter.

Speaking of the voluble Schultz mouthpiece, Davis testified that he went to Hines during that fruitless 1935 swipe at policy by the Dodge Grand Jury and protested that the District Attorney was hounding him. "Hines said 'We won't worry about him,' " the lawyer went on. Was this so? Dodge, a staid 58-year-old New Englander suddenly floundering in the muddy waters of Manhattan but testifying in a firm and forceful voice as he tilted with the young prosecutor who had succeeded him when he elected not to seek another term in 1937, swore that Hines never once dared to tell him to keep his mouth shut.

As far as policy went, the burden of Dodge's recital was that in his time in office the sun barely set on a day when he wasn't pulling out all the stops to bring down the numbers mob. He said that policy arrests had tripled during his administration. Dewey didn't need to challenge that handsome statistic, since the record by then was bulging with testimony about the booming prosperity the racket enjoyed until Arthur Flegenheimer's outside troubles took his firm hand off the tiller.

Prosperity? The ever-thoughtful Dutchman found a way in 1933 to increase his own take from policy in the face of ever-rising costs. That was the Year of the Fix—Abbadabba Berman's time, a good time for the Combination and a bad time for the poor people of Harlem.

Abbadabba originally came around with his $10,000-a-week proposition in the fall of 1932. He said he could go to the tracks and fix it so that the pari-mutuel totals would hardly ever wind up to coincide with any heavily played numbers. Now that sounds ridiculous, but who could doubt the guy with the adding machine mind? Nobody. Schultz listened with a fine glow—color it green—in his bedroom eyes but turned the deal down. With millions rolling in and relative peace among the natives in the ranks, he said he thought it would be best to keep policy honest and give the players a better shake.

Come June 1933, however, adversity had eaten away at the man's less-than-Puritan moral fiber. Apart from all the bites Jimmy Hines was putting on, his legal bills were running up because he had a small army jogging between New York and Washington trying to buy off his tax case with a $100,000 settlement. You could not expect the guy to cover all those grunts with the grand a week he customarily took from each of the policy banks for walking-around money, could you? Of course not. George Weinberg said that within a period of months while the boss was on the lam and fussing over that tax headache he had to haul no less than $275,000 out of the

Combination's strong box for him in dribs and drabs of, oh, $25,000 to $50,000. So it was indeed time to tap the loyal Harlem masses a little harder. It was time to call in Abbadabba and cut down on them winning numbers.

To see how easy this was, you start with the method by which the daily policy number is arrived at. The winner is derived from the third digit in the pari-mutuel payoff totals for the first three races, then the first five races, then the first seven. Thus if the payoffs on the winning horses in the first three races added up to $315.60 and then went to $731.60 after the fifth race and $913.40 after the seventh the winning number (the one before the digits) would be 513. Well, all Abbadabba had to do was to go to the Coney Island track in Cincinnati, or to the New Orleans tracks or Florida's Tropical Park when their pari-mutuel totals were being used, and set himself up at a telephone. Just before the seventh race he would call George Weinberg in New York and tell him which two winning numbers had emerged from the first five races —5 and 1 in the example used here. Weinberg would riffle through the day's play, all collected from the various drops and neatly sorted out by then, and tell Abbadabba which digit or digits from one to ten on the seven-race totals would produce the most winning tickets. Let's say that in this instance Weinberg reported that 513 and 517 would hurt the most.

This is where the lightning brain comes in. Just as the windows were closing for the seventh, Abbadabba would go over the payoffs on the sixth-race winners and then study the odds on all the horses in the next one to see whether the probable returns on the top three were apt to produce a total which would cause a 3 or 7 to come up in the seven-race summary. Again for purposes of our example, let's say that

Abbadabba found that the indicated payoff on the top-heavy favorite in the race—the chalk, as the high players call it—was going to cause the seven-race totals to come out to $913 and change, thus making 513 the numbers winner for the day.

Once Abbadabba had that figured out—we're down to split seconds now, mind you—he would have to throw some fast bets into the window to alter the odds and change the payoffs. Abbadabba, only Abbadabba, could do that, and at Coney Island, moreover, he enjoyed a singular advantage. There he had a way to get his bets down *after* the seventh started and while the field was still battling for the finish line. A sure system. He was exercising the final say on the payoffs and maybe now and then snaring himself a winner in the process—and collecting $10,000 a week for the strain all this put on his mental processes.

It sounds impossible, but it worked because of the sheer mechanical wizardry of Mr. Biederman-Berman, compounded, of course, by the privileges he enjoyed around the friendlier tracks. You understand, it couldn't have been done without the rare benefit of that outside telephone line and the collaboration of the world's most congenial track officials and mutuel clerks.

How well did it work? George Weinberg said that "pretty near every day was a winning day" after Abbadabba began to toil in the Dutchman's cause because the banks seldom got stung for anything worse than small hits. In simple terms, the rigged payoffs almost invariably steered the pari-mutuel totals away from the more heavily played numbers, and this happy process, in operation whenever the right tracks were running, ran on and off from 1933 into 1935. How much it may have enriched the individual banks in the Combination

New York *Post,* Louis Liotta

Polly Adler, the peppery little madam, numbered Dutch Schultz among her steadier clients. He even showed up at her Manhattan bordello when he was a fugitive, supposedly in full flight from the federal men and police. This is a 1953 photo of Miss Adler, long after her retirement from the flesh trade.

is something else. To begin with, the Dutchman made them ante up $2,500 a week apiece to pay that initial overhead item of $10,000 to compensate Abbadabba for his exhausting labors. It is a fair assumption that the lion's share of policy's new-found wealth wound up in the pockets of the game's white master.

Strangely, it wasn't enough.

In the same year, Schultz found it necessary—or perhaps the word is advisable—to cut the commissions of his runners and controllers to put some more bulge into the Arthur Flegenheimer Defense Fund against that inevitable rainy day in court. How much of a cut? A round 50 percent, down to 10 percent for the runners and 5 percent for the controllers, seemed about right, and in a move of such dimensions the proper executive breaks the news himself even if he happens to be the nation's most wanted (or is it "wanted") fugitive. So, with New York clearly exempt from the worldwide search for him, the Dutchman around Decoration Day of 1933 showed up in person at his Lenox Avenue GHQ to break the bad news.

This session, combining the agony of a pay cut with the ecstasy of a rare visit with the big boss, was aired early in 1935 in the course of a bail bond investigation conducted by Paul Blanshard, Mayor LaGuardia's vigorously incorruptible Commissioner of Accounts. Irving Ben Cooper, Blanshard's Seabury-trained counsel, elicited the story from the lips of Max Romney, a tall and elegant East Indian Negro who went back to 1920 in policy. Romney, a controller for the Combination, told Cooper that the Dutchman's poverty plea fell on universally deaf ears even though his less charming helpers, such as Abe Landau, were talking rather freely about breaking some heads if any serious resistance developed. The mobsters evidently had never learned the aphorism that in unity there is strength. Now they found out about it. The runners and controllers hired a hall and held a mass protest meeting, like any labor stiffs going against a skinflint employer, and declared a strike of sorts. All of a sudden fewer and fewer bets were being delivered to the banks, reducing the vast policy inflow to a mere trickle as the Dutchman's street soldiers lost their zeal for shaking the nickels and dimes out of the pockets of their Harlem neighbors.

How effective was this? Alexander Pompez told the Hines trial that his bank's volume dropped from $9,000 a day to $186 in the first week of the strike. The lesson, naturally, was not lost on Dutch Schultz. The cut in the commissions was swiftly revoked. The aforementioned Romney, for his part, quit policy in the wake of the unseemly labor-management dispute and stayed out in the face of an apparent death sentence. "I got threats that if I didn't come back and behave myself they'd pick my body out of the river," Romney told the Blanshard investigation.

The significant item in the Romney-Pompez disclosures, of course, is the timing. The weight of their testimony, among others, was that the Dutchman was in the Lenox Avenue command post at least once a week during 1933 and well into 1934—even with that tough new administration downtown. One has to wonder why some lowly foot cop on patrol along the avenue never went into that storefront and picked himself up a promotion and some instant fame by putting the cuffs on that long-missing fugitive.

Didn't anybody in the city of New York want Dutch Schultz brought in? If the men in blue couldn't be bothered (the tax case was federal, after all), how about the government sleuths? There were all kinds of stories about the intrepid T-men trailing the guy to dark and dangerous hideaways outside the city and just missing him by a whisper. Beautiful, but why didn't they ever take that nickel subway ride up to Harlem and see if Arthur Flegenheimer might perchance be around there minding the store?

"All I ever did was to sell beer and whisky to our best people."

—AL CAPONE, 1930

"I never did anything to deserve that reputation (Public Enemy No. 1), unless it was to supply good beer to people who wanted it."

—DUTCH SCHULTZ, 1935

CHAPTER XVI

HEAT, WASHINGTON-STYLE

THE RISE AND FALL OF ALPHONSE CAPONE IS TOO WELL known to be retold here, but two of its more engaging aspects bear repeating in any biography of Arthur Flegenheimer; he had quite the same experience.

When John Torrio left Chicago in 1925 because some other delinquent types were firing bullets at him (and worse, hitting him), Capone built the nation's flagship racket empire into a $105-million-a-year operation fed by beer and bathtub gin, gambling holes, dog tracks, brothels, dance halls—name it. But while the streets were strewn with bodies in the process, Scarface Al enjoyed a splendid immunity from any serious prosecution. He did take a year in a Philadelphia jail on a contrived gun charge when enemy artillery was being rolled into place for him back home after the St. Valentine's Day Massacre. And he did stand an occasional bust by the Windy City cops which sometimes took as much as an hour or two out of a busy day. Otherwise, like Dutch Schultz running his beer monopoly and later his policy "business" in New York, Capone wasn't bothered much.

But then something happened in Washington—and we shall see, revealed here in all its glorious detail for the first time, that the same kind of bad luck would in time befall the Dutchman.

In Capone's case, the long journey down from the heights was set in motion in the spring of 1929 when Walter A. Strong, publisher of the Chicago *Daily News,* led a delegation of troubled fellow citizens into the presence of Herbert Hoover in the White House and begged for some relief from the seat of government.

The President, moved by the hair-raising tales his visitors had brought, summoned Andrew Mellon, Secretary of the Treasury, and asked if perchance the T-men might have the necessary weapons to break the Capone stranglehold on Chicago. Mellon turned the assignment over to Elmer L. Irey, chief of his Enforcement Bureau. Come winter, with nothing more impressive in the record than a tax case against the wrong Capone, Al's brother Ralph, called Bottles by his intimates, the Secretary called Irey in again.

"Mr. Irey," Mellon said, "do you know about President Hoover's medicine-ball cabinet?"

Irey said yes, he had heard about it, and Mellon went on:

"Well, when the exercising starts, Mr. Hoover says, 'Have you got that fellow Capone yet?' And when exercise is done and everybody is leaving, the last thing Mr. Hoover always says is, 'Remember, now, I want that man Capone in jail.' "

And so that man Capone went to jail.

This brings us to Arthur Flegenheimer again. Bear in mind that the first tax indictment against him was handed down in January 1933, and that a goodly portion of his long travail as a "fugitive" after that was spent in the friendly haven of his very own town. Now let's see what prompted the Dutchman

—almost two years later—to give himself up and stand trial.

To begin with, you can throw out all of 1933 because New York was still in the hands of Tammany Hall. It was rotten through and through, from the top down. It had a Police Commissioner, Jim Bolan, remember, who years later would swear under oath that while he had "heard" about Dutch Schultz he didn't know that the man was a big gangster except for some "newspaper talk" about him.

Now with the dawn of 1934 the flaming torch of reform, held firmly aloft in the grip of Fiorello LaGuardia, threw its cleansing light over the sin-drenched metropolis. The word went out to the furthest precincts: "Muss 'em up." The streets weren't going to be safe for the bad boys after that; on the newspapers, we were so carried away that overnight Sodom and Gomorrah-on-the-Hudson began to take on the look of a sleepy Amish village in Pennsylvania.

The rackets, of course, continued to thrive.

And Arthur Flegenheimer was still loose in the streets, surely passing a police precinct here or there on his rounds.

As the months wore on, Franklin D. Roosevelt's Secretary of the Treasury, the dignified, patrician Henry Morgenthau Jr., a New Yorker himself, took to brooding about the outstanding tax case against the long-time fugitive only to find his repeated inquiries all leading down the same dead-end streets. Finally, on November 1, he picked up the telephone and made two calls. One went to Mayor LaGuardia in New York and the other to J. Edgar Hoover, right there in the capital. Here, published for the first time, is the text of both those conversations, opening when LaGuardia picked up the first call with a cheerful "Good morning, Mr. Secretary"—

H. M. Jr: How are you?
Mayor LaG: Fine.

H. M. Jr.: Mr. Mayor, I think you and I have got a common interest in Dutch Schultz.

Mayor LaG: Yes.

H. M. Jr.: And I think I saw last week that you made a statement that you're anxious to get him.

Mayor LaG: Yes.

H. M. Jr.: Now I've been told and I—I mean I feel I can talk very frankly and confidentially to you.

Mayor LaG: Yes.

H. M. Jr.: That there's been a feeling between the New York Police Department—

Mayor LaG: Yes.

H. M. Jr.: —and J. Edgar Hoover. And on account of that there's been a crossing of wires. I don't know whether it is true or not.

Mayor LaG: I don't think so—not on the top it may be down below.

H. M. Jr.: Yes.

Mayor LaG: Because I talked to my Commissioner about that and you see Edgar and I are very good friends.

H. M. Jr.: I see.

Mayor LaG: And we worked together many years when I was a member of Congress, so that the feeling up on top is alright if there is any sabotizing down below.

H. M. Jr.: Yes. Well now the point is the Treasury wants this fellow.

LaG: Yes.

H. M. Jr.: And he's the last of the big gangsters that are out.

Mayor LaG: Yes.

H. M. Jr.: And if there is anything we can do to work with you I want to let you know that.

Mayor LaG: Why absolutely and and—

H. M. Jr.: But it's the Treasury that wants him you see.

Mayor LaG: —anything we can do to cooperate with Department of Justice we'll do.

H. M. Jr.: Yes, yes. Well it's our own people—Elmer Irey has been out for him now for about a year.

Mayor LaG: Yes.

H. M. Jr.: You know Elmer Irey?

Mayor LaG: Yes.

H. M. Jr.: And so if there is anything that the Police Commissioner has or there is anything we can do if you tell him that Elmer Irey is ready and anxious to cooperate.

Mayor LaG: Well as long as you tell me I wish that either Hoover or Irey would tell me frankly if there's been any lack of cooperation in any way—

H. M. Jr.: Yes.

Mayor LaG: —so that I can straighten that out immediately.

H. M. Jr.: I see.

Mayor LaG: You see? Because I think it's a defiance not only to the city but to the whole government that this fellow is at large.

H. M. Jr.: No question about it.

Mayor LaG: But my hunch is that he is not very far from this city.

H. M. Jr.: Yes. Well I'll ask Irey—I mean I can't ask Hoover because he doesn't work for me but I'll ask Irey if he does feel there is any and if there is I'll call you again myself.

Mayor LaG: Will you please?

H. M. Jr.: Yes.

Mayor LaG: And you can tell me very frankly because at the top it's alright. If there's any feeling then it's down below and then I would suspect that it isn't one of irritation or jealousy but one of rather protecting this particular person.

H. M. Jr.: I see.

Mayor LaG: And I want to get right to it.

H. M. Jr.: I knew you would.

Mayor LaG: So don't hesitate to let me know.

H. M. Jr.: Thank you.

Mayor LaG: And is it alright if I talk to Hoover and tell him that we've had this little talk?

H. M. Jr.: Well you could use your own judgment on that.

Mayor LaG: Yes because I want to get any little snag eliminated and as I say some of these things that I've observed I think that this gentleman has very strong connections.

H. M. Jr.: Yes.

Mayor LaG: I want to break that down And if—anything that Irey wants to talk to me, tell him to come right in.

H. M. Jr.: I don't think it would serve any particular purpose for the moment if you did talk to Hoover but you—

Mayor LaG: Alright.
H. M. Jr.: —but you can use your own judgment.
Mayor LaG: Alright. I—I won't because this thing is very very important.
H. M. Jr.: Yes.
Mayor LaG: And just let me know if there is anything you want the whole—any part of the Department to do and it will be done at once.
H. M. Jr.: Thank you.
Mayor LaG: Alright, Mr. Secretary.
H. M. Jr.: Good-by.

The next call went to J. Edgar Hoover.

Hello.
Hello, this is Hoover talking, Mr. Secretary.
H. M. Jr.: Yes, how are you?
Hoover: Fine, thank you, hope you're the same.
H. M. Jr.: Mr. Hoover, I think I can take a chance on the telephone.
Hoover: Yes, this is the through wire—confidential wire.
H. M. Jr.: Oh. We're particularly interested in Dutch Schultz.
Hoover: Yes.
H. M. Jr.: And I was just talking to Mayor LaGuardia and told him that the [word missing] was that the New York police really weren't very keen about it, see?
Hoover: Yes. I've heard that same story.

H. M. Jr.: And he said whether I could substantiate it and I said I doubted it.

Hoover: Yes.

H. M. Jr.: And he said that—well I've heard about some jealousies between yourself and down there. I don't know whether it is true or not.

Hoover: Yes.

H. M. Jr.: But just purely gossip.

Hoover: Yes.

H. M. Jr.: But—so he said anything that we could do or he could do to let us know but I just wanted to tell you personally as far as the Treasury is concerned that that's the last of the big income tax gangsters who are out and I am particularly interested in it myself.

Hoover: Oh, I am very glad to know that. We haven't been making any first—what they might call first-line drive on trying to find him because we thought that naturally it was a matter the Treasury would give its first attention to but, if you would like to have us do so, I would be very glad indeed to instruct our New York office to just bring all pressure to bear on that. We've heard a lot of unsavory rumors. They may be without a scintilla of foundation. I don't know.

H. M. Jr.: You say you have not been giving it particular attention?

Hoover: No, that is we've only been looking for him as we would for any other general fugitive.

H. M. Jr.: Yes.

Hoover: Because he was not one of the cases that we've worked on and we've been looking for some of these kidnapers primarily and have had him more or less in what we would call the secondary class because I assumed that the Special Intelligence Unit were bearing down themselves on it.

H. M. Jr.: Well they are.

Hoover: Yes.

H. M. Jr.: And—they are—but I don't—I just—and—

Hoover: Well, I—I really think, Mr. Secretary, that a case of that size being as important we ought to more or less pool our assets so to speak.

H. M. Jr.: That's the point.

Hoover: And everyone of us kind of just put our shoulders to the wheel to try to find him.

H. M. Jr.: That—that's the attitude.

Hoover: And I'll be very glad indeed to see that that is done at once. I'll see that our New York office and we here will just put him down as kind of Public Enemy No. 1 secretly so we can find him.

H. M. Jr.: Yes. I don't think the publicity on it will help find him.

Hoover: Oh no, no indeed, I think the thing to do on that case, from what I have known of

Wide World Photos (Morgenthau)
New York *Post* (LaGuardia)
Wide World Photos (Hoover)

Wanted for tax evasion on a 1933 indictment, Dutch Schultz enjoyed a perfectly tranquil existence as a fugitive for 22 months. Then one day President Roosevelt's Secretary of the Treasury, Henry Morgenthau Jr. (left), made a couple of phone calls. One went to Mayor LaGuardia of New York and the other to the FBI's J. Edgar Hoover—and, lo, feeling the sudden heat, the gangster surrendered. LaGuardia is shown on the steps of New York's City Hall (right), Hoover on the FBI firing range in Washington (next page).

took the Congressional Special to Washington once again. That trip proved most unnecessary. The word that came down from the frosty Morgenthau, whose son Robert would later become the most effective United States Attorney in the history of New York's Southern District, was on the crisp side. "We don't do business with criminals," Morgenthau said, and somebody remembered that Al Capone, a bigger spender than Arthur Flegenheimer, had offered the Treasury $400,000 on the tax claim against him (a piddling $215,-030.48) only to be turned down.

There was nothing left for Dutch Schultz to do except to come in and get it over with.

"Why should I drag another guy into my tax troubles?"

—DUTCH SCHULTZ, when he was asked about the tax case against Andrew Mellon.

CHAPTER XVII

THE SURRENDER—AND A BODY IN THE SNOW

ON THE VERY DAY THAT HENRY MORGENTHAU ANNOUNCED in Washington that the government wasn't interested in any cash settlement from the Treasury's most wanted man, a prominent attorney in Albany, James M. Noonan, had a visit from two strangers.

Noonan's callers outlined a "hypothetical" tax proceeding and asked the counselor what he thought of it. Noonan pondered the matter for a split second or so and then expressed a most disdainful view of the prosecution's case as it had been set before him. Accordingly, he was told that he would hear presently from a potential client described as a person of some means. The call came two mornings later, on November 28. Noonan happened to be available for an immediate audience, and very shortly there stood before him a broken-nosed, sallow-looking man in a black topcoat, a baggy blue suit, and, of course, a gray fedora.

Noonan said he recognized his visitor from his picture in the Albany Post Office.

A brief conference ensued and then, at 10:30 A.M., the two men appeared at the nearby office of United States Commissioner Lester T. Hubbard.

"I'm Arthur Flegenheimer," said Jim Noonan's new client. "I am under indictment in the Southern District of New York. I wish to surrender."

The Commissioner did not recognize the name and did not stand up and do a song and dance, for that matter, when it was translated to Dutch Schultz. So they started all over, with some interpolations by Noonan, and in due course the federal official was persuaded that the chain-smoking gorilla in the fedora was nobody less than J. Edgar Hoover's Public Enemy No. 1, come to throw himself upon the mercy of the bar. This so impressed the Commissioner that he set bail at $50,000 and doubled it later at the formal arraignment. Schultz thereupon was packed off to the state capital's new $2 million escape-proof jail in time to catch a belated pre-Thanksgiving dinner with 16 local malefactors of considerably lesser prominence. This repast—fresh ham, potatoes, vegetables and pie and coffee—left the refugee from the Big Town with a decidedly low opinion of Albany's facilities for the oppressed.

Except for his meals and an occasional turn around the 150-foot exercise corridor, Schultz confined himself to his cell to catch up on his reading. In the evening papers, he would find quite a few things about Arthur Flegenheimer. Down in Manhattan, Commissioner Valentine was quoted as saying that the Dutchman had surrendered only because he had found himself just "one jump"—a short jump, presumably—ahead of his suddenly relentless pursuers. In truth, a band of New York police and federal agents, no doubt spurred on by those nagging calls Henry Morgenthau had made to Messrs. LaGuardia and Hoover, had swarmed into upstate Newburgh only to hear that the fugitive had slipped away to a cottage somewhere between Saratoga and Lake

George, supposedly with a revved-up plane at hand in case the enemy got too close. Maybe so, but while the fuzz was beating the bushes in that scenic country, Schultz happened to be in Albany offering his body to the law, like any good citizen should, after a while, when he knows the law wants to see him. Valentine speculated that the Dutchman might have chosen that course because rival underworld types were looking to throw some lead at him. Then the gruff Commissioner added an observation which the prisoner would have to view as unfriendly at best.

"I wish they were bringing him back in a box," he said. "That's what the bum was afraid of—that he'd be brought in dead. That's why he surrendered. The trail was getting too hot for him."

Mayor LaGuardia was more restrained. "It is a sad commentary on the police department of every city in which Schultz had been hiding," he said of the Dutchman's 22 months of freedom, perhaps unmindful of the fact that New York City itself had served as the gangster's primary host during most of that period.

Valentine's suggestion that Schultz might have sought the sanctuary of a jail to escape enemy guns quickly washed out when the man's barristers hastened into court to get his bail reduced so that he could walk the streets again. J. Richard Davis, noting that his client had suffered but one conviction in his 33 years and had posted bail in 11 other cases without ever running away, put the case this way:

"Schultz is not a Dillinger. He is not a Baby Face Nelson. He is indicted for failure to pay income taxes. Is this a serious crime to man?"

Without waiting for an answer, Davis went on to submit that his much-abused client had a perfectly good reason for not filing tax returns during the three years listed in the indictment. "He had no income," said the attorney. Later on, Jim Noonan would observe that Arthur Flegenheimer's situation was really something like that of J. P. Morgan, who had paid no tax in 1929 "because he had no taxable income." There was something amiss in this argument, actually. The financier, unlike the beer-and-booze magnate, had filed a return, but it showed no taxable income because of the heavy losses Mr. Morgan had sustained in that very bad year for non-bootleggers.

The Dutchman's bail eventually was reduced to $75,000 but the process of posting it took several weeks, inflicting upon him his longest incarceration in all the years since he had done that 15-month stretch for unlawful entry as a 17-year-old apprentice thief in The Bronx back in 1919. Breathing free air again but under an injunction not to leave the jurisdiction, he repaired to a hideaway outside Troy, just a few miles from Albany, to await his trial, which was months away.

Only one minor inconvenience occurred during this hiatus —a quick trip into town on March 9, 1935, to see Troy's District Attorney, Charles J. Ranney, about a case of murder.

The victim happened to be Jules Martin, the Schultz enforcer in the restaurant shakedown racket. Martin, nee Modgilewsky and known as "Modgilewsky the Commissar" because he was a very rough customer, had been found dead in a snowbank up that way the week before. Ranney had reason to believe that Rensselaer County's other distinguished guest from New York might know something about the violent departure of his associate, but the command appearance produced nothing more than a blanket of silence. The Dutchman even refused to say that he had nothing to say, letting his attorney, Jim Noonan, convey that to the District Attorney. Well, did Schultz know the deceased? Ranney couldn't even get that harmless question answered.

Accordingly, the murder lay dormant for another three years, until two cons in Atlanta Federal Penitentiary started peddling a story that Bo Weinberg had done in Julie Martin. When that tale got around, Dixie Davis, his pipes loosened by his extended singing role in the Hines trial, suddenly remembered that Martin had been dispatched by the Dutchman himself. Davis's story is worth telling first, because he submitted that, much to his own revulsion and disgust, he had witnessed the whole thing with his very own baby blue eyes.

In the barrister's account, the unpleasantness began when Schultz, short of cash, phoned Martin one day and told him to dig $21,000 out of the accounts of the Metropolitan Restaurant and Cafeteria Association, the polite name for the shakedown operation, and dash upstate with it at once, if not sooner.

Well, the busy little subsidiary's bank deposits happened to be rather low at the time of the hurry-up call from Troy and Martin was said to have remarked to Philip Grossel, its secretary, that "the Dutchman's got some nerve coming around to draw that kind of dough when we're almost broke." The Commissar spoke with considerable authority, since the anemic condition of the exchequer derived principally from the fact that he had been going South—or rather West—with small but regular stacks of the association's receipts in order to operate a factory which he had set up in Elkhart, Indiana, for the purpose of turning out a fleet of rebuilt taxicabs. Anyway, within a day or two after making that crack about the Dutchman's avarice, Martin found himself on a train rolling toward Albany with $21,000 and J. Richard Davis riding shotgun.

Davis said the trip wasn't his idea. He said he had orders to deliver Martin and the cash to the Harmony Hotel, a decrepit installation in the little town of Cohoes, near the capital, where Mr. Schultz would be waiting. The confrontation between the errant strong-arm man and his employer evidently was exceedingly bitter from the very outset. Davis said the Dutchman maintained that there was $70,000 missing from the association's accounts, while Martin, even after absorbing a hard sneak right to the eye, insisted just as vehemently that he himself hadn't heisted more than, oh, maybe $20,000. This is how Davis described the conclusion of the debate:

"Dutch Schultz was ugly; he had been drinking and suddenly he had his gun out. The Dutchman wore his pistol under his vest, tucked inside his pants, right against his belly. One jerk at his vest and he had it in his hand. All in the same quick motion he swung it up, stuck it in Jules Martin's mouth and pulled the trigger.

"It was as simple and undramatic as that—just one quick motion of the hand. The Dutchman did that murder just as casually as if he were picking his teeth."

Davis said that even as Martin tumbled to the floor, moaning, Schultz turned to him and advised him that he was free to leave at once, adding, "Dick, you must hate me for this." That made sense, of course, since the peace-loving barrister was hardly accustomed to that kind of untidiness in hotel rooms and, in any case, Lulu Rosenkrantz and a party named Danny Dale happened to be on hand to dispose of the expiring guest for the ill-tempered Dutchman. Davis said his mental anguish increased immeasurably the next day upon learning to his horror that Martin's body also bore twelve stab wounds, all in the chest, when it was found stiffening in the snow. Davis said that when he asked his client about this unseemly item at a later date, Schultz replied, in his irrepressibly direct way, "I cut his heart out." The counselor said he never really liked Dutch Schultz after that—a rather slow footnote, since it came almost four years after the man had expired.

In the interest of fair reporting, especially since the Martin demise was the only one ever so directly credited to the Dutchman and his constant companion, the .45 Colt, the Davis story should be weighed against the earlier account from the Atlanta gaol.

That one came mainly from a disreputable character named Hyman (Hymie the Painter) Berger, then idling away his time in federal custody on an endlessly long sentence, like life, for an auto theft which had compounded a series of other indiscretions. Berger submitted in February 1938, six months before Davis opened up, that he happened to be in Troy on March 2, 1935, to see one William Dooley in connection with a little painting racket he had going for himself in Brooklyn. He said he ran into Dutch Schultz, Bo Weinberg, Dixie Davis and Jules Martin, saw the quartet go into a house around 2:00 A.M. and presently saw Martin stagger out in evident haste, only to be overtaken by the hulking Weinberg. He said he saw Weinberg slip a revolver between the outmatched Martin's molars and fire it.

Dooley, in Atlanta himself because he had been caught impersonating a federal officer, a social lapse frowned on by most federal officers, actually had spilled the Weinberg story first, but he had to admit that he had not actually witnessed the deed himself. Thus the tale rested on Hymie the Painter, known here as Hymie the Storyteller because the author is inclined to go along with Tom Dewey's expressed view that Dixie Davis had the Martin murder right. While no knowledgeable observer could list the dandy mouthpiece on any roster of the more dedicated searchers after truth, there is no gainsaying that his account had more merit on every score, starting with the fact that he had the locale right—Cohoes, not Troy.

Beyond that, one wants to remember that among the sudden departures with which he became acquainted in the service of the mob the Martin slaying was one of the very few that Dixie Davis did not charge up to Bo Weinberg. That had to count for something.

Even so, it is necessary to report that if the Dutchman himself had the blood of Jules Martin on his hands or his conscience, it hardly showed a month later when he presented himself in Syracuse, on the eve of his tax trial, for that celebrated meet-the-press session of his. The man of the hour was in reasonably good humor all through the long session, which even contributed some tidbits to his scant biography.

A reader of Horatio Alger (not to mention Mr. Shakespeare, Stefan Zweig, Emil Ludwig, Ambrose Bierce and some guy named Plato), he managed to come out in the Alger mode: Born of impoverished immigrants, lost his father at a tender age, had to quit school to help support his mother and kid sister, worked at any job he could get, lifted himself up by his own diligence, enjoyed a modest success—and now had the damned government on his back trying to tear it all down. Sort of a typical American success story.

The Dutchman strove in other ways to strengthen the image of the respectable burgher. Thus on another occasion, talking to Meyer Berger of The New York *Times*, he professed some anger over a reference to his private life.

"Ain't you the one who wrote that I was a pushover for blondes?" Schultz asked the celebrated reporter.

"I was *told* that you are a pushover for a blonde," Berger replied. "Someone told me that."

"That is beside the pernt," the Dutchman came back in one of his few pronunciation lapses. "I only remember it made me feel bad when I saw it in the *Times*. I don't think 'pushover for a blonde' is any kind of language to write for a newspaper like the *Times*."

Berger stood corrected. At last he had an editor who really appreciated the niceties of that time in history.

An old hand on the Schultz story, Berger, by the way, was disappointed by the racket overlord's appearance. To him the Dutchman always came off as "an ill-dressed vagrant," or at best a guy with "a special talent for looking like a perfect example of the unsuccessful man."

Schultz, for that matter, made no secret of the frugality that governed his wardrobe. He said he never spent more than $35 or so for a suit or more than $2 for a shirt. "You take silk shirts now," he told the assembled press in the big Syracuse session, "I think only queers wear silk shirts. I never bought one in my life. Only a sucker will pay $15 or $20 for a silk shirt."

But, then, there were matters of substance on that day's agenda as well.

Had he surrendered in November because the FBI seemed to have turned a little trigger-happy when all those agents chopped down John Dillinger? And then Homer Van Meter? And then another Dillinger playmate, Pretty Boy Floyd? And then, on the very day of the Dutchman's surrender,

Wide World Photos

Having turned himself in late in November 1934, Schultz, in a second hearing before U.S. Commissioner Lester T. Hubbard in Albany, hears his bail set at $75,000.

Wide World Photos

Ordered into the Albany jail while his bond is checked, Schultz was shy about having his picture taken in such unaccustomed surroundings.

Baby Face Nelson, who had taken two G-Men to eternity with him when he was trapped in a Chicago suburb? "Naw," said the Dutchman. "I wasn't wanted for murder or kidnapping like the guys that were getting shot. They only wanted me for a minor offense—this income tax stuff."

Did he consider himself a public enemy? "I'm no public enemy. I'm a public benefactor." In what way? No answer.

Was he the Beer Baron of The Bronx until Repeal? "I'm no beer baron. I never was a beer baron. That'll all come out at the trial." But hadn't he made a couple of million selling beer? Dixie Davis, on hand in the hotel room, rescued his client. "He never was in beer," the lawyer said, although the defense was prepared to concede at the trial that Arthur Flegenheimer was up to his neck in the forbidden brew.

Why was he in trouble? "I think they've picked me out—the government. I mean—because a certain group of individuals, some of them still in the government and some actually prosecuting this case, had a personal grudge against me. And they wanted the publicity out of it, too. That was mostly it."

Did he know Jimmy Hines? "I know of him and I hear he is a grand man. Not that I can recall that I ever spoke to him, though." All that with a bland, expressionless face, despite a trace of nervousness, while he waited for Davis to close out this line of questioning. "He doesn't know Hines," the lawyer said, also with a straight face.

Had he known the late Vincent Coll? "I knew his sister. She's Florence Redden. I just received a letter from her wishing me luck in my trial." But weren't he and Coll good friends once? "Sometimes," came the cryptic reply. Was Coll looking for him the day the Vengalli baby was gunned down in East Harlem? "I wasn't the target. The police know who the target was. They know who shot and was shot at and it wasn't me. I believe I was in court that day."

How did he feel about cops? "They're overgrown bullies. They're too lazy to work—that's New York cops I'm talking about."

Was he worried about the trial: "Worried? No, I'm not worried. I've been in worser spots than this."

Even so, the Dutchman in a single day accepted a set of rosary beads from one well-wisher and a murmured "Good luck" in Yiddish from another. "I guess I'm gonna need all the luck I can get," he said, "so I ain't passing anything up."

All the flanks were covered.

"Any guy who can lick the government can lick anybody."

—DUTCH SCHULTZ in Syracuse

CHAPTER XVIII

DAY IN COURT

WHEN HIS TRIAL BEGAN ON APRIL 16, 1935, DUTCH Schultz offered his army of attorneys his own advice and counsel in the selection of the jurors. "You can't read faces," he told the reporters, "but you can tell an intelligent man when you see one. This jury appears intelligent to me, judging from their answers to questions—but don't say it looks good to me."

We shall see how good it was.

The prosecution was mainly in the hands of John H. McEvers, special assistant to Attorney General Homer Cummings and the bearer of rather impressive credentials: he came off the prosecution team that had won the Capone conviction. Now he was armed with a case assiduously put together by Tom Dewey, then wearing among his garlands a mint-fresh tax conviction which had put Waxey Gordon, that formidable bootlegging contemporary of the Dutchman's, behind bars under a sentence carrying ten years and a fat $50,000 in fines. With Schultz, Dewey got off to a flying head start when Hugh McQuillan, chief of the Treasury's intelligence unit in New York, turned up a dummy bank account in which the Beer Baron had deposited a round $856,000 in the last six months of 1930. On this item alone, if you followed the book, Schultz owed $44,000 in back taxes and another $29,-000 or so in penalties. The drawback in the case against him, of course, was that his legal battalions were to prevail in their view that he had to be tried in the Northern District—up-state, out of sight of possibly hostile New York City jurors—because his business was in The Bronx and his tax returns, if he had taken the trouble to bother with that sort of trifle, would have been filed in Albany.

The interval between 1929–31 and the time of the indictment in 1933, compounded by the fact that the errant non-taxpayer spent so much time debating whether to stand trial, had pushed the Dutchman's asserted $92,103.34 deficiency up to $180,000 with the accrued interest and fraud penalties. There was an item of consolation, however: while the cash cost had gone up so precipitately, a severance of seven of the counts before trial reduced the potential penalty from 43 years and $110,000 in fines all the way down to 16 years and a pittance of $40,000 in fines. If, that is, a jury of graying farmers and merchants in the very wet state of New York could be persuaded that a kindly bootlegger deserved to be punished just for cheating on his taxes; it is well to remember that the Democratic Party's 1928 standard bearer, Alfred E. Smith, Governor of New York, ran against Herbert Hoover on a dripping-wet platform even in the face of the natural burden he had to carry as the first Catholic candidate for the Presidency.

There wasn't much question in the Schultz trial about the generous flow of income derived from the banished juices during Prohibition by the defendant and the army around him. While the government had to show only that Arthur Flegenheimer had taxable income of almost a half million dollars in the period under question, McEvers regaled the upstate jurors with a towering assortment of figures. From a nine-day procession of witnesses, heavily weighted with delegates from the 18 banks that accommodated the bulging Schultz accounts, the prosecutor drew testimony purporting to show a three-year gross of $2,863,000 and a net of $1,352,000. These telephone numbers did not inspire much argument in the courtroom. Indeed, deposits of $1,600,000 in two of the three years under an assortment of Flegenheimer aliases—Joesph Harmon (he used the name Harmon in a 1921 pinch for grand larceny), Charles and Arthur New (his mother's maiden name was Neu) and George Schultz—were conceded by the Dutchman's legal battery. The line of the defense was fairly clear: of course there was money in beer, nobody gave it away, but how much of it stuck to Arthur Flegenheimer's own hot little hands?

Thus, for example, the defense dwelt at painful length on ledger items of $236,026.96 carried alongside the initial *S*. The government labored to persuade the jury that *S* stood for Schultz and the defense in turn implied very heavily that *S* in any illicit operation might also be short for "*S*hakedown." A particular December listing of $22,991.50 alongside the familiar *S* drew special attention from William J. Hughes Jr., an attorney imported from Washington by Jim Noonan for his special background in tax matters. Hughes made the point that Christmas comes in December and the Dutchman addressed himself to the same piece of wisdom during a recess. "The best definition of Christmas I ever heard," he said, "came from out West, where some professionals were testing gangsters with the Binet test. One of the questions they asked was, 'What is Christmas?' and the answer was, 'Something a cop thinks comes every day.' "

This sort of thing, naturally, was not calculated to improve the angry disposition of the Mayor of New York. Mr. La-Guardia said that any cop shown to have accepted any cash gifts from the likes of Schultz would be dealt with severely. This was not followed, as you might have guessed, by any mass exodus from the Police Department.

The government's case was somewhat hindered, although not at all critically, by the shyness of no less than 20 subpoenaed witnesses. On this roster, in terms of prominence, the name of Heinie Zimmerman, star third baseman of John McGraw's Giants until he fell from grace in a small bribery scandal, led all the rest. Zimmerman had been banished from baseball for passing along an offer of $100 apiece to three teammates—Benny Kauff, Fred Toney and Rube Benton—to throw a game to the Chicago Cubs on the last Western trip of the 1919 season. The slugger's story was that he just delivered the message and then played his own heart out in the game, foiling the dishonest gamblers by helping to win it with his own bat. A brother-in-law of Joey Noe, Zimmerman in due course drifted into that other national pastime, bootlegging, enjoying a partnership with the Dutchman himself in at least one Bronx speakeasy. McEvers wanted to ask him about a bank account he shared with Schultz but couldn't find him, although Zimmerman had testified before the Grand Jury that indicted the Beer Baron. Henry Margolis, Frank Ahearn and George Yarlas (Yarlasavetsky), much larger Schultz associates, indicted with him, were just as scarce. They had vanished the day the true bill was handed down and they weren't going to come in until the Dutchman's case was out of the way. Another key witness, Daniel (Deafy Dan) McCarthy, a partner in Schultz's Hub Social Club in The Bronx, did show up for the trial but failed to wait around to testify. Due on the stand one morning but told that he wouldn't be needed until the afternoon session, he asked McEvers, "Will it be all right if I go for a walk?" McEvers made the mistake of saying yes—and Deafy Dan never stopped walking, not even when a bench warrant was issued for his arrest.

Bo Weinberg was on hand. So was Rocco DiLarmi, another Schultz partner. So was Peter Donohue, skipper of the Dutchman's beer fleet. But they all pleaded a combination of faulty memory and the Fifth Amendment and cheerfully held still for the contempt sentences dealt out by Federal Judge Fredrick H. Bryant rather than help the government persecute their old buddy.

Still, amidst the endless procession of bank officials and accountants, McEvers managed to come up with a decent sprinkling of ex-speakeasy operators to give the jury the flavor and evident financial rewards of the Schultz operations. One of the more qualified prosecution witnesses was none other than Otto Gass, who had hired Li'l Arthur as a mere boy to work on his horse and wagons, delivering beer, only to suffer an unfortunate confrontation with him a few years later. Gass testified that Arthur, moving along in the trade, came into one of his drops one night and said to him, "I'll give it to you in three ways—get out, stay out, or be rubbed out." Horrified by this show of ingratitude, Gass withdrew from the beer business.

The prosecution even turned up its own pinup girl in Marguerite Scholl, a brave Bronx lass quickly dubbed the Little Girl in Blue by the tabloids. Marguerite had gone to work for Wolf & Yarlas, one of the Schultz fronts, as a stenographer and bookkeeper at 17. Now she felt no compunction about taking the witness stand and describing the financial transactions she had recorded for the beer cartel. She even produced the most critical ledger book used by the government.

McEvers also brought in Julius Salke and Stephen DiRosa, the detectives who had tangled with Schultz and Danny Iamascia in the shootout on Fifth Avenue. You will recall that the two sleuths said the Dutchman had offered them $50,000 apiece to let him off that morning. The inference to be deduced from their testimony was clear: If the man had $100,000 to spare for that kind of little favor in 1931 then he must have had some money left over for taxes as well. The defense, of course, ridiculed the notion that Schultz would have offered any cash rewards to two cops who had just shot down one of his best pals.

To add a touch of color to the government's case, McEvers put George S. Tarbell, a former Assistant United States Attorney, on the stand to testify about a strange incident that had occurred on February 27, 1933. On that day in history, just a month after the indictment, some cad broke into Tarbell's office in the Post Office Building in New York and made off with a bulging file of records, including wiretaps, bearing on the case against Arthur Flegenheimer. It wasn't a total loss: McEvers had some taps left, including a few showing that now and then the honest beer-and-booze merchant had occasion to do business with such nefarious racketeers as Ciro Terranova and Joey Rao, the men to see in Spanish Harlem, and even, in happier days, with a lowlife like Chink Sherman.

The Dutchman's side brushed it all aside—the beer, the booze, the money, the naughty associations.

The defense, a crisp three-hour affair, rested on three witnesses—two Schultz attorneys, Edward H. Reynolds and David Goldstein, and the faithful Schultz accountant, Milton Bernard. The burden of it was that (a) the defendant failed to file tax returns only because he had expert legal advice to the effect that he didn't have to and (b) when that advice turned out to be grievously wrong he made the most strenuous efforts to pay his debt to Uncle Sam only to be rebuffed at every turn. Reynolds, a former United States Attorney with considerable experience in Prohibition cases, accepted full responsibility for the faulty advice. He testified that he had assured Mr. Flegenheimer back in 1926 that no citizen of the republic was obliged to pay taxes on anything illegal, like selling beer while the Volstead Act was on the books. Reynolds said that when he ran into the Dutchman in Dinty Moore's restaurant in Manhattan five years later his ex-client scolded him rather severely. "You're a helluva lawyer," helluva lawyer quoted Schultz, "I'm in a fine fix on the income tax."

David Goldstein, the same attorney who helped Schultz beat the assault case growing out of that Fifth Avenue confrontation, then described how no stone had been left unturned to square the tax thing once it turned out that Arthur Flegenheimer really should have taken Uncle in as a partner, like any true-blue American entrepreneur, even though he was making his money by violating one of Uncle's newer laws. Goldstein submitted that he himself had gone all over New York and Washington trying to settle the overdue account for that big $100,000, no questions asked, but nobody would listen to him. Milton Bernard, also in the battalion of couriers employed in this noble patriotic cause, told the same story, and the tall, broad-shouldered Noonan, an impassioned courtroom orator, summed it all up for the jurors: "It shows that he was on the level—that there was no willfulness in his heart. The government wouldn't take his money."

McEvers had another view of it: "He went to a lawyer and

was told that although a court had ruled otherwise income from an illegal business was not taxable. This big Beer Baron of The Bronx said, 'I'll take a chance,' and he continued running his $2-million-a-year business in defiance of the government. But when he saw that others of his kind had been sent to Alcatraz and other prisons, he hurried to pay his taxes."

The defendant himself, outside of court, put it this way: "I offered $100,000 when the government was broke and people were talking revolution and they turned me down cold. You can see how that at least I was willing to pay. Everybody knows I am being persecuted in this case. I wanted to pay. They were taking it from everybody else, but they wouldn't take it from me. I tried to do my duty as a citizen—maybe I'm not a citizen?"

The Dutchman passed over another testimonial he might have included in his self-portrait as a citizen so profoundly dedicated to his country's welfare. The fact is that at one stage he was prepared to dish out a good deal more than $100,000—like $200,000—to help things out in Washington. In 1932 one of his agents approached Hugh McQuillan in New York and offered to slip the extra 100 Big Ones into the Democratic kitty for the party's upcoming drive to evict Herbert Hoover from the White House in favor of FDR. The offer was spurned. Looking back, one had to wonder what had ever prompted Citizen Schultz's political brain trust to believe that Mr. Roosevelt was going to need any help from *them* to win that election, but that's beside the point here.

With the rhetoric out of the way, Judge Bryant gave the case to the jury on April 26—and then the man of the hour had some anxious moments.

The jury got the case at 11:50 A.M. on April 27 and deliberated for the rest of the day, with the Dutchman pacing the corridors nervously, puffing on cigarettes and confessing that "the suspense is awful." Just a few days before, exuding confidence and good cheer, he had kidded the reporters about their writing talents. He told them he was reading Ambrose Bierce's *Write It Right* in his spare moments—"all about how you newspaper fellers misuse the English language"—and enjoying it immensely. Now he was a little more grim. "There's a certain amount of strain but I can stand it," he said in one of his seemingly more assured moments, but that surely was a mild way to put it. Never mind the tax bite or the certain fines, Schultz was a cinch to trade in his ill-fitting low-cost civvies for prison denim for quite a stretch if the jurors happened to bring in the wrong verdict; there was nothing in the charge to the jury to suggest that Judge Bryant suffered from any lighthearted attitude toward gangsters who chiseled on taxes.

The first day's deliberations produced nothing closer than a six-to-six tie and the judge ordered the jury locked up for the night after the foreman, a rawboned giant named Michael J. Shea, who had been a bank appraiser, insurance man and operator of a general store, assured him that the panel would be able to reach a verdict the next day. But at 3:00 P.M. that afternoon the jurors came up empty once more. It was seven to five for conviction now, but hopelessly deadlocked. The judge discharged the panel with thanks. It was evident that in the town of Syracuse, New York—hardly Bible country—the sins of Arthur Flegenheimer were not regarded as at all opprobrious.

The Dutchman, positively exultant over the hung jury, had

a thing or two to say later when he repaired to Bridgeport to await his second trial. He was also somewhat critical of the press:

"You newspaper birds are to blame [for his troubles] but I don't hold it against you. I was a little shaky when I read some of your stuff but when that jury disagreed I knew you couldn't fool the people too much. You've made me Public Enemy No. 1 and the jury didn't believe it. And it will be better than seven to five when the next trial comes up. I ain't admitting anything but the record will show that I tried to pay my income tax and the government refused to touch it. Sure I got dough. I'd be a sucker if I didn't have some.

"Now you take Capone. He was supposed to be a smart guy. But the jury didn't disagree when Al got the works, did it? I ain't never going to Alcatraz or Leavenworth or nowhere. I'm no gorilla. I never killed anybody or caused anybody to get killed. They say I was a Beer Baron. Well, what if I was? We got Repeal, haven't we? I get a laugh out of anybody calling anybody who gave the people beer a public enemy. If that is the case, how about Roosevelt?"

There being no immediate motions for a summary indictment of the President, the victory statement went on:

"This tough world ain't no place for dunces. And you can tell those smart guys in New York that the Dutchman is no dunce and as far as he is concerned Alcatraz doesn't exist. I'll never see Alcatraz. Al Capone was a dunce for going to Alcatraz."

It was a portrait of an arrogant winner, hardly a suitable companion piece for the earlier, pre-trial view from that meet-the-press session in Syracuse. This was Dutch Schultz, the gangster, telling 'em all off. The guy in the Syracuse hotel room was Arthur Flegenheimer, up from the streets, good to his mother, hard working, suddenly persecuted by unseen and unnamed enemies.

The second trial was set for the little backwoods town of Malone in July. The Dutchman set himself up there a week in advance and went on a social rampage calculated to show the burghers up North that he was just another regular fellow and anything but the bum they might have read about in the papers. This buttering-up process, with the wine and beer flowing freely and all the tabs picked up by the openhanded stranger in town, brought forth some instant protests.

The Reverend John R. Williams, pastor of Malone's First Congregational Church, took to the pulpit to deal with the matter. "I have even heard," he said, "that men in high places will fawn over a gangster and hail his advent because it will bring money to the community." What had provoked the clergyman was the Dutchman's appearance at a local ball game with Mayor Ralph Cardinal and a pair of leading businessmen in his entourage. Schultz had an answer for that. "After all," he said, "I like baseball. Because I happen to have some income tax trouble doesn't mean that I have to bury myself ."

Judge Bryant, a native of Malone himself, evidently thought there was more merit in the pastor's view. He revoked the defendant's bail just before the trial got under way, shaking off the anguished demands of counsel for an explanation; he said he did not have to furnish any reasons for what he was doing. So Arthur Flegenheimer went behind bars again, effectively removed from the higher social life of Malone while he was facing a Malone jury.

Martin Conboy, Special Prosecutor in the government's new effort to clap some more permanent iron bars around the Dutchman, put it to the second jury in a rather elementary way. Conboy started by noting that a married man with one exemption was entitled to an exemption of $1,900 on his tax returns. Had Arthur Flegenheimer made more than $1,900 a year? "Well," said Conboy, "here's his income: In 1929 it was $131,522.41. In 1930 it was $202,021.92. In 1931 it was $147,693.02. His gross business for those three years was not at the rate of $5,000 a year. The total was almost $3,000,000. Yet he never filed an income tax return and never paid a cent of income tax."

The government's two-week case included the same array of talking witnesses—Marguerite Scholl and all the bankers and speakeasy operators and accountants—and pretty much the same array of non-talking witnesses. Bo Weinberg again, his memory in no way improved. Rocco DiLarmi again. Moe Margolese and Samuel Rasnoff, two other tongue-tied Schultz henchmen. Nothing had changed; the loyal inside men all preferred contempt sentences as an alternative to betraying their employer's secrets. Still missing, of course, were such Schultz associates as Heinie Zimmerman and Deafy Dan McCarthy.

The prosecution suffered another blow when the Dutchman's ledger book, admitted in the first trial, was barred by the court as inadmissible. This was after the defense, correcting an earlier oversight, conceded that the book was the property of the defendant and thereby won its argument that it could not be put into the record because the government's illegal seizure of it violated his Constitutional rights. Even so, Conboy managed to get in an impressive array of facts and figures to support the indictment's contention that the defendant Flegenheimer had enjoyed considerable prosperity between 1929 and 1931.

Jim Noonan produced his familiar trio of star witnesses to show that his client had failed to file tax returns only because of some misguided legal advice. He added a fourth, Frank Wagner, a home-grown tax consultant, to testify that there was nothing in the government's presentation which showed any distinction between gross income and net income. It was the same old tried and true Syracuse formula: of course money came in from the sale of beer, but how much could the proprietor have kept?

And once more, as in Syracuse, great pains were taken to let the jurors know that the $100,000 offer from Schultz not only stood in perpetuity but would be paid to Uncle even if the jury deemed the defendant to be innocent of the tax evasion charges. "I will do my duty as an American citizen," Schultz himself was careful to tell the newspapers, evidently forgetting an earlier proclamation to the effect that the government had no right to go after him in the first place but should have had its bloodhounds on "the big swindlers who steal millions of dollars from the widows and orphans."

Lest there be any doubt about the nice stranger in town who was being persecuted by them bluenoses in Washington, a local attorney, George Moore, carried the ball much of the way for the Dutchman. When the prosecution suggested that the defendant was not only a tax evader but a gunman on the side, Moore asked his Adirondack neighbors to observe for themselves that the defendant "hasn't a wicked countenance." And as for getting filthy rich peddling spirits in the dry days, Moore, speaking as "one home-towner to another," reminded the jurors that "the beer business was a hazardous business—our local bootlegger never made much money."

The message did not fall on deaf ears.

The jury, nine to three for acquittal on the very first ballot, deliberated 28 hours and 23 minutes and on August 2 brought in a verdict of not guilty.

Judge Bryant sat bolt upright, disbelief on his face, banged his gavel angrily over an outburst of cheering in the courtroom, and then addressed the jurors in a low, quivering voice:

"You have labored long and no doubt have given careful consideration to this case. Before I discharge you I will have to say that your verdict is such that it shakes the confidence of law-abiding people in integrity and truth. It will be apparent to all who have followed the evidence in this case that you have reached a verdict based not on the evidence but on some other reason. You will have to go home with the satisfaction, if it is a satisfaction, that you have rendered a blow against law enforcement and given aid and encouragement to the people who would flout the law. In all probability, they will commend you. I cannot. The clerk will give you your vouchers."

The tall, gray Conboy, equally shaken, had nothing to add to the stinging rebuke from the bench, but in Washington Attorney General Cummings went even further than the judge. He called the verdict a "terrible miscarriage of justice."

The jury foreman, Leon Chapin, Director of the New York State Dairymen's League, took the searing blast from the bench with aplomb. "We feel that the government just didn't prove its income tax evasion charge," he said. "We feel the government utterly failed to show that he earned so much as a nickel of tax income and we based our verdict on that belief. If the government had shown us only $5,000 gross income we would have convicted."

It made one wonder what that mountain of evidence was

Wide World Photos

Schultz thanks his attorney, James M. Noonan, after winning a hung jury in his first trial, in Syracuse, for cheating the government on taxes in his bootlegging days.

Wide World Photos

Sweating it out: the gangster had some anxious moments while the jury was out in his second trial. The Malone panel deliberated for 28 hours and 23 minutes before finding that the ex-Beer Baron hadn't done anything bad.

all about. It certainly sounded like income when so many of those 67 prosecution witnesses were reeling off the numbers. It sounded like income when the prosecution showed beer money, or some kind of money in any case, flowing into 18 bank accounts in the names of Arthur Flegenheimer or his associates. And it sounded like income when Martin Conboy exhibited to the jury a notebook which showed the Dutchman pocketing $23,600 in a single eleven-day period.

The cascading dollars—could it have been stage money?—also vanished, quite naturally, in the appraisal of the jubilant Dixie Davis. Not in the least disturbed by Judge Bryant's acid-tipped remarks, the counselor rushed right into print with an endorsement of the kindly jurors. "It was the only verdict under the circumstances," he said. And Schultz, shaved to a pink glow all during the trial but ashen white when the jury came in, seconded his mouthpiece's words. "You can say I said so too," he told the reporters.

Were they really going to pay that 100 grand to the government, win or lose, as they said? "We intend to pay," Davis said.

Were they going to pay the $36,937.18 tax claim New York State had outstanding against the Dutchman (not counting the penalties): "We intend to settle all taxes," Davis said.

As it happened, no undue haste was expended in the process of reducing the Flegenheimer national debt but Milton Bernard did get right on the pipes to square things in the Empire State before anybody started dragging his boy into court again. Bernard drew a blank because he didn't quite want to pay the whole $36,937.18; he wanted to "discuss" it first. New York just wanted the money and didn't want to kill a lot of time talking about it.

As far as the city was concerned, the Malone verdict failed to endear Fiorello LaGuardia to the victorious defendant. "Dutch Schultz won't be a resident of New York City," said the Little Flower. "We have no place for him here."

This did not please the Bronx boy-in-exile.

"So there isn't room for me in New York?" he said. "Well, I'm going there."

"Don't forget to split all my infinitives."

—DUTCH SCHULTZ to Walter Lister,
October 1935

CHAPTER XIX

GANGSTER ON HORSEBACK

DUTCH SCHULTZ DID NOT GO BACK TO HIS NATIVE HEARTH from Malone, even though there was a new son, born during his trial, waiting for him in Frances Flegenheimer's modest apartment in Queens. While he had said that it was "absurd" and "ridiculous" for Fiorello LaGuardia to imagine that he could keep him out of the city, he had some excellent reasons for staying away: He was still the city's Number One fugitive on a newly upholstered tax rap, there was still an outstanding federal tax warrant out for him on the counts which had been severed in the Syracuse and Malone trials, and the state had a warrant ready to serve in the event that Milton Bernard kept filibustering for a negotiated settlement instead of coming around with a check for $36,000 and change.

So the Dutchman repaired to the rolling green acres of Connecticut, where the Fairfield County horsy set not only embraced him like a long-lost son, home from the legal wars, but even detected a certain long-dormant charm in his gunbearer, Lulu Rosenkrantz.

Operating first out of a modest suite in Bridgeport's Stratfield Hotel and later from a $12.50-a-day room in the same city's Barnum Hotel, the gangland duo took at once to the bridle path, where one caustic observer was immediately reminded of Don Quixote and Sancho Panza. Without the windmill, that is. In any event, the pair soon found themselves sorting out invitations from one hostess after another in the shore society of Westport, Fairfield, Belle Island and Stamford. One of the bedazzled socialites summed it up this way for a New York *Sun* reporter some time later: "My dear, Arthur was the answer to a hostess's prayer. When it became known that he had been invited to your party, you had nothing to worry about. Everyone came. . . . And, really, he was charming. It was hard to believe all those horrid stories."

The Dutchman had an easy entree in that part of the woods because he was an old client of Dudley Brothwell, a Fairfield riding master. Brothwell rated Schultz an excellent horseman but he must have been exaggerating ever so slightly, since he never let him accept any bids to ride to hounds with the lifted pinky crowd, evidently counting this exercise too dangerous. The riding master, by the way, turned up later as one of the witnesses Tom Dewey used to corroborate the hidden kinship between Schultz and Jimmy Hines. Brothwell testified that the political muscleman had dropped in on the policy overlord at his stables. From the accounts of Dixie Davis and George Weinberg, the stable summit, even apart from its fragrance, was something less than a joyous reunion. The way the verbose Davis told it, Fairfield's new social lion—fresh off a brisk canter on his very own steed, Sun Tan, presumably—greeted his political buddy this way: "You know, I have got a lot of trouble and a lot of expense and everybody is being cut. Until this case is over I will have to cut everybody and, Jimmy, I am sorry I will have to cut you along with everybody else. I will make it up to you when this case is over. When I beat the case, I will make it up to you." Davis said the chop was from $500 down to $250 a week and Weinberg furnished the quotes from the cooperative Hines' assent: "Well, if things are tough, I suppose I will have to take a cut."

Tom Dewey, with his case resting on the testimony of such questionably repentant sinners as Davis, Weinberg and Harry Schoenhaus, had another respectable witness behind Brothwell to help him nail down the connection between the mob and Hines. Charles W. Hughes testified that when he was assistant manager of the Hotel Barnum in the summer of 1935 he saw Hines with the Dutchman and some of his troops.

The Connecticut idyll—not all fun and games, obviously—ended on September 24 when Schultz checked out of the Barnum and casually announced that he was going to New York to join the SRO throng taking in the Max Baer–Joe Louis fight at Yankee Stadium. This had the sound of an unlikely surrender in the old stamping ground, of all places, but it didn't happen that way. Instead, the next day, U.S. Commissioner Morris Spritzer in New Brunswick, New Jersey, had a call from State Senator Toolan inquiring whether he could hope for reasonable bail, like $10,000, if Arthur Flegenheimer chanced to drop in on him. Spritzer told the counselor he could not give him any such assurance. Then the Commissioner called J. Howard Carter, Chief Assistant to Francis W. H. Adams, the new United States Attorney in Manhattan, and asked him what he would consider a proper neighborhood for bond in the case at hand. Carter said he thought $75,000 would be about right. This dour piece of intelligence must have been conveyed in unmistakable terms to Mr. Flegenheimer's authorized spokesman, the Senator, for New Brunswick was denied the distinction of accepting the second surrender of Dutch Schultz and the scene switched to Perth Amboy.

There, the next morning, the Deputy Chief of Police, John F. Murray, received an anonymous phone call inquiring whether he would like to make a "good arrest." Murray said he always liked to make good arrests and the caller told him to wait at his desk. Half an hour later the phone rang again and the officer was advised that if he proceeded to Room 407 of the Packer Hotel he would find Dutch Schultz there. Murray went to the hotel with Detective Lieutenant James Nolan, ascertained that Room 407 had been rented a few minutes earlier to "Morris Golden and party," and hurried upstairs. "Morris Golden and party" proved to be Dutch Schultz, just like the man said, and his favorite bondsman, Max Silverman. Two other gentlemen who had accompanied the pair to the little Jersey town, quite possibly two men who looked a lot like Lulu Rosenkrantz and Abe Landau, were not in the room but did turn up—riding shotgun, so to speak—in a sedan that followed the car in which Murray and Nolan escorted the Dutchman to Police Headquarters.

Booked on suspicion of being a fugitive, the prisoner was taken before Acting Recorder Harry S. Medinets, who proved to be most kindly disposed toward him. Medinets had a wire from Frank Adams imploring him to hold the Dutchman without bond because of the long-standing warrant, but he wasn't impressed at all. "You are entitled to the same treatment every prisoner gets before this court," the Recorder told Schultz. "I will permit bail in this case."

How much? Why, $10,000, the very amount Senator Toolan had tried to arrange in New Brunswick, and it was promptly furnished. Asked later why he had set such low bond, Medinets said, "I was not going to keep a man in jail just because he has a bad record. He is a human being just as anyone else."

Frank Adams did not quite agree with that assessment. He sent Howard Carter scurrying over to Newark to get a bench warrant from Federal Judge William Clark calling for the Dutchman's rearrest on the untried income tax counts. Pretty soon the darling of the Fairfield County hunt set, a symphony in soft brown, found himself before Judge Clark surrounded by as diverse an aggregation of lawyers as had ever been assembled in that courtroom: ex-Governor Silzer, Senator Toolan, J. Richard Davis (of course), and a third local man, Harry Weinberger.

This powerhouse legal battery, citing the government's interminable "persecution" of the citizen before the bar, submitted that any bail in the tax case higher than, say, $25,000 would be oppressive. Carter, in turn, advanced the view that $75,000 really would be more like it. Judge Clark, noting acidly that the surrender in Perth Amboy apparently had been arranged with a pre-set low bail in mind, went along with Carter. The Judge then cast a cold eye on the surety bonds put before him and, lo, the Dutchman found himself behind bars once more, this time in the rather low-class Hudson County Jail in Jersey City.

Four days later the legal battalions won a $25,000 cut in the bail from the Federal Circuit Court of Appeals in Philadelphia and on October 1 their client emerged into the free air again. The reporters were waiting, as usual, and Schultz turned to them after slipping a $5 bill to the doorkeeper and telling him to go buy himself a cigar.

Where was the Dutchman going? "I don't know," he said, "but I do know the Federal Government is hounding me. They tried me on the same charge in New York, and now they dug up a new trick to repeat the maneuver."

Actually, the government hadn't quite run out of "new tricks."

Lest there be any arguments about double jeopardy in the use of the old indictment, the Adams office had come up on October 9 with a brand new true bill. This one cited Arthur Flegenheimer on eleven counts of failing to file tax returns for 1929, 1930 and 1931—all misdemeanors by contrast with the felony of willful tax evasion cited in the original case. Now the government charged that Schultz had earned a nifty $928,707.35 in the years in question and that his failure to file returns had cheated Uncle out of $200,726.62. He faced a possible sentence of eleven years in prison and $100,000 in fines on the new grunt.

Would he run again?

No. The Dutchman simply settled down in Newark while the new round of legal maneuvering got under way. He was going to fight extradition, of course, but it was apparent that he wasn't quaking in his boots over the prospect of going into a fresh courtroom battle again so soon after the protracted Syracuse and Malone trials.

Why? Well, for one thing he knew now that he had an infinitely stronger legal hand than Al Capone. The case against him was confined to his beer operation: nothing about policy, nothing about guys getting knocked off, nothing about any other racket. The case against "that dunce" in Chicago involved all kinds of dirty money, down to the killer wood alcohol to extortion and strong-arm stuff to gambling and, horrors, flesh-peddling. But needle beer? Hell, Prohibition had just been repealed as the most colossal legislative blunder in the nation's history; it was still a burning memory. What jury in the mid-Thirties was going to hold still for a moth-eared tax case against a reformed bootlegger who had labored against so many adversities, paying off crooked cops and all that, to wet the parched throats of his neighbors? How many juries, for that matter, were going to convict anybody for cribbing on his taxes? This sport had achieved a national acceptance by then.

Either that or Arthur Flegenheimer knew that you didn't need twelve good men and true to beat a law case. One juror would always be enough.

In Newark, the Dutchman turned rather gregarious, mounting a private public relations campaign in the process. One night, over a bagatelle game, he put his case before Vic Hamerslag, a reporter for the Newark *Star-Ledger.* It came out this way:

"Get this straight. I am not afraid to go back to New York to face that indictment. But I'm not exactly pleased at the prospect of going back and being slapped into jail without bail. That's what they want to do to me.

"If I knew I would be given the same rights as any other citizen against whom there are charges and would be admitted to a reasonable bail, I wouldn't hesitate a minute to go back.

"I've never failed to answer bail. The fact of the matter is that I'd appear even if I were paroled in my own custody. Of course I realize that's impossible, but I do feel I'm entitled to reasonable bail."

Hamerslag asked why he didn't think he could get reasonable bail. The answer:

"Because that wouldn't be in keeping with their policy. They're after me and they're not going to leave anything unturned to embarrass and harrass me."

Why?

"They're after me now because some puny individuals in the government service can't stand up and take a licking like a man. By licking I mean they can't swallow that I was acquitted once and another jury disagreed on exactly the same charges they've got against me now. The only difference between the charges now and then is that they slapped a different name on them. . . . Now right here I'm going to tell you something, and I wouldn't give you a bum steer. Perjured witnesses were used against me in both trials and the government knew it.

"With all this, they're still at me. They couldn't take those lickings. . . . You want to remember that they got a new indictment against me since the arrest (in Perth Amboy), a sort of afterthought, you know. We have the prisoner, now we'll put some charges against him."

What about the Public Enemy No 1 label?

"I never did anything to deserve that reputation, unless it was to supply good beer to people who wanted it—and a lot of them did."

What about the future, Hamerslag asked.

"I want to settle down and be a plain citizen and be given a chance to earn a living," Schultz said. "I want to be plain Arthur Flegenheimer and forget there ever was a Dutch Schultz. That bird has had too much trouble."

The Dutchman neglected to say—was it modesty or shyness?—how he meant to earn his living. He surely wasn't abdicating his rule over the Harlem policy racket.

In the same period, holding court in the Palace Chop House with Lulu Rosenkrantz and Abe Landau on hand to keep any disorderly strangers away, Schultz granted a rather curious interview to Isaac McAnally, a New York *Post* reporter he had come to trust over the years. This was the audience in which the Dutchman first told his story of the alleged miscarriage of justice in the execution of Toughy

Odierno and Frank Giordano in the slaying of Joe Mullins back in 1931, an item touched on in this narrative in the account of the Schultz-Coll war [Chapter 12]. McAnally, chosen for the red-hot disclosure because the *Post* "might go after it stronger," said that Schultz professed to be very deeply concerned about the fate of Odierno and Giordano even though they were defectors from his own gang.

"I don't say they didn't do a lot of other things," the gangster said, pounding the table with the flat of his hand, "but they didn't do *that* job."

You will recall that Odierno and Giordano, himself even then facing trial with Coll in the Harlem baby killing, were convicted on the testimony of two Edison Company repairmen who had a clear view of the Mullins spot killing. Schultz elected to skip that detail. In his version, the Coll gunmen could not have committed that deed in The Bronx because at that very moment they had their hands full elsewhere with two of his own beer truck drivers—snatched out of one of his speakeasies, he said, under the eyes of an off-duty police sergeant who happened to be tending bar for him. Schultz said the drivers, released unharmed, had assured him that Odierno and Giordano were their captors. He said he sent word to a man connected with the prosecution that the District Attorney had the wrong killers in the Mullins case and that he could prove it. "I told him," he said, "that if he sent those boys to the chair he would never be easy in his conscience again as long as he lived. But nobody ever came around to me."

McAnally pressed the Dutchman as to why he hadn't done more. Now there was a switch in his story.

"As a matter of fact," Schultz said, somewhat lamely, "when I sent the word I didn't say that I could prove *both* guys were innocent. I only said that I knew Odierno didn't do it. I always liked that Toughy Odierno. He was an amusing little guy and I felt sorry for him. I didn't give a damn about Giordano."

McAnally asked the Dutchman how he could have had any tender feelings in the case when the Coll torpedoes undoubtedly were gunning for him, too.

"Well, that didn't matter," he said. "When little Odierno was in the Death House I sent him dough so he could have cigarets and stuff. Hell, you can't be mad at a guy when he's in that place."

Schultz offered no explanation for the fact that the doomed men might have beaten the rap by producing the two truck drivers with whom they were supposed to have idled away that fateful afternoon. Nor did he say why *he* hadn't produced the drivers, especially since he had such warm feelings towards his pal Toughy. The fact is, Odierno and Giordano, during an all-night sweating by police and Assistant District Attorney Breslin, had come up with a terribly defective alibi. The hoodlum pair said they were on a train coming down from Albany the day Joe Mullins was shot, but a crumpled dining car check stub found in their hotel room hideaway, supplemented by all kinds of testimony from New York Central trainmen, established that they had come down on a Pullman the day before the guns were aimed at the Schultz beer checker. Ed Breslin told the author that the mobsters caved in when their alibi was blown apart; besides, he noted dryly, Giordano couldn't quite explain how the revolver that killed Mullins happened to be in his possession. The retired Judge also described an amusing exchange between Police Commissioner Mulrooney and Vincent Coll when the Mick, swept up with the others in the Mullins dragnet, had to be turned out for lack of evidence.

"If we don't get you on this one we'll get you on another one," Mulrooney told the gangster.

"Commissioner," Coll replied, "that isn't nice to say."

Why did Dutch Schultz wait three years to tell his "inside" story of the case? He had no adequate answer when McAnally put the question. Why wouldn't he let the reporter acquaint the masses immediately with his hidden concern about the flagging eyesight of Lady Justice? Schultz said he didn't want to get involved in the thing until his tax troubles were over; then, he said, he might even put the reporter in touch with the friendly cop who was tending bar for him the day Odierno and Giordano were supposed to have staged that kidnapping. "You understand," he added, "the cop wouldn't say anything for publication. That would crucify him." To say the least.

When McAnally brought the tale back to his office the *Post*'s City Editor, Walter Lister, decided that he would like to have a chat with the talkative Dutchman himself and maybe get something the paper could print—on any subject. The reporter arranged the interview for the night of October 17—again in the Palace Chop House and at the very round table where assassins' bullets would close out the saga of Arthur Flegenheimer just six days later. The unsigned story by Lister, later Managing Editor of the Philadelphia *Evening Bulletin*, furnished the last close-up of the gangster in the twilight of his immensely successful career. Here it is:

DUTCH SCHULTZ WEEPS IN HIS JELLO FOR GANG WIDOWS AND ORPHANS

By a Staff Correspondent

NEWARK, Oct. 18—Here is Dutch Schultz sitting at a table in the back room of a side-street bar. He is eating a dish of raspberry jello.

"This is lovely," he says between spoonfuls of the stuff. "Have some? Have something to eat? Have a drink?"

Personally, Schultz is on the wagon.

"I don't want to get my feet tangled up," he explains, "until I get over this headache. I might forget to show up in court some day."

The Beer Baron is on his good behavior these days. He is fighting removal proceedings in Federal Court. If he loses—and he may know by Tuesday—he will have to face another income tax trial in the Southern District of New York.

So he is glad to buy you a drink, or a sandwich, or a dish of jello.

Does he miss the big town? Sure.

"Anybody would miss a place as big as that," he rumbles hoarsely (he caught a touch of laryngitis the night before).

"I never found any place as good as New York. I never used to go away on vacations. I never went to Florida—though they gave a couple of cops a swell vacation, sending them down to Miami to look for me."

What does he miss most, now that he is just across the river, but doesn't feel like using the tube?

"I don't know. People. Things." Perhaps an income, although he doesn't say so.

Schultz is smaller than his pictures make him look. He is under average height, swarthy, black-haired, with a worried pucker between his eyebrows. He is wearing a neat brown suit, with light tan shoes. There is a star sapphire in a ring on the little finger of his right hand.

"It isn't worth much," he says, "but a friend gave it to me."

Wide World Photos (top)
United Press International (bottom)

At top, a jubilant Schultz leaves the courtroom in Malone after his acquittal. Behind him, all aglow, is Dixie Davis. At bottom, the gangster was much less cheerful as he was brought to Newark for a bail hearing after having surrendered in Perth Amboy on an outstanding fugitive warrant from New York. He was shot down a month later.

New York *Post*

Police Commissioner Lewis J. Valentine. He wanted Schultz rather badly—but the policy overlord had little to fear from the men in the ranks.

It doesn't take long to discover what is most on his mind. Schultz feels injured. He thinks he has been badly treated. His complaint, boiled down, is that they have him on a wrong rap.

Maybe he wouldn't mind so much if he faced court on a charge of beer-running or some outcropping of gangsterism—not, of course, that he admits knowing anything about beer or gangsters. But he argues that it's unfair, technical, and just plain mean to try to send him to prison on an income tax charge, especially after he has been acquitted of a similar charge in Malone, N.Y.

"I offered to compromise on my tax," he repeats. "I thought the Government was going to let me do it. But somebody decided to make a football out of me.

"It's always a good popular play for the Government to go after racketeers. It keeps folks' minds off bank closings and widows and orphans being swindled."

Justice, he philosophizes, is sometimes pretty cockeyed.

"Coppers and courts can be wrong," he says. "Why, right here in Jersey—remember the time five guys stuck up the Public Service? No, it was the Reid Ice Cream job, years ago. Five guys got the payroll. Then after they made the touch they are in a room, splitting the dough, when five other guys come in and heist them."

Schultz jabs the table with a stubby, well-polished forefinger.

"Well, they get those last guys. They burn. They burn the guys that heisted the guys that heisted the dough."

The papers, Schultz also insists, keep getting him wrong. He doesn't say this angrily. He says it wearily, as a man might who has long ago given up hoping that anything will be done about it.

"Why," he says, "they've got me in a war right now. I see by the papers that two Schultz lieutenants have just got killed.

"Schultz lieutenants!"—and he achieves a fine, hoarse scorn. "If you can show I ever knew these guys I'll beg or borrow all the money you'll ever want and give it to you.

"The papers can sure hurt you. I remember that baby killing. (The accidental shooting of five-year-old Michael Vengalli on East 107th Street in July, 1931, during what was referred to as a Schultz–Vincent Coll feud.)

"I was the first to realize," says Schultz, "how bad that thing was. I got the papers that night and I see that they got me, and my picture, as doing it. Oh, Jeez!

"Then next morning I buy more papers and now I see that they got Coll and his picture. Augh!"

After a while, Schultz drifts toward the door. One of his boys pays the bar check. Schultz and a pal who has just come in start down the street toward a barber shop. But they stop on a corner to talk about how crazy justice is these days.

"Look," says the pal, "they won't let Dutch alone, will they? Why? Because he has income tax trouble.

"Well, J. Pierpont Morgan stands up and they ask him, 'How much tax did you pay the United States?' And he says, 'Not a cent.' And what do they do? Nothing.

"And look at these judges we have got. I know a judge who leans down from the bench and says, 'My good man, you have admitted stealing $7. You are a disgrace to society.' But that same judge has taken $3,000,000 away from the widows and orphans in lousy mortgage certificates.

"I know another judge—God rest his mother, I haven't a thing against her—who will put on a black robe and set himself up in judgment. But I would like to ask him what he did with a little girl from Connecticut. And I would like to know how his father got so much money from the widows and orphans that his son could get to be a judge.

"Dutch here never robbed any widows and orphans. So what?"

That's THEIR story.

There was a footnote to this interview. As Walter Lister left the Chop House, the Dutchman shook his hand and said, "Don't forget, when you write your piece, to split all my infinitives for me."

A man of good cheer at that moment, obviously. Nothing much on his mind beyond his image as one of gangland's more cultured—and more misjudged—citizens. He could not have known that a death sentence had been passed upon him by his own kind and there wasn't enough time left to repair the tattered Flegenheimer name. There wasn't enough time left because a guy named Workman had a contract to kill him.

"Gee, what an experience I had!"

—The Man Who Shot Dutch Schultz

CHAPTER XX

THE GUNNER— AND HIS COMMANDING OFFICER, LEPKE

CHARLIE WORKMAN CAME OUT OF NEW YORK'S TEEMING Lower East Side. He was the second child of Samuel and Anna Workman and besides his older sister he had two other sisters and three brothers. Charlie was born on September 15, 1908—a date no one else in the large brood would have much occasion to celebrate after a while, because he was the bad one. He was bad from the beginning. He wouldn't stay in public school long enough to go on to high school. He quit in 9A. "At the age of 17," says an old police report on him, "Workman became known as 'Handsome Charlie' and was feared in the neighborhood for his rough tactics." There would never be any doubt about the "rough tactics" of Handsome Charlie, man and boy. The lessons of the hard East Side streets were never lost on him. He followed the familiar pattern, starting off, like Arthur Flegenheimer in The Bronx, with petty thefts. His first arrest, at 18, involved the wholly unglamourous charge of stealing a $12 bundle of cotton thread off a truck on lower Broadway. He got off with probation but within a year he was back in custody, charged with shooting a man behind the ear in an argument over $10 or

$20. He beat that case when the complainant developed memory trouble and refused to identify him as his assailant, but he wound up in the New York City Reformatory for violating his probation in the theft case. Out in seven months, he was ordered back for associating with "questionable characters" and failing to find legitimate employment. He was paroled again in three months but then resentenced on the same charge of evil associations. That took another four months out of his youth but he wasn't going behind bars again, not for any length of time, for another twelve years. This, however, did not mean that he was going to be a total stranger to the police. He would beat a gun charge in 1932. He would pay a $25 fine for bashing in the face of an off-duty cop in a traffic argument in 1933, plus the usual $2 fines for items like passing red lights. He would suffer the small inconvenience of a pinch for vagrancy in 1939, hauled in because the cops thought he might know something about Lepke and Gurrah, then on the lam from a Dewey racket indictment; in that pinch, in character, Workman would just turn his fierce black eyes on the detectives and tell them to go to hell. What would he know about those guys?

The fact is, Handsome Charlie knew a lot about the Garment Center racketeers. For all his tender years, he was around the fringes when the strong-arm twins, who got their start shaking down pushcart peddlers on the Lower East Side, made their debut in the big time as musclemen in the summer-long garment strike of 1926. In that classic confrontation, death knell of the sweatshop, the employers called in one set of goons and the labor giants, Sidney Hillman's Amalgamated Clothing Workers and David Dubinsky's International Ladies Garment Workers Union, both beset by hard-line Communists within their own ranks while fighting the manufacturers, called in another. Lepke and Gurrah, interested neither in the labor-management conflict nor in the higher internal politics, came out of it with their eyes opened up to the incredible riches waiting to be plucked in a billion-dollar-a-year industry simply rife for the kind of protection and extortion operations which would become their specialty.

Off his artistic performance as a bruiser for the mob, the little curly-haired Workman was graduated, summa cum laude, to a full-time spot on the Lepke payroll, available at all times to the Brooklyn gun-for-hire ring. The salary was $125 a week, just a mildly lush stipend for the early Thirties, but there were extras. In Murder Inc.—so christened by Harry Feeney, dean of the Brooklyn police reporters—the resident gunslingers enjoyed an interesting fringe benefit. They had the right to sweep out the pockets of their victims, and it's a fair assumption that Handsome Charlie drew many lucrative assignments, because he rapidly became one of the execution cartel's top killers. He was right up there with Abe (Kid Twist) Reles, Albert (Allie) Tannenbaum, Martin (Buggsy) Goldstein, Harry (Pittsburgh Phil) Strauss, Harry Maione, called Happy because he never smiled, and Frank Abbandando, known as Dasher because he showed great speed of foot when he starred in the Elmira prison infield one season. In this incredibly mindless company, something of a Kamikaze troupe without the risks, Workman took a back seat to nobody.

Lepke, who adored the guy, used to say he had so much guts he was "bugs," so after a while he came to be called Charlie the Bug. He was called by some other names too, all highly flattering for a man in his chosen profession. There were some inside the mob who referred to him as The Powerhouse. The author once asked a hardened police inspector how he would characterize the Bug, and the answer was:

"The same as a regiment." Burton B. Turkus, who was District Attorney William O'Dwyer's chief assistant in the investigation that stripped the veil from Murder Inc. and spread it across the front pages in 1940, called Workman "one of gangland's most deadly executioners." Allie Tannenbaum, no slouch himself in that league, deferred to Workman as "one of the best killers in the country" and said he was so good that at one time he was on three different payrolls—Murder Inc., the Bug & Meyer mob and, yes, Dutch Schultz's. The plaudits appear to have been well earned.

Turkus, the workhorse in that Augean housecleaning in Brooklyn and the man who took the wrapped-up cases to court and put seven of the Murder Inc. cast in the electric chair, credited the swarthy Workman with no less than 20 hits, coast to coast. In private practise now, Turkus insists that this had to be a conservative figure, because his information was that mobs all over the country made demands on the Bug's lend-lease services. O'Dwyer himself never went beyond the phrase "at least five murders" when he talked about Workman's known accomplishments, but he was confining himself to the cases in which he believed the requisite corroboration existed for conviction in the state courts.

If there ever was any lingering doubt about the measure of Handsome Charlie, the assignment to knock over Dutch Schultz had to dispel it for all time. For sheer magnitude, nothing compared with it but the executions earlier in that decade of the warring Cosa Nostra dons, Joe the Boss Masseria and Salvatore Maranzano. Those were family affairs, of course, in the struggle for power inside the Italian underworld federation. The case of the Dutchman was quite different; now all the mobs were getting together to dispose of a maverick contemporary who had suddenly become a dangerous nuisance to the whole community of crime.

The Big Six had two and possibly three impelling reasons to vote the death sentence on Schultz. The first—and the best, from all the available information—had to be the man's obsession about killing Tom Dewey to turn off the heat. A second reason had to be the common fear, probably well grounded, that Schultz had turned so irrational that he wouldn't stand up if Dewey managed to nail him for something worse than the old tax rap—say the restaurant racket; the mobs were afraid the Dutchman would trade off some information about their operations—and he had to know a thing or two—to beat any unconscionably long stretch up the river.A third reason was the one advanced by Joe Valachi in the parts of his story that survived the Department of Justice's blue-pencil screening when Peter Maas put together *The Valachi Papers* in 1968. In this version, perhaps out of ethnic pride, Lucky Luciano rather than Lepke got the credit for disposing of the Dutchman. Valachi told Maas that he had heard about it at the time from Vito Genovese, who was then so close to Luciano that he was being groomed to step into his shoes if anything bad happened. Valachi said Luciano's motives extended a little beyond any concern over the possible ramifications of a Dewey assassination. He said the Cosa Nostra boss, casting loving eyes on the Schultz policy empire ever since the 1933 tax indictment made something of a lamister out of him, had seized on the Dewey thing as the ideal opportunity for disposing of the Dutchman and taking over. But Valachi, bear in mind, also mentioned the plot on Dewey as one of the irritations bestirring the Big Six and its execution arm, Murder Inc., just before Schultz went on the spot.

While Burt Turkus got the Dewey story from his two favorite blabbermouths, Abe Reles and Allie Tannenbaum, a piece of independent corroboration came from quite a separate source. This was the hulking Seymour Magoon, called Blue Jaw because he practically invented the 5 o'clock shadow, a Reles buddy with an even 25 entries on his arrest record. Even as Reles and Tannenbaum were doing their nightingale act, Magoon happened to be in custody in The Bronx as a material witness in the Brooklyn cartel's slaying of Benjamin (Benny the Boss) Tannenbaum, knocked off while babysitting for a friend because he was the babbling type and he also knew about that super-special Workman mission in Newark. It's all in the book Turkus wrote with Sid Feder in 1951, *Murder, Inc.*, with the new twist—the Luciano-policy angle—nailed down 12 years later after the Valachi concert hit the nation's television screens.

The Dutchman began to brood about Tom Dewey when the Special Prosecutor started putting together his airtight case in the restaurant shakedowns (seven men, a combination of Schultz minions and crooked labor leaders, eventually went to prison in that one).

Schultz was so frantic that he slipped into town from his Newark retreat to put the case before the other mobs—an ethical requirement of the breed in an undertaking of such monstrous proportions—but couldn't quite make the case. Turkus said he came away with nothing more than a week's grace while the Big Six agreed to ponder the logistics of the proposed mission and its probable implications.

Reles, Tannenbaum and Magoon all said the man delegated to the on-the-spot study of the Schultz proposal was nobody less than Albert Anastasia, Murder Inc.'s Lord High Executioner. The story was that Anastasia set himself up a four-day stakeout on Dewey's Fifth Avenue apartment house, patrolling the sidewalk in the guise of a neighborhood father taking his small son (on loan, apparently) out for an airing. There was just one variation here. Reles and Tannenbaum said that Anastasia used a boy on a tricycle; Magoon said he had a baby in a carriage.

Either way, Anastasia supposedly satisfied himself that the Dutchman had proposed an entirely feasible hit, apart from the complexities which would surely follow a mission of such awesome proportions.

Dewey followed the same routine every morning. He would leave the house at 8:00 A.M., pick up his bodyguards and Paul Lockwood, his towering assistant, and go around the corner to a drugstore to have a cup of coffee before starting downtown in his car. The guards generally waited outside the store. If a couple of marksmen with silencers on their pistols followed the Special Prosecutor in they might well be able to dispose of him, Lockwood and the druggist—Anastasia never spotted any others customers in the store at that hour—and slip into their getaway car before the Dewey gunbearers knew what had happened.

Splendid, but the Big Six turned thumbs down.

Turkus was told that Lepke had registered the heaviest "No" vote, saying, "This is the worst thing in the world. It will hit us all in the pocketbook because everybody will come down on our heads." Lepke surely was thinking about something well beyond the mob's own extensive local operations. He wasn't the only one in the syndicate who understood that if Dewey were rubbed out the ensuing crackdown on organized crime would have to be devastating all the way from Maine to California—and Murder Inc. itself was handling contracts in a raft of cities between those ocean-to-ocean boundaries.

Elsewhere, Lepke is quoted as having said, "We will all burn if Dewey is knocked off." Beyond this, according to Turkus, the little merchant of mayhem also entertained the confident notion that the mobs did not have to worry too much about Dewey as long as they could keep knocking off any turncoats who were disposed to help him. "No witnesses, no indictments," Lepke was quoted as saying, and there was clearly some substance behind it.

In any case, the oral communiqué that went out to the Dutchman in Newark said that the underworld, thanks, would rather have a live Tom Dewey to stand off than a corpse that might bring down upon the house of crime the combined law enforcement forces of the city, state and federal governments. "I suppose they figured that the National Guard would have been called out, or something like that, if Dewey had been killed," Frank S. Hogan, District Attorney of Manhattan, told the author, looking back on that time, "and I guess they wouldn't have been far wrong."

No such fears troubled Dutch Schultz, apparently, for the word that came back to the mob was that he was still saying that "Dewey's gotta go" and that he was going to attend to it whether the Big Six wanted a piece of the action or not.

There was one flaw in the story, of course, that had to trouble any thoughtful observer, and that was the use of Albert Anastasia as the man to case the proposed assassination setup. While "Mr. A's" puffy features might not necessarily have been familiar to Tom Dewey or Paul Lockwood, it surely was conceivable that any detectives on the guard detail might well have recognized a familiar underworld map such as that one.

When the story broke, Bill O'Dwyer quickly denied that any Schultz plot to murder Dewey had been unearthed by his investigation, and Dewey himself in turn insisted that he himself had never heard of any such nonsense. Turkus always said, and still does, that he passed the story on to Dewey when he got it; he says he still marvels over the way the man listened to the chilling details without any show of emotion.

The author put the question to Dewey and got this answer: "I had no personal information about the reported Schultz plot against me but it is interesting that Valachi tells the same story as Burt Turkus with a slightly different emphasis."

You can read that, 28 years after the strong initial denial, as neither a denial nor a confirmation, but Dewey's answer to the question which flowed from it was quite interesting:

> Q. If there was no Schultz plot against your life, what other reason would the Big Six or Syndicate have had for killing him in your view?
> A. The *only other* [italics the author's] reason I can think of would be that he was a loud-mouthed bully who became too self-important.

On the matter of Lepke Buchalter's confident "no witnesses, no indictments" dictum, there is a disparity between the O'Dwyer-Turkus researches and Dewey's view. The Brooklyn investigation pointed to a whole flock of spot killings of suspected Dewey informers. O'Dwyer put the figure at seven but Dewey now terms that a "gross overstatement," saying he knew of only two or three. From the number of corpses turned up, O'Dwyer's count always appeared closer.

The fact is that the big heat went on Lepke, still a fugitive in the summer of 1939, 17 months after his indictment on racket charges, because the bodies of witnesses were dropping in too many places. It was at that point that Dewey, by then District Attorney and carrying even more muscle than he had enjoyed as Special Prosecutor, took Police Commissioner Valentine into a hush-hush session with J. Edgar Hoover and Harry J. Anslinger, Federal Commissioner of Narcotics, and laid it all on the line. "If the killing off of witnesses continues," Anslinger quoted Dewey in his autobiography, *The Murderers,* "there will soon be no one left to testify when we finally catch up with Lepke. If the four of us together can't land Lepke, we might as well turn the job over to the mobs."

It was then that a $30,000 price tag—$25,000 from the city of New York and $5,000 from the FBI—was put on the 42-year-old underworld boss, dead or alive, and a million circulars went out on him. Within the week, Lepke emissaries —Frank Costello? Albert Anastasia?—were on the phone with Walter Winchell setting up the terms of surrender: the columnist delivers Lepke to J. Edgar Hoover, who had called him "the most dangerous criminal in America," so that he can be tried on federal charges and stay out of the clutches of Mr. Dewey, or, maybe worse, Bill O'Dwyer and that Murder Inc. mess.

The reasoning was pretty elementary.

Lepke and the mobs had satisfied themselves by then that the long-time underworld kingpin had to go "inside" because the heat, local and federal, was too much to stand off any longer. What were the alternatives? Lepke had an idea that a spell in a place like Leavenworth—there were ten handy narcotics raps pending against him—might be much more palatable than what he faced on his home grounds. Dewey was talking about a somewhat outlandish sentence like 500 years—a small exaggeration, although he had built up an imposing case in his racket investigations. O'Dwyer appeared to be in a position to ticket the fugitive for one of those perfectly awful three-minute dates in that oversized chair at Sing Sing.

Here Lepke's vaunted cunning abandoned him. He chose what seemed to be the softest alternative, letting Winchell deliver him to J. Edgar Hoover, in the flesh, on a Manhattan street corner on August 24, 1939.

After that, nothing went according to the script.

The FBI Director's prize catch was found guilty of trading in narcotics—his only serious conviction after eleven arrests dating back to 1915—and drew a 15-year federal sentence. Not bad. It meant about ten years in the cooler, hardly a prohibitive price for all the notches on the man's hired guns, but Tom Dewey wasn't buying that at all. He made Lepke stand trial as the Mahatma of the bakery and flour trucking rackets and got another 30 years tagged on to the federal grunt. And then it was Bill O'Dwyer's turn. He brought up the savage 1936 murder of Joseph Rosen (only 15 bullets) in his Brooklyn candy store.

A former garment industry truckman driven out of business by the mob because he was carrying goods to non-union shops in Pennsylvania, which was bad for Sidney Hillman's Amalgamated Clothing Workers, Rosen was another one of those soreheads who wouldn't listen when the Lepke-Gurrah delegates came around and told him to keep his big yap shut. O'Dwyer had evidence that the finger went on him after Lepke had observed, in his soft-spoken way, that "Rosen is shooting off his mouth that he is going down to Dewey." O'Dwyer even had under lock and key the Lepke confederates charged with the actual killing—Louis Capone and Emanuel (Mendy)Weiss. So that case was all wrapped in ribbons when Burt Turkus took it into court in the winter of

1941 and Lepke (his mother called him Lepkeleh for "darling Louis," but he was credited with giving the signal for as many as 80 murder expeditions over the years) was pointed toward the little green door with Capone and Weiss. Capone, no relation to Alphonse, was more than a just a gun hand in the Borough of Churches. He was high up in Murder Inc.'s inner councils. Mendy Weiss was an even more interesting figure, as will be seen, because he knew a thing or two about the assassination of Dutch Schultz.

Lepke and his handymen, as it happened, were not going to sit down in that ridiculous contraption at Ossining for another three years, thanks to appeals and reprieves. And there's some irony there, too. When the matter of life or death came down to the wire, if you'll pardon the expression, the man in the Governor's chair at Albany was Thomas E. Dewey. Think of it: Lepke Buchalter may have saved Tom Dewey's life in 1935 when he delegated Charlie Workman and two helpers—was one of them Mendy Weiss?—to wipe out Dutch Schultz. Nine years later it fell to Dewey to make the ultimate decision about Lepke and Weiss. Should he spare them? Well, the Governor did cling for a long time to the forlorn hope that a living Lepke might turn troubadour and clear up some items of unfinished business in the Manhattan District Attorney's office.

But Lepke either couldn't find the key or decided that he would rather be dead than lose the good name he had built up in his killer's trade—or perhaps he reasoned that the long arms of his confreres, bearing shivs fashioned in the prison metal shop, surely would reach out to him in Sing Sing if he started doing business with the law to save his own backside from getting singed.

The unholy trinity from Murder Inc. finally was set to go

on March 2 but Dewey granted a 48-hour reprieve to give the Lepke barristers time to petition the United States Supreme Court to review the mob king's conviction. Once the new stay was granted, Lepke emissaries slipped the word to Albany that the Death House's all-time celebrity guest felt like talking for a change. This pulsating message was passed at once to Frank Hogan and he lost no time piling into his limousine with Sol Gelb, his Chief Assistant by then, and Joseph A. Sarafite, moved up to head of the Rackets Bureau in the New York County District Attorney's office just the day before. The prospect of a heart-to-heart chat with the doomed five-foot-five-and-a-half-inch giant of the rackets made that trip up the river quite eventful.

Aflush with excitement, Hogan and his men were still putting together questions for the law's imposing new ally when the chauffeur called out, "We're here, Chief."

The way back was—well, kind of flat.

Lepke did want to talk, but he didn't want to say anything, as will be seen here in the first authoritative account of that momentous session ever published.

Frank Hogan dipped back a quarter of a century into an action-filled career to reconstruct that drama-charged afternoon in the Death House.

"We spent two or three hours with Lepke," he said. "We had been given to understand that he would talk about some unsolved homicides, that he would cooperate if he could beat the chair. But actually he had little to offer for us to be at all sanguine about obtaining indictments—not enough, in any event, to merit postponing the execution again. He did mention two or three cases, but they were typical Lepke cases. All we could say was that Lepke talked about those cases but there was no corroboration and no accomplices. They had a technique of knocking off people like that, you know. When we were finished, we couldn't point to anybody and say here, 'Lepke gave us a case, let's go before the Grand Jury with this one.' And we couldn't say that Lepke had given us any information about the other higher-ups of the underworld; he was very careful on that score. We reeled off one name after another and just drew blanks. Lepke knew what he was doing every minute, even though he was two days away from the electric chair. He did answer some other questions—about the garment racket, for example—but he didn't tell us a thing we could have done anything with. He knew just how far to go—and we knew pretty fast that we weren't going to get anywhere with him.

"We did go over our notes pretty hard when we got out of there. We didn't want to dash all the man's hopes that very afternoon, but there was no basis for recommending another stay to the Governor. We simply had nothing of any substance to go on."

The big question about that closely kept session, of course, had to do neither with any unsolved murders nor with any glittering underworld names on the rarified Lepke level. No, it had to do with the burning whispers—never quite stilled—about Lepke's asserted relationship with Sidney Hillman, co-director of President Roosevelt's wartime Office of Production Management, in the years when the world-famous labor leader was running the Amalgamated Clothing Workers Union.

To this day, Frank Hogan won't say whether the gangster mentioned the since-deceased Hillman, "There were so many names," he told the author. "I wouldn't want to single out any one. It's too far back."

Sol Gelb, in private practice now, was less reticent. "I

asked about Sidney Hillman," he said, "and I have a vivid memory of Lepke's answer. He said he hardly knew Hillman. I don't know whether he was telling the truth, but that's what he told us." Gelb said the name of David Dubinsky, head of the International Ladies Garment Workers Union until his retirement in 1966, also came up as the racket titan, chain-smoking nervously, sat across a small wooden table from his interrogators in a Death House reception room. "Lepke mentioned Dubinsky," Gelb said, "In connection with some incident a few years back in which a non-union shop in the garment district had been busted up, but it was an entirely vague reference. It was a tidbit Lepke was dropping on us to whet our appetites, but it was meaningless. He didn't have to tell us about the rough stuff in the Garment Center unless he was really going to open up. We knew there were goons on both sides—goons brought in by the manufacturers and goons working for the Hillman and Dubinsky unions."

Did the names of any political figures or high police officials come up? Gelb was certain that no police brass had been mentioned but said that Jimmy Hines did come into the conversation. He said that Lepke conceded that he had come to know Hines somewhere along the way but did not say that he had ever done any business with the protector of the Dutch Schultz policy empire.

"I got the impression," Gelb said, "that we were talking to a man who was utterly desperate and frantically trying to save himself but at the same time would only tell us things we already knew. When he did say anything—about a murder, for example—it was always information about people below him, his own underlings. I concluded that he was so high in underworld ranks that he couldn't give us anything because he was the boss. He would have to talk about himself to give us anything and after all he couldn't very well talk about murders *he* had ordered. He was anything but open and frank on that score. There certainly was no basis for another reprieve."

Joe Sarafite, on the Supreme Court bench in New York for many years now, remembered Lepke as a man "*in extremis*—scared, worried, frightened, pathetic"—but so crafty that he never even came close to a slip-up. "He talked a blue streak," the Judge said, "but he gave the clear impression that he was telling only what he wanted to tell, not the sort of things we had gone up there to get from him. We were interested in evaluating anything he said in the light of possible prosecution but how much weight could you put on his words without corroboration? He was a tarnished witness. He did so much himself that the only one he could implicate was himself, but he never came forth with anything worth a nickel in any case. He just wandered. He talked about all kinds of people but there wasn't a shred of admissible evidence in any of it."

The Judge, without disputing Sol Gelb, said he did not recall any discussion of Sidney Hillman. "There were so many names," he said.

When Burton Turkus was completing *Murder, Inc.* in 1951, he submitted a series of written questions to Frank Hogan about the Death House interview. Among other things, Turkus wanted to know whether the condemned man had mentioned an offer of a "deal" from Bill O'Dwyer "or anyone else" in return for talking, whether he had mentioned Fiorello LaGuardia (then deceased) or Sidney Hillman, whether he had talked about Lucky Luciano, Salvatore Maranzano, Frank Costello, Longy Zwillman, Albert Anastasia or such lesser racket figures as Joey Adonis, whether he had mentioned the nationwide purge of the Mafia in 1931, or whether he had talked about any underworld political alliances. Another question dealt with the unsolved 1931 murder, in Brooklyn, of a clothing manufacturer named Guido Ferrari, gunned down while he was undergoing some unpleasantness with the Hillman union. Had Lepke mentioned the case of Mr. Ferrari?

Turkus did not get an answer from Hogan. Instead, he received a letter from Joe Sarafite simply saying this:

"The District Attorney did not request the Governor to grant any reprieve of Buchalter, nor was any other official action taken by him which could be used as a justifiable basis for revealing what Buchalter said. Beyond this statement, we are unable to answer the questions."

In an appendix to his book, Turkus quoted Sarafite's letter and observed, pointedly, that while Hogan had not replied "affirmatively to the queries—neither did he deny them." The obvious inference was that Lepke had indeed reeled off a glittering array of names on both sides of the law when he took that last shot for clemency.

That was seven years after the 1944 Death House session. Why is Hogan still loathe to discuss any of the names that may have crossed Lepke's lips? "It wouldn't be fair," he says. "After all, Lepke had nothing to lose—he could have mentioned anybody he wanted."

For purposes of this book, however, both Sol Gelb and Judge Sarafite went over the Turkus list. Apart from Gelb's saying that Sidney Hillman's name had been mentioned, both men expressed an absolute certainty that none of the other figures cited by Burt Turkus had come up in the limited Lepke songfest.

This should lay to rest, once and for all, the raft of speculative stories which ran in the newspapers during that last 48-hour reprieve of Lepke's. These high-octane accounts covered a great deal of ground.

The *Herald-Tribune* said that "Lepke made and signed a death cell statement about a 'deal' freighted with political dynamite, which was proposed to him when he was a federal prisoner more than three years ago."

The *Sun* said that Lepke had "sought to escape the chair by involving a number or prominent persons in his long career of crime."

The *Daily Mirror,* least shy of the New York gazettes in that time, said that Lepke had named "30 politicians, high police officials and racketeers as principals in alleged offers of 'deals' to save his life. Lepke was said to have declared, many of these individuals sought to induce him to 'frame' others for political purposes."

It stands to reason, of course, that if there was a smidgen of truth in any of those blockbusters, then Governor Dewey, who loved inside stories when he could prove them, might well have found it advisable to stay the executioner's hand one more time. He didn't, and the Supreme Court sounded the death knell for Lepke on Saturday morning, March 4, when it turned down his eleventh-hour appeal. And so at 11:00 P.M., that night—unusual because Sing Sing traditionally staged its electrical lynch parties on Thursdays—the State of New York collected on its long-overdue final payment from Murder Inc. On the long-departed heels of such minor players as Happy Maione, Dasher Abbandando, Buggsy Goldstein and Pittsburgh Phil Strauss, Lepke went to the chair with Mendy Weiss and Louis Capone.

Capone, chewing gum as the guards strapped him into the Empire State's medieval instrument of eye-for-eye justice and applied the cathodes to his legs and shaved head, was the first to go. He said nothing.

Weiss, named as the actual triggerman in the Rosen murder, made a brief statement for the 24 assembled witnesses, exercising the privilege of the doomed. "I'm here on a framed-up case," he said, "and Governor Dewey knows it." On the credit side, Weiss thanked Chief Judge Irving Lehman of the State's Court of Appeals for expressing some reservations in the verdict which upheld the convictions.

Lepke, deemed to be the strongest of the trio and thus the last one to come through the door, did not utter a word. The only sound in the chamber as the triple charges snuffed out his life was the singsong prayer of Rabbi Jacob Katz, the prison chaplain.

But Lepke had taken the precaution to leave behind a last will and testament of sorts—or possibly two—for his underworld cohorts. The *Daily News* came up with this 45-word statement which it said had been passed out by the condemned man three and a half hours before the execution:

"Louis Buchalter has spoken to Hogan about one particular man and one man only. The man who is responsible and who was in back of several crimes is a high political power and these charges should be given every consideration before it is too late."

The *News* said Lepke was talking about a labor leader. No name was mentioned, but the only man in the United States who then fit that description—labor leader and "political power"—happened to be Sidney Hillman.

The author, not here as an advocate of the long-time shepherd of the clothing workers, is constrained to note that Frank Hogan says no such thing, that Sol Gelb says that Lepke passed over the name of Sidney Hillman as a mere

New York *Post*

Charles (Lucky) Luciano, then top man in the Mafia, cast a large vote in the underworld's death sentence on Dutch Schultz. He happened to be moving in on the policy racket himself at the time.

New York *Post*

Louis (Lepke) Buchalter, the smiling figure on the left, furnished the Murder Inc. guns for the Schultz assassination. He is shown in Kings County Court in 1941 in his trial in the murder of Joseph Rosen, a Garment Center truckman who wouldn't stay in line. Lepke went to the chair in this case.

New York *Post*

Jacob (Gurrah) Shapiro, Lepke's lifetime ally in the rackets, is shown in 1941 after he was transferred out of the federal penitentiary in Atlanta for slashing a cellmate. He died in Sing Sing six years later, when he was 56, while serving 15 years to life on an extortion conviction.

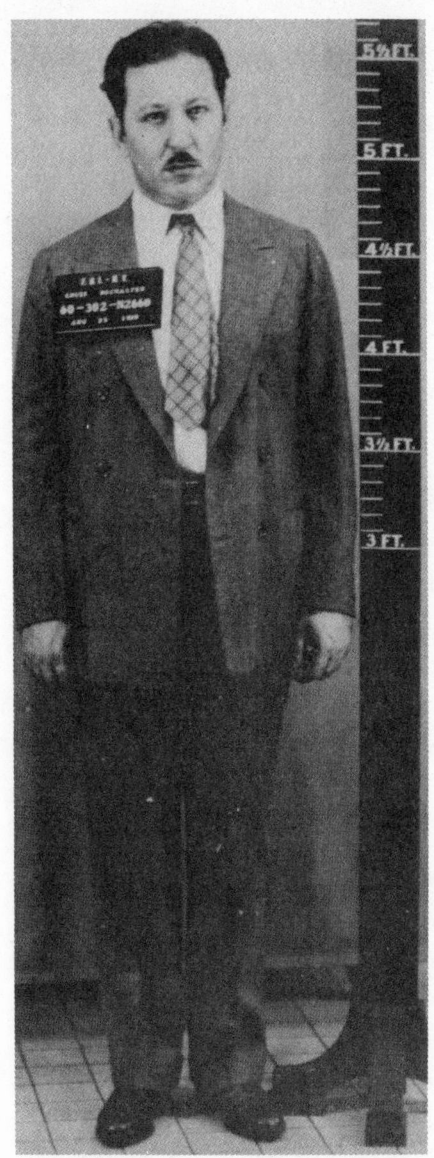

Federal Bureau of Investigation

The FBI put out this lineup shot while Lepke Buchalter was on the lam in 1939 for trading in narcotics and for bribery and conspiracy. Lepke later turned himself in to Walter Winchell, the Broadway columnist, in the hopes of staying in federal hands instead of having to face Tom Dewey's racket charges or Brooklyn District Attorney Bill O'Dwyer's murder case. The strategy backfired.

$5,000 REWARD

On November 8, 1937, Homer Cummings, Attorney General of the United States, under authority vested in him by law, offered the following rewards:

$2,500 for information furnished to the Federal Bureau of Investigation resulting in the apprehension of **JACOB SHAPIRO;**

$2,500 for information furnished to the Federal Bureau of Investigation resulting in the apprehension of **LOUIS BUCHALTER.**

The photographs and descriptions of the above named persons are hereinafter set out.

Jacob Shapiro was convicted in Federal Court at New York, New York, on November 8, 1936, of violating the Federal Antitrust Laws, and was sentenced to serve two years in a Federal penitentiary and to pay $10,000 fine. On appeal, this conviction was affirmed, and on June 14, 1937, upon his failure to surrender to the United States Marshal, as ordered, his bail in the amount of $10,000 was declared forfeit and a warrant issued for his arrest.

An indictment was returned by the Federal Grand Jury at New York, New York, on November 6, 1933, charging Shapiro and Buchalter, and others, with violating the Federal Antitrust Laws. Both Shapiro and Buchalter failed to appear in Federal Court for trial on July 6, 1937, and bail in the amount of $3,000 for each was forfeited and warrants issued for their arrests on July 7, 1937.

No part of the aforesaid rewards shall be paid to any officials or employees of the Department of Justice. The right is reserved to divide and allocate portions of any of said rewards as between several claimants. The offer provides that all claims to any of the above described rewards and all questions and disputes that may arise as among claimants to the foregoing rewards shall be passed upon by the Attorney General and that his decisions shall be final and conclusive.

Photographs taken February 16, 1936.

JACOB SHAPIRO, with aliases: "GURRAH," CHARLES SHAPIRO, MORRIS FRIEDMAN, SAMUEL DISHOUSE, SAMUEL DISNAHUSEN.

DESCRIPTION: Age, 41 or 42 years (born in Russia about 1895); height, 5' 5½"; weight, 200 lbs.; build, stocky; nationality, Russian, Jewish; hair, medium chestnut; eyes, blue, wears glasses occasionally; complexion, medium - inclined to be flushed; features, large mouth, thick lips, nose somewhat flattened - appearance of having been broken (possibly remodeled by plastic surgery) - large ears; dress, rather conservative - well tailored; speech, very gutteral, Jewish accent; mannerisms, gesticulates with hands when speaking; peculiarities, thick hands and short stubby fingers; fingerprint classification, 11 11 R O 7 Ref: 9, 3, 1
26 R 1 26 26 26

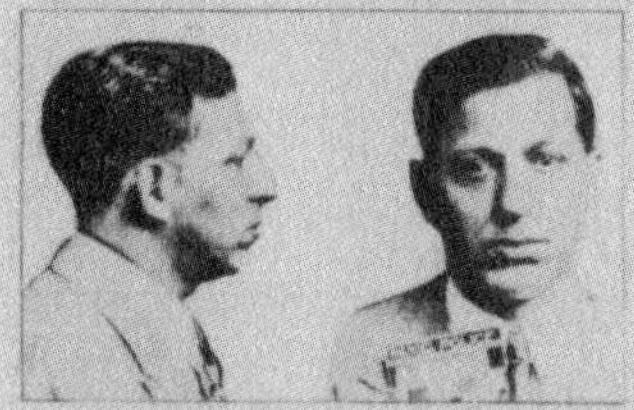

Photographs taken June 12, 1933.

LOUIS BUCHALTER, with aliases: "LEPKE," LOUIS BUCKHOUSE, LOUIS BUCKHALTER, LOUIS KAWER, LOUIS COHEN, LOUIS BUCKALTER.

DESCRIPTION: Age, 40 years (born February 12, 1897, at New York City); race, white - Jewish; height, 5' 5½"; weight, 160 lbs.; build, medium; hair, dark brown or black; eyes, brown; complexion, dark; peculiarities, nose - large, rather straight and blunt - ears - prominent - eyes - alert and shifting; marital status, married - one son, Harold, aged about 17; fingerprint classification, 25 11 17.
27 0

Information may be communicated in person, or by telephone or telegraph collect, to the undersigned, or to the nearest office of the Federal Bureau of Investigation, United States Department of Justice, the local addresses and telephone numbers of which are set forth on the reverse side of this notice.

JOHN EDGAR HOOVER, DIRECTOR,
FEDERAL BUREAU OF INVESTIGATION,
UNITED STATES DEPARTMENT OF JUSTICE,
WASHINGTON, D. C.
TELEPHONE, NATIONAL 7117.

November 8, 1937.

Federal Bureau of Investigation

The FBI's wanted card on Lepke and Gurrah.

New York *Post*

Rudolph Halley, counsel for the Kefauver crime investigation, questioning ex-Mayor Bill O'Dwyer in the big TV hearings of 1951. O'Dwyer by then had resigned his office to become U.S. Ambassador to Mexico, courtesy of President Truman.

acquaintance (surely an understatement, considering the warm relations between the mobs and the garment unions), and that Judge Sarafite has no recollection whatever of Hillman's name having come up at all.

So much for the farewell aired by the *News.* The more consequential Lepke sign-off, which was at variance with the tabloid's 45-word gem, came in something he had dictated to his wife, Betty, on that last afternoon. Carefully recorded on a crumpled piece of yellow scratch paper, this missive said that (a) Louis Buchalter was innocent in the murder of Joseph Rosen, and (b), more important, Louis Buchalter never tried to buy back his life by squealing to Frank Hogan. On that score, all the wheels turning even on the edge of eternity, Lepke said he was "anxious to have it clearly understood that I did not offer to talk and give information in exchange for any commutation of my death sentence."

If that was so, of course, then Hogan and his assistants, all able men, must have been talking to some other guy in the Death House. The simple truth is that Lepke offered to talk and did talk but just didn't say anything, preferring to adhere to the unwritten code of the underworld. He took the secrets of his three decades in crime into the execution chamber with him—and all manner of men, in the inner councils of crime, in politics, in the garment unions, in law enforcement, had to sleep easier that night. As Burt Turkus said, "When Lepke's life ended, life just began for a great many other people he could have named." Don't ever doubt that.

There's a final piece of irony in this saga. If Joe Valachi was right, Lucky Luciano furnished even more inspiration for the killing of Dutch Schultz than Lepke, although it will be seen that Lepke surely did supply the gunbearers, But whatever his role, large or small, the now-dead Luciano deserved to be counted as another of the saviors of Tom Dewey, who lived to have two chances at the White House and then to settle down into a high-powered Wall Street law firm. Fine. Now bear in mind that Dewey was the man who won the conviction of Luciano on 61 counts of compulsory prostitution in 1936. Dewey got the 38-year-old Cosa Nostra boss stuck away on a 30-to-50-year sentence but Luciano, who won his nickname in the early days when he survived a gangland ride in which he had been left for dead on Staten Island, got lucky again. He came out in 1945 when his reputed contributions to the war effort, of all things, earned him a commutation. The story, never fully explained by any of the government authorities involved, was that Luciano—an American above all, even without the citizenship papers to prove it—had come to the aid of the Navy when it found itself beset by sabotage and other bad things on East Coast docks. From his cell in Dannemora, so it was said, Luciano had graciously passed the word along to his criminal bedfellows on the waterfront to start showing a little less greed and a little more patriotism so that our side could win the war.

The author put the endlessly debated question of the racket king's early release to Tom Dewey when this book was in preparation and got this answer: "In the Court of Appeals one judge dissented from Luciano's conviction on the ground that the sentence was too long. Thereafter, an exhaustive investigation by William B. Herlands established that Luciano's aid to the Navy in the war was extensive and valuable. Ten years is probably as long as anybody ever served for compulsory prostitution, and these factors led the Parole Board to recommend the commutation combined with the fact that Luciano would be exiled for life under the law."

Going back to Luciano and Dutch Schultz, there is ample

evidence that for some time preceding the Newark spot murders the Italian mobster and the Dutchman's man, Bo Weinberg, had become fairly chummy. This accounts for the fact that Weinberg's disappearance in September 1935 was attributed to Schultz long before Dixie Davis began to tie the pieces together three years later.

The full details of the Weinberg murder have not come out to this day, of course, and for that matter no *corpus delicti* has ever turned up. In the one this book is about, however, there were hardly any secrets. The inside of the Newark story began to get around even while the Dutchman, Lulu Rosenkrantz, Abe Landau and Abbadabba Berman were still in that excruciatingly vain battle for their lives in the hospital, because for all his vaunted craftsmanship, Charlie Workman proved to have an uncommonly loose tongue once he had made the biggest score of his life.

The Bug came away from the scene of the carnage babbling like a kid off his first heist. He did everything but take an ad in the New York *Times* to make sure nobody else, especially that awful Mendy Weiss, would purloin the credits. He made the case against Charlie Workman all by himself.

God hath yoked to guilt Her pale tormentor, misery

—WILLIAM CULLEN BRYANT, *Inscription for the Entrance to a Wood,* 1817.

CHAPTER XXI NIGHT IN CHELSEA

DANNY FIELDS, FORMERLY ISIDOR FRIEDMAN, WAS A PRELIMINARY fighter who went from the ring to the easier combat of the Garment Center mob (no third man and no Marquis of Queensbury rules). The husky ex–light heavyweight, a six-footer, was one of the assortment of handymen in the brass knuckle set Lepke Buchalter kept on hand for his labors in the service of Sidney Hillman's Amalgamated Clothing Workers Union. Away from the strains of his new career, more violent than the old even though he never got hit anymore, Danny Fields liked girls more than almost anything. He kept a sultry young divorcée— out of a quiet hamlet on the Hudson but now caught up in the perilous tides of the Manhattan underworld—stashed away in a low-cost love nest on West 21st Street in the Chelsea district.

On the afternoon of October 24, 1935, towards four o'clock, Danny called the girl—known here as Ruth Sands because she would find her way out of the depths once this was all over—and told her that he was bringing company home. It was the kind of call any husband in the other world might make so close to dinner. The shapely brunette was used to it, except that this night would be something very special indeed.

Danny Fields' "company" turned out to be nobody less than Charlie Workman.

Ruth Sands, tall and comely and hardly the gun-moll type, knew something about "Handsome Charlie" but the man who came in with Danny didn't live up to his advance billing at all. He was nothing like the slick and flashy figure she had heard about, nothing like the collar ad who made all those other Murder Inc. triggermen look like so many Pier Six hoodlums. He was filthy dirty and all messed up. He had no topcoat or hat. His shirt was a sight—there was some talk about blood on it, but this was never explained—and his suit looked as though he had slept in a garbage dump, which in fact he had. But Workman wasn't interested in the SAME DAY dry cleaner down the street. He said everything, every last stitch, would have to be dumped into the incinerator as soon as Danny could go down to his place on the Lower East Side and get Mrs. Workman to wrap him up another outfit. It was as if the smell of death was on him, down to the shoetops, but Ruth Sands didn't know it then.

The girl did know that it was no time to ask questions, for Workman appeared violently angry, bursting with an unspoken rage, all this time. He was so tense and upset that it took some persuasion before she was able to get him to sit down to her hastily prepared dinner—and the steaks did not improve his disposition one bit. He kept fidgeting because he wanted to see something in the early editions of the next morning's tabloids, and as soon as she had the dishes cleared away the girl was sent over to the newsstand at 23rd Street and Eighth Avenue, two blocks up the street and just a few steps away from the drugstore where Vincent Coll made the last telephone call of his short life.

Well, the papers tore it for Charlie the Bug.

He blew what was left of his cool and started talking about the bloodletting in Newark the night before.

He said that he had shot Dutch Schultz.

"He must die," he said, desperation showing clearly now in his voice.

He said that he had shot some of the others, too.

"They must all die," he said. He said it that way even though Abbadabba Berman and Abe Landau already were dead—this was in the news stories, but way down because nobody cared about the supporting players in that melodrama—and the doctors in Newark were quoted as saying that the Dutchman and Lulu Rosenkrantz had no chance at all, not even a whisper.

But that wasn't really what the Bug was raging about.

He was spilling his guts because he had been left behind after the massacre in the Palace Chop House. He said the other two guys skipped and he had to run through some creepy park and hide in a goddamn swamp somewhere and sleep on a garbage dump and then walk along the railroad tracks in the dark night and find his way to the Hudson Tubes and get back to Manhattan all by himself. He said he could never understand how anybody could do that to him, and nothing Danny Fields said could calm him down. Charlie said they were a pair of yellow bastards and they had no right to do that to him.

Ruth Sands fretted and held her tongue. She had been in on some mob stuff before. Danny in his time had used the apartment to shelter not just an occasional minion of the Lepke-Gurrah gang who had to lie low but even a stray lamister or two from Dutch Schultz's band, because Danny had friends all over the place. Now it occurred to Ruth Sands that everything that had gone before was just child's play compared to this. Now Charlie the Bug was in her apartment and the toll of the dead was ticking away in Newark. The Dutchman went at 8:35 P.M.—they got that on the radio—and in another seven hours they would be drawing the sheet over Lulu and before another dawn Ruth Sands would have to come to grips with a terrible fact: she would have to live the rest of her life with the awful secret of the biggest mass spot killing since the St. Valentine's Day massacre.

After all, the commander of the new mission was her very own house guest, and it was quite obvious that he hadn't just dropped in for dinner.

The Bug was there to stay.

Indeed, he regained his composure after awhile and had Danny give him an alcohol rub with those strong fighter's hands because his back was stiff from the time he was in that swamp over in Jersey. Then Paul Berger, another Lepke trooper, dropped in for a visit and the three men killed two or three hours playing cards and there wasn't much talk about Newark. And then it was late and the Bug flopped on the living room sofa and slept like a man at peace with the world—his world—at last. He would take care of that runout, especially the bum who went into the barroom with him and shared the artillery chore and then scrammed without him, on another day. There would be plenty of time for that.

In the morning, refreshed, Workman announced that he would like to see his wife and baby. He had been married the year before to Catherine Delewin and they had just had a baby son, Solomon. Danny was ordered to go fetch them—and bring back them clothes while you're there.

The dutiful Fields nipped off across town to East Fourth Street and Avenue A and quickly observed that the area around the $68-a-month Workman apartment seemed to be crawling with policemen—a scene duplicated that day wherever the top guns of Murder Inc. might have been in residence. Danny, not exactly anxious to mix it with the law, since he was known as a Lepke helper himself, whisked back to his own place and reported failure. "I couldn't go in, Charlie," he said. "The joint's lousy with cops."

The Bug, disconsolate, then asked Danny to drop all of his garments into the incinerator and trot out some of the Fields models. This was done, with the smaller man hardly emerging like a guy who was waiting for the photographer from *Esquire*, and then a fresh visitor rapped on the door. This was Henry (Heinzie) Teitelbaum, bearing greetings from the boss himself. "You gotta go away, Charlie," he said. "Lepke's orders." For Heinzie Teitelbaum, a court jester of the mob noted for his fractured English, that crisp message could not have been more explicit, but the Bug turned it down cold.

Danny Fields tried some soft persuasion on his house guest.

"Charlie," he said, softly, "Lepke's only saying you gotta lay low three or four days and then go to Florida. What's wrong with that?"

The Bug said no.

He said he wasn't going anywhere without Catherine and the baby and he wasn't going anywhere without $2,000. He said he was entitled to that much—was it too much to ask?—for the "work" he had done in Newark in the face of all that adversity. He said he was goddamn angry and he didn't care who knew it, not even Lepke.

Ruth Sands never knew just what happened after that,

because there were also some whispered conversations in the bedroom, but the man who came to dinner did leave that very day. And he was indeed heading for the surf and sun of Florida, just like Lepke said, but he had his way on at least one count. Catherine and Solomon went along.

For Ruth Sands, the nightmare was over for the moment. She no longer would have to get the jitters every time she heard a footstep in the hallway or shake with fright when she heard a police siren down on Eighth Avenue. Indeed, another three years and three months were to pass before she would have to relive those fright-filled two days, and that would come under tragic circumstances.

The man she loved went on the spot on January 28, 1939. Tom Dewey was hot on the heels of the Lepke-Gurrah combine then and Danny Fields, one of the troopers named in the burgeoning rackets investigation, suddenly found himself in some rather extensive sessions with Murray I. Gurfein, the prosecutor's Chief Assistant. Danny, then on the payroll of one of the garment firms operating as a Lepke front, had moved well beyond the muscleman stage. As a highly ranked Lepke lieutenant and collector for the terrorist combine, he had to know lots of interesting things about where the mob's loot was coming from. He had to know who was being shaken—and how. Gurfein found Danny pretty tight-lipped, but he could have helped Tom Dewey an awful lot once Lepke and Gurrah—fugitives at the time in the same 14-man jumbo indictment—were taken into custody. He could have helped, that is, if he had lived to open up to Gurfein.

Instead, just turned 40, Danny Fields died under a hail of bullets on a Lower East Side corner where he happened to be standing with Louis Cohen, also known as Kushner, a fabled figure of the underworld. You had to go back to the early Twenties for that name to ring a bell, but the cops had no trouble with it at all. Louis Cohen, undersized but a very tough guy, was the man who had killed Louis (Kid Dropper) Kaplan, much larger in the criminal trade at the time. Kaplan was a bully-boy thug who had come up from the East Side in the company of such notorious delinquents as Big Jack Zelig, Dopey Benny Fein, Little Augie Orgen and—hold on here—the inseparable Lepke and Gurrah. On August 1, 1922, Gurrah Shapiro, a slow-moving hulk, tossed a few errant shots in Kaplan's direction and got arrested, despite his atrocious aim. Gurrah beat the case on two counts: there were no witnesses who could remember seeing the gunplay and the defendant submitted that Kaplan had popped a shot at him, too. In the end, the Kid himself wound up in the hands of the police. The charge—murdering one Louis Schwartzman, an ex-fighter, for pilfering his best girl. Our Mr. Cohen happened to be a Lepke-Gurrah loyalist in whatever unpleasantness was afoot in the underworld society of the Lower East Side then, and this is where he comes in. When Police Captain Cornelius Willemse took Kaplan to Essex Market Court by taxi for his arraignment, Little Louis turned up in the welcoming delegation on the sidewalk. There were all kinds of cops on the scene, but Cohen paid no attention to them. He had something to do. He went around to the rear of the cab, aimed a pistol through the heavy glass panel, and killed the prisoner, taking care not to hurt the rather bulky Willemse in the process. Thus Kid Dropper was removed from the Lower East Side scene without the nuisance of a prolonged and costly trial and Louis Cohen was permitted to redeem himself with a sentence of 20 years to life which, serving fast, he was able to pay the state in 15 years.

Now, 17 summers later and just a short walk from the old

courthouse, Louis Cohen would fall with Danny Fields.

It might have been a mistake, at that. The word around later was that Cohen was supposed to finger Danny for the executioners but had made the mistake of standing too close to the line of fire. Charlie Workman, talking to Allie Tannenbaum once, had it another way. He said Louis was there to knock off Danny himself but everything got fouled up that day.

Could Ruth Sands shed any light on the murder of her boy friend? No. Packing her things to go back home and shake off the hard memories of the city, she had no idea how the mob had found out that Danny had been talking to the District Attorney. Gurfein, a partner in his own Manhattan law firm today, has his own theory. "They must have trailed him down to my office," he said, "and I suppose they figured he was spilling his guts; he really wasn't."

Later that year, in April, Ruth Sands was to have a much more momentous session with the authorities, set in motion when a Newark narcotics agent, J. Ray Olivera, came into the Dewey office looking for some help on a drug angle he was trying to run down in connection with the Lepke-Gurrah operation. Vic Herwitz and Dave Worgan, two Dewey assistants, were assigned to help Olivera and it occurred to them, on a long shot, that Ruth Sands might have picked up some information about the mob's traffic in dope while she was living with Fields. She was working as a waitress then in Glens Falls, and the D.A.'s men went to the upstate hamlet with Olivera, talked to her there, and then, for her own comfort, took her to the DeWitt Clinton Hotel in nearby Albany. There, still not quite over the shock of Danny's death, Mrs. Sands lost her reserve and started to talk about the night Charlie Workman dropped in for dinner in that

Chelsea apartment and did all that blabbing about the Newark murder mission.

That was quite a bombshell, but nothing happened, and Mrs. Sands was to testify in the Workman trial that nobody seemed to be interested in it when she told the story. The fact is, it was Newark's case, and Herwitz passed the information along to the Essex County prosecutor, Bill Wachenfeld, while Olivera also submitted a written report on it. That report, still in the files in Newark, also says that Mrs. Sands named Mendy Weiss as the "directing head" in the Fields murder. Herwitz himself doesn't remember Mrs. Sands' saying anything about that spot killing which could have been followed up profitably. There was no corroboration available on it, of course, and no corroboration on the Workman tip. On the latter score, the necessary supporting evidence would not be forthcoming for another year, as a matter of fact, but then it would come in large helpings. Here this chronicle takes on some even more forbidding hues as a new pair of underworld charm boys enter the picture. First, Abe Reles, called Kid Twist.

"What's the difference who shot him? He's shot. Let's forget about him."

—LEPKE BUCHALTER, talking about Dutch Schultz.

CHAPTER XXII

THE TWIN SONGBIRDS OF MURDER INC.

FOR A GUY WHO NEVER REACHED BEYOND FIVE-FEET-TWO IN his cashmere socks, Abe Reles walked very tall in his set. Pound for pound, he had to be listed as an even more formidable instrument of destruction than a cold-blooded killer like Charlie Workman. He enjoyed every minute of it; just to kill some time, he went along "for the ride" the night three of his Brooklyn colleagues went out to Long Island to knock off some bum named John (John the Polack) Bagdonowitz for walking out on Murder Inc. It was never clear whether he counted that one as one of the eleven execution missions on his personal list of credits, since it wasn't like him to make idle boasts.

You could throw out Reles' unfortunate height defect. He was wide, squat, dark and menacing. He had piercing black eyes, long arms all out of proportion to his body, and remarkably strong hands. Always firm and trim in his good days, he looked as if he could strangle another man or beat him to death with his grubby fists—and he could. Burt Turkus says he was the closest thing he had ever seen to a monster—"a small monster."

Reles did six months for juvenile delinquency in 1920, when he was 13, and in the next two decades acquired a dossier that filled three police yellow sheets. He had 42 arrests, covering everything in the book up to drugs and homicide (just five cases), and if he didn't hold the record for the most arrests he surely could claim it for beating the most cases. Oh, he did the inevitable short stretches in the Elmira Reformatory and the City Prison. Once he even stood a 30-day contempt rap for losing his head and assaulting a court officer, but that was about it; none of his seven convictions involved anything serious.

When you asked the kinky-haired Reles how he made his living between arrests he would mention things like bookmaking, running crap games or helping out a labor union here or there. He never liked to talk about the stable of whores he had once, or about busting heads in the Shylock trade, but when they broke him in the Murder Inc. investigation he added roles in a large assortment of killings, either as a star or a bit player, to his spotty employment record. He never even blushed describing his execution chores, although he did get angry once when someone suggested that after one such mission he surveyed the results to his complete satisfaction and then turned to a colleague and said, "Hey, who was this guy anyway?" No, said Kid Twist, he never killed anyone whose name—the last name, anyway—he didn't know.

Abe Reles fell into the O'Dwyer dragnet on February 2, 1940. Used to walking through the law's swinging doors, he came in voluntarily, oozing confidence, when he heard that Harry (The Mock) Rudolph, a minor sinner doing a misdemeanor bit in the Workhouse on Rikers Island, had implicated him in a seven-year-old slaying. For no apparent reason, Rudolph suddenly had remembered that Reles and two playmates, Buggsy Goldstein and Anthony (Dukey) Maffetore, had murdered a 19-year-old hoodlum companion of his, Albert (Red) Alpert, in an East New York yard in some argument over a batch of stolen jewels. The reason he remembered it so well, Rudolph said, was that the Murder Inc. trio put a slug into his own belly at the same time and it hurt like anything. Well, Goldstein (34 arrests) and Maffetore (15 arrests) also were picked up and stashed away in separate jails. The cops had Maffetore talking after a while, and behind him Turkus had another wayward Brooklyn boy named Louis (Pretty) Levine who also felt like talking around the same time and happened to know a thing or two about Alpert's demise.

Tossed into the creepy, bug-infested Raymond Street Jail, Reles spent 47 days telling Turkus to stop bothering him with the Alpert murder—"you got no corroboration." But it all changed on March 22. The gangster's 25-year-old wife, Rose, mother of his five-year-old son, dropped in at the District Attorney's office and announced that "my husband wants an interview with the law." Taken to Turkus, who was chief of the Homicide Division, she said she had to see Mr. O'Dwyer or no one. Turkus accordingly ushered her into the big man's presence, and Rose Reles laid it on the line. "I want to save my husband from the electric chair," she said, "because there's another baby coming." O'Dwyer said he had to have it in writing and the woman said that was no problem, Abe was ready. Turkus thereupon dashed over to the home of a nearby judge to get the necessary court order permitting him to remove the penitent from his unseemly Raymond Street quarters to Brooklyn's comparatively luxurious Hotel Bossert (clean sheets, room service and all that).

Since the law's new-found friend happened to be blessed with total recall, even unto the goriest anatomical detail in instances where the conventional heaters had been supplemented with such things as meat cleavers, ice picks, tire irons and nooses, this was the break that would turn the key on a sizeable portion of the murders ascribed to the Brownsville-East New York-Ocean Hill mobs. How many murders? Turkus always said it was around 200, coast to coast; the more conservative O'Dwyer never pegged it at any more than 83 or so, but he may have been confining himself to the more local contracts. Abe Reles talked about 85 that *he* knew about.

Naturally, the name of Charlie Workman turned up very quickly as the Reles memoir began to unfold. The O'Dwyer songbird remembered the Bug borrowing a car for a journey to Sullivan County the night a certain party who had lost his credentials with Murder Inc. was due to go on the spot. He remembered Lepke saying to him only the year before, "Charlie has a tough assignment—I hate like hell to have to do it, but we've got to take Feinstein." That was Samuel (Tootsie) Feinstein, the Bug's very own sidekick, fallen from grace either for flubbing an easy assignment (it was just to kill some guy) or because he fell in love with his own wife and started talking about the straight and narrow. He said that not long after Lepke made that plaintive remark to him the Bug drove off with Tootsie one night and then for a long time the Bug would take $50 to Mrs. Tootsie Feinstein every week and tell her that Tootsie would be home soon, but Tootsie never came home again. He remembered that Workman picked up a package of hardware from the Murder Inc. arsenal the night in January 1939 when a punk named Albert (The Plug) Shuman, suspected of whispering things to Tom Dewey, caught a fatal bullet in the head—from one of the guns in that package. He remembered Red Levine beefing to him once that "any time I've got a contract Charlie is around to do the killing"—meaning that the greedy Workman was grabbing off all the choice jobs. He remembered that the Bug had the assignment to steer Danny Fields—mind you, Danny Fields—to a Brooklyn garage to meet his maker, but he wasn't saying that the Bug fulfilled that mission, because Danny got his in Manhattan. (There is also a record, furnished by Allie Tannenbaum, of the Bug expressing "disappointment and sorrow" over the demise of Mr. Fields.) He remembered the Bug telling him he set up a party named Morris (Mersh) Schlermer to finger a certain Max Rubin in a bungled shooting party in The Bronx.

And oh, yes, he remembered a 1939 New Year's party at his own house in Brooklyn, just a bunch of the boys getting together with their wives and in-laws, when Charlie Workman started talking about Mendy Weiss. Charlie was very bitter about Mendy Weiss, who wasn't among those present at the festive table. He said Mendy Weiss was no damn good and after a while he took his host aside and said, as Reles told it:

"If I didn't go into the shithouse and kill the Dutchman, he wouldn't have been killed."

This undignified treat, pointing a way to a solution of the Dutch Schultz assassination after it had been gathering dust in Newark for three and a half years, was slipped to Bill O'Dwyer and Detective Captain Frank C. Bals on Good Friday. Reles went on to say that the Bug told him that Mendy Weiss and Piggy, the forever mysterious wheelman borrowed from Willie (Willie Moore) Moretti's gang in Jersey, ran off after the shootings. "Charlie," Reles recalled, "said he had to go out by hisself and find his way back by following the railroad tracks."

The Reles recitation was so impressive that the word went

out to go find Charlie Workman, and two days later, on March 24, two detectives from the Manhattan Grand Jury squad, John J. O'Brien and Abraham Belsky, had the good fortune to run into the Bug coming out of an apartment in Brighton Beach with Allie Tannenbaum, of all people. The cops took both gentlemen in on a charge of vagrancy, always handy in those situations. It must have seemed trivial to Charlie Workman, but he would always regret that he went along so cheerfully. The rap quickly went from vagrancy to the equally handy "material witness"—Abe Reles was in excellent voice at the time, so pick any old murder—and the bail turned out to be $75,000 per man, too much to raise in that delicate time for Murder Inc.

Workman couldn't know it, of course, but almost a quarter of a century was going to pass before he would walk the streets again—and the guy handcuffed to him on that pinch in Brooklyn would have more to do with that item than even Abe Reles. Tannenbaum was going to furnish the key testimony once he decided, with the help of the persuasive O'Dwyer, that sometimes it's better for a man to polish up his singing voice than to face a rap that might land him in that horrible little green room at Sing Sing. But that's ahead of the story.

On April 8, O'Dwyer and Burt Turkus called Bill Wachenfeld over from Newark and told the prosecutor that it was a man called Charles Workman who fled the Palace Chop House on that night of painful memory and traded shots on the sidewalk with one of the Dutchman's wounded soldiers. O'Dwyer said he had that information from an informant and he thought that perhaps Mr. Wachenfeld might want to bring over the woman who had seen the fleeing gunman. The D. A. cautioned his New Jersey colleague that if his eyewitness was indeed able to identify Charles Workman she would thereafter need a round-the-clock bodyguard or somebody might kill her. Wachenfeld suggested that perhaps it would be safer if he just took home a picture of the suspect and let the woman, Marion Seaberg, try to pick it out from among a small selection of other Rogues' Gallery luminaries. This was done, on the instant, and Wachenfeld reported back, in some sorrow, that Miss Seaberg had failed to pass the test. She said she had never seen Mr. Workman before. O'Dwyer was in no way dismayed. He suggested that Wachenfeld start extradition proceedings and get the Bug salted away in one of his prisons while the case was being tied together by other means. Apprised of the fact that corroboration for Reles' story was now available from the suddenly talkative Allie Tannenbaum, Wachenfeld did that. On his home turf, of course, he found Workman no more communicative than he had been in New York. Turkus had told the prosecutor that nobody was ever going to get so much as the time of day from that guy, and Turkus was so right. Here is a report Detective Captain Joseph Cocozza made on June 12, 1941, after Wachenfeld hustled him over to Essex County Jail to have a chat with the prisoner:

"I asked Workman if he could tell me who was with him on the night of October 23, 1935, when he and two or three others killed Dutch Schultz.

"Workman shrugged his shoulders and said 'Listen, Mr. Cocozza, I don't want to cut you short but I won't answer any questions. I have been framed.'

"Then I asked Workman if he had committed any other crimes in Essex County or in New Jersey alone or with anyone else.

"Workman replied, 'I was never in Newark or in Jersey and I never committed any crimes here.'

"I asked Workman if he knew anyone in Newark or in Essex County or in New Jersey and he replied 'No.'

"I then asked Workman if Tannenbaum and Reles told the truth and he replied, 'Why don't you ask them?'

"I asked Workman if Ruth Sands told the truth and if Danny Fields was his friend and Workman replied 'Ask the girl about it.'

"Then I told Workman that I would probably be up to see him again before he moved or that perhaps I would see him later on and he replied, 'Don't waste your time, Mr. Cocozza, you and everybody else here in Jersey are swell guys but I don't want to see you any more. There is nothing more that I can tell you.' "

As it happened, the Jersey police didn't need any help from the Bug, because by then all the blanks had been filled in by Mr. Tannenbaum. The lovable Allie, who had progressed from a $50-a-week slugger, strikebreaker and stinkbomb thrower to $75 to $100 and finally to a $125-a-week graduate killer in the Lepke murder school, had been talking a blue streak ever since mid-April.

The manner in which this classic case of underworld lockjaw was cured, by the way, came straight out of a Grade B movie. To start with, Tannenbaum's lawyers got him out of Bill O'Dwyer's clutches on a writ of habeas corpus only to find a delegation of lawmen from Sullivan County waiting to claim the guy on an old Murder Inc. contract up that way. Then one day O'Dwyer made the 100-mile journey to the land of lakes, hills and sour cream, dropped in on the prisoner and suggested a brief change of scenery, like an automobile ride. The District Attorney, never faulted for any lack of humor, didn't tell the big fellow where they were going, but he was taking him to see one of the fellows Abe Reles had mentioned, Hyman Yuran, a wealthy young dress manufacturer and a buddy of the Murder Inc. hired guns. Tannenbaum began to catch on all by himself after a while because he knew that country like a book.

The winding backroad course of O'Dwyer's limo took the grim party to a swimming pool drain behind the Loch Sheldrake Inn and there were some workmen there with spades and pick axes and a character named Sol (Sholem) Bernstein, also out of the old crowd, was telling them where to dig. It didn't take long. Hyman Yuran, also known as Yoell Miller, was waiting in a shallow grave of limestone and Sholem Bernstein said that Allie Tannenbaum was one of the gentlemen who had put him there. O'Dwyer, an ex-judge with a built-in concern for the rights of the accused, wanted Tannenbaum on hand to face the backslid Bernstein and affirm or deny. Well, the gruesome tableau failed to produce the desired result. Yuran, named with Lepke and Gurrah in the garment racket indictment and suspected of switching over to the enemy Dewey when he was building his extortion case against the pair, had been in his improvised resting place since the summer of 1938, more than a year. Naturally, he was hardly in the pink of condition, so O'Dwyer's guest just took a quick look and turned pale. All he said was, "I demand my constitutional rights."

Tannenbaum was going to need more than that, because behind Sholem Bernstein the man from County Mayo had Abe Reles, author of the Yuran squeal in the first place. So the prosecutor was in no way dismayed as he headed back alone to his busy office on the Gowanus. Even if Tannenbaum sounded as if he thought he could beat that case, O'Dwyer had an even better one up in that same verdant Murder Inc. dumping ground. This case, the one Tannenbaum was being held on in the first place, involved the 1936 demise of Irving Ashkenas, like the equally unfortunate Yuran a Lepke defector. Ashkenas, who operated a jitney service for Catskill-bound vacationers, had been found sprawled alongside one of his own hacks near the Paramount Manor Hotel in Loch Sheldrake, not very far from the quicklime pit where the mysteriously slain Chink Sherman had reposed a few months earlier. Ashkenas was very dead because someone had fired five bullets into his head.

Between the Yuran and Ashkenas missions, Tannenbaum had a right to guess that he was in bad trouble for the first time in his life. So, blessed with a trifling formal record for his 30 summers up to that time and evidently not wishing to dirty his police yellow sheet with any homicide convictions, he had a change of heart.

A courier brought the word to Bill O'Dwyer that Kid Twist's playmate would like to come home to Brooklyn and tell him some things. One may assume that it came as something of a wrench to the guy to leave the good green Catskill country, becuase there were warm memories there, perhaps even enough to counteract the scenes of horror that came later. Consider his history: Allie Tannenbaum was born in Nanticoke, Pennsylvania, but the family moved to an Orchard Street tenement on the Lower East Side when he was three, and then to Brooklyn. Allie made it to the fifth grade at Bushwick High School and quit at 17 to go to work as a stock boy in the Garment Center. He moved on to an Upper Broadway haberdashery after a while and then became a salesman for a paper and twine jobber. In the interim, his father acquired the Loch Sheldrake Country Club and Allie began to put in weekends and summer vacations there, helping out. That had to be the good time, maybe the best time —but one summer Allie attracted the attention of a burly resort guest named Gurrah Shapiro (Gurrah for the way he said "Get out of here," which came out "gurrah dahere"). The coarse, bullnecked Shapiro, impressed with Tannenbaum's brawn and muscle, arranged his introduction to that fun-loving crowd in Brooklyn. That was around 1931, when Allie was 25, and from then on the road dripped with blood.

Somewhat more literate than his Murder Inc. co-workers because of his better schooling and his formative years in the square world, Allie Tannenbaum actually proved more helpful to Bill O'Dwyer than Abe Reles. In the matter of the Dutch Schultz assassination, it turned out that he had more information to start with because Charlie Workman, by contrast to his passing remarks to Reles, really had spilled his guts with him. What is quoted here, without editing for the refinements, is a confidential report which emerged from one of the numerous sessions with high New York and New Jersey police brass once Tannenbaum began to hit the high notes as O'Dwyer's featured canary:

> Albert (Allie) Tannenbaum states that the first he knew of the Dutchman's death was the day after the fatal shooting, when he read the newspaper accounts of the killing. Allie knew of no motive for the shooting aside from the fact that Special Prosecutor Thomas E. Dewey was after the Dutchman which caused great concern in the ranks of the Lepke mob. Allie also states that bad blood existed between the Lepke and Schultz factions, as a result of the rubbing out of Bo Weinberg,

which in addition to the pressure of Mr. Dewey, might have served as a motive for the end of the Dutchman.

Aside from learning of the shooting in the newspapers, Allie also heard of it on the same day when he went to the meeting place of Lepke's mob. At this time Lepke wanted to know from Allie where he had been the night before, as he was wanted by Lepke to "go to work on Marty Krompier." Allie told Lepke that he was at the movies the night of the Dutch Schultz killing. Allie did not know that Lepke was looking for him that night. This conversation with Lepke took place in the back office of 500 Seventh Avenue, in Manhattan, a cloak and suit place conducted under the name of Fierman & Kolmer. During the conversation with Lepke at this time, Allie inquired if there would be further trouble with the Dutchman's men as a result of the shooting of Schultz. Lepke said no, that it would all be taken care of.

The next time Allie got information regarding the shooting was a few days after the actual occurrence when he had a conversation with Charlie Workman, at a certain place in New York City.

Workman told Allie about the shooting of Dutch Schultz, stating that he went to Jersey with Mendy Weiss and one known as Piggy. These three were instructed to go to Newark for the purpose of killing Dutch Schultz. They first stopped at a "flat" where they were to await a telephone call or message as to when the Dutchman would be in the tavern. As soon as he got the message, Charlie took two pistols and put them in his coat and they went to the tavern where Dutch Schultz was. The three of them were walking together—Charlie,

Mendy and Piggy—and about a block away from the tavern, Piggy said "I better not go near the place." Piggy told Charlie and Mendy he wasn't sure he knew the Dutchman, and said, "Maybe the Dutchman's men will recognize me." Then, from what Charlie told Allie, he started getting cold feet, and at this point both Charlie and Mendy edged up closer to Piggy and said to him, "What do you mean? What did you tell us before that you knew him? Come on, you, walk along with us," and when everybody got a few feet from the tavern they saw one of Schultz's bodyguards in front of the place and stuck him up and walked into the tavern where they saw some men at the table but didn't see the Dutchman there. Mendy ran towards the back, Piggy stood at the entrance, and Charlie went walking towards the back and he couldn't find the Dutchman. Then Charlie went and opened up a little door and saw a man taking a piss and didn't recognize him as the Dutchman but figured it was one of his men. Charlie told Allie that he took one shot at him with his .45 revolver. Workman figured it was one of Schultz's men and shot him once so that he wouldn't bother him.

At this point, Workman walked out and saw Piggy wrestling with one or two of the Dutchman's bodyguards and he butted in and started to help Piggy. After that was straightened out he still didn't know who shot the Dutchman. Again he walked towards the back and finally there was a lot of shooting there and he started to run out. He came out and he didn't see the car there, neither did he see Mendy or Piggy around. He was left stranded and he started to run. As he started to run one of the bodyguards started shooting; and he turned around and emptied both pistols and shot one of the bodyguards in the street.

This was all told to Allie by Charlie Workman. They had a shooting match in the street. Charlie then started to run and when he got a few blocks away took off his coat, his jacket, and threw it away. He walked a few miles to some little town where he saw a railroad station. Here he sat down and waited for a train, and when a train finally came along he boarded the same and came back to New York. During the course of his story to Allie, Workman mentioned about running through a little park where he lost himself, and this was the point where he threw his coat away. He dropped nothing but his jacket. Allie is not sure if he threw the coat away in the park or not.

Workman didn't tell Allie how they got to Newark, whether by car or train, and when Allie asked Charlie why he didn't go back to the flat he was told that he didn't know where the flat was located, except that it was not far from the tavern. Allie says when Workman left the tavern he saw that the getaway car was gone. There was a shotgun in the getaway car to be used just in case they were pursued. Mendy told Allie about the shotgun.

At a later date, Allie relates, there was some friction in the ranks due to the fact that Mendy and Piggy left Charlie behind at the tavern. Charlie said that Mendy shouldn't have left him stranded, and that as long as he didn't see him right away he should have waited for him. That was the opinion held by Charlie, that Mendy should have waited. Thus, about a few months after the shooting, Lepke was present at a meeting and smoothed things over. This meeting took place in Workman's house, somewhere on Ocean Parkway, Brooklyn. At this meeting were present Charlie, Mendy Weiss, Allie Tannenbaum, Lepke, Toots Feinstein, and others whose names Allie doesn't recall. The purpose of the meeting was to iron out all this friction and bad blood that existed. The meeting was held in he living room. Mrs. Workman was not present. Lepke asked Mendy for his version as to why he didn't wait for Charlie in front of the tavern. Mendy said "Well, I ran out and didn't see Charlie there, that only two minutes before I saw Charlie run towards the back. I thought he got out through the kitchen. I thought he got out through the back way, and there was no sense in me waiting for him. If I knew he didn't get out I wouldn't have rode away from there."

At this point Charlie Workman spoke up and said "Well, as long as you were doing so much bullshitting that you shot the Dutchman six times when he was only shot once you shouldn't know I was back there. You claimed you were shooting in the back, and you claimed you saw him running towards the back. If you didn't see me how do you come to say I got out the back way?"

Mendy says "Well, that's what I thought," and they were talking back and forth, and Lepke said "All right, forget it, forget all about it, it was a mistake and tell everybody not to talk about it."

That was all that Allie heard about the matter.

Allie also relates conversation held between Charlie Workman and Charles (Lucky) Luciano in Miami, sometime after the Schultz shooting. Workman told Allie he was going over to see Charlie Lucky to borrow

> $1,000 from him. When Workman came back, he told Allie he saw Luciano and borrowed the money from him. He also started talking about the Dutchman's killing, Workman told Allie, and stated to Luciano how he was left behind, stranded, with no car, and that he didn't like the idea at all. He stated that Luciano said, "All right, forget it. I'll straighten it out."

While the essentials were fairly uniform, some of the details in Tannenbaum's recital did vary in the telling. Once he said he heard Workman's account of the shooting not "a few days after the actual occurrence" but the very next night. He said he was summoned then to Ruth Sands' apartment (which she would deny) and saw the Bug alone there and "very angry." He said he asked Workman, "Where were you the last couple of days?" and the Bug replied, "Gee, what an experience I had." He said Workman followed that mild understatement with a full account of the bloodbath, touched off with a punch line that seemed mingled with more pride than horror. "It looked like a Wild West show," the Bug was quoted as saying.

On the motive for the death sentence, Tannenbaum departed from the Dewey assassination plot in another singing session. "The Combination," he said, "received information that the Dutchman was about to be indicted by the District Attorney of New York County and feared that, in that event, the Dutchman would not stand up but would tell what he knew about the different mobs." Here, of course, Tannenbaum had to be referring to Dewey, then Special Prosecutor, rather than Bill Dodge, the District Attorney who had been helped into office by the Schultz mob. Dodge did have a Grand Jury looking into policy in 1935 but the Syndicate,

New York *Post,* Stein

Abe Reles, one of the top Murder Inc. guns, was the first to put the finger – six years later – on the man who killed Dutch Schultz.

New York *Post,* Toots Haberman

Allie Tannenbaum, another high-ranked toiler in Murder Inc., furnished the rest of the testimony that nailed the Schultz assassin.

New York *Post*

Burt Turkus, Bill O'Dwyer's homicide chief, got the credit for persuading Abe Reles to talk. Turkus sent a whole assortment of Murder Inc. killers to the chair.

always attuned to this sort of secret proceeding, must have known that this investigation was pure flimflam; the newspapers all duly recorded it when that Grand Jury, led by Lee Thompson Smith, a real estate man, bolted and led Governor Lehman to supersede Dodge with the mustached racket buster that June.

The reference to the Schultz bodyguard encountered outside the Palace Chop House and "stuck up" remained a mystifying item. What happened to him? Did the kindly execution duo simply slap the outside triggerman on the wrist and send him off with a mild reprimand? It would hardly seem so. More likely, the Bug added the outside man to his narrative for purposes of adornment. The reference to the timid Piggy wrestling in the tavern "with one or two of the Dutchman's bodyguards" is also open to question. Schultz's trio of gunbearers all had been trapped at the table in the back room; there was never any evidence of any others in the tavern and, again, Workman and Weiss would have had to slip some lead to any such strangers instead of letting them stay alive to identify them either to the remnants of the Schultz mob or to the authorities.

The matter of Workman's failing to recognize the man trapped in that embarrassing position in the Palace men's room also raises a question. Tannenbaum's interrogators were delinquent for letting that statement go unquestioned, because elsewhere he had said that the Bug at one time or another had worked for the Dutchman. Thus one would have thought that some recognition had to occur, even though the gunner had nothing better than a side view because the victim was facing the urinal.

On the item of the kangaroo court presided over by Lepke, Tannenbaum also was able to recall, in still another session, a fuller text of the pint-sized mob boss's opinion. It went this way: "What's the difference who shot him? He's shot. Let's forget about him. It doesn't make any difference. Why don't you fellows forget the whole thing?"

Well, now, who could quarrel with that when it came from the underworld's "Judge Louis," who had the kindest, softest brown eyes and the manner of a Solomon with a machine gun under his robe? Obviously, nobody did, because the quiet that immediately settled over the assassination of Dutch Schultz and his cohorts kept the whole thing in cold storage until first Ruth Sands talked, after Danny Fields went on the spot, and then, two years after that, Abe Reles opened up.

"Nobody ever commits a crime without doing something stupid."

—OSCAR WILDE

CHAPTER XXIII

THE BUG COPS THE PLEA

IN HIS TRIAL IN JUNE 1941, CHARLIE WORKMAN RAN INTO a well-stacked deck, aged in the telling.

Beyond the glib and slickly polished Allie Tannenbaum, sporting an ensemble of Death House green for his role in Newark's Common Pleas Court, the state had Abe Reles, an even more assured witness. And beyond Lady Justice's two newly enlisted acolytes, the prosecution roster included the woman known as Ruth Sands.

The chief defense counsel, Samuel I. Kessler, had an understandably difficult time trying to shake Tannenbaum and Reles loose from the stories they had been reciting with such fastidious attention to detail since the year before. The best Kessler could do was to establish for the benefit of the jury that they had been very bad boys indeed before their switch to the forces of light. Big Allie readily conceded a personal role in "about six" murders—something akin to Jack the Ripper saying he had once kissed a maiden against her will. Little Abe, more candid about his work record, confirmed that the roster of the dead came to "about eleven" in his case. Had he killed all those innocents himself? Heavens to Betsy, no. "I was just part of the picture," said the baby gorilla. Part? What part? Reles answered that one with no sweat: "Two of us shot a fellow, but how you gonna know who murdered him? Sometimes there was maybe three or four doing the shooting." Splendid. Now about those eleven instant stiffs. Wasn't there one who was strangled in Abe Reles' own home, with the whole family, in-laws and all, on the premises? No. "They were way in the back," said the witness, showing more impatience than anger. "They were five rooms back."

With that kind of testimony, no juror needed to be hit over the head to conclude that the prosecution's stars, given to so much naughtiness before their nobler instincts took hold, might well be the types to tell a fib in the courtroom. But there was another side to that coin, too. The jurors would have had to come from Mars not to know that the man on trial wasn't exactly a model citizen himself. Even without hearing an ounce of evidence on his background, it had to be pretty clear to them that Charlie Workman had come from the same Brooklyn murder co-op as the men who were now trying to put him in the hot seat at Trenton.

There was a question from the start, then, about how much good the defense could do for itself by dwelling too much on the tawdry characters of Tannenbaum and Reles. The trick was to knock their stories down, and on that score Kessler had a little luck with the forlorn state's witness in the black dress, Ruth Sands, brought over to Newark by Vic Herwitz because he had remembered that she seemed to know so much about the murder of the Dutchman.

While the paramour of the departed Danny Fields could not be shaken from her account of Workman's bitter two-day confessional in his Chelsea apartment after his perfectly rude intrusion on Dutch Schultz in that *pissoir* in the Palace, she did knock down Allie Tannenbaum's testimony that he had heard the Bug's account of the shooting expedition in her place. This was a curious item in the trial. Back in 1939, Mrs. Sands had told Vic Herwitz that Tannenbaum had seen Workman in the apartment. Now she testified that her house guest's only visitors on those two days were Paul Berger, the Lepke husky who was in the card game set up to soothe the triggerman's tattered nerves, and Heinzie Teitelbaum, the relay runner who had brought that get-out-of-town message from Mr. Buchalter. As for Tannenbaum, who would walk away clean as a jaybird and become an honest lampshade salesman in Atlanta once he sang his last aria for Bill O'Dwyer, it is well to note that he had told the story both ways himself. In some sessions with the Brooklyn interrogators he said he had seen Workman in the Sands apartment; in others he said he had seen the Bug about a week later.

Kessler produced a bombshell witness of his own in the person of Marty Krompier, even then still showing lingering signs of the slugs he took in the Hollywood Barber Shop on that night when all the guns went off. Krompier had a brand new version of the Newark bloodletting. He said the man who shot the Dutchman wasn't the defendant Workman but the witness in the green suit, Allie Tannenbaum. How did he know that? Well, he said he had the misfortune to run into Tannenbaum in a Broadway bar in February 1938 and one thing led to another and he said to the big guy, "Why don't you let me alone? Haven't you done enough harm to me already?" And—

Q. (by Kessler) Just what did he say?

A. He said, "I know the rumor's going around that I hurt you. It's a lie. As a matter of fact I was on the other thing in Jersey."

Q. What happened then?

> A. I didn't want to talk to Tannenbaum. I grabbed my hat and coat and started for the door. He grabbed me by the hand and whispered, "Let's get this thing straight. I hit the Dutchman."

On cross-examination, Prosecutor Wachenfeld could do no more than establish that, like his own stars, with that juicy minimum of 17 murder missions between them, Marty Krompier was no altar boy either. Krompier had to admit that apart from his endeavors as a manager in the honest sport of boxing his varied career had brought him into contact with people like Dutch Schultz, although he insisted that the Dutchman was more like a good buddy to him than a business associate.

Workman's case was helped considerably by such Newark eyewitnesses as Jack Friedman. The Palace's co-owner swore that the Bug was nothing like the menacing guy in the topcoat who ordered him to hit the deck just before the heavy action began. And Marion Seaberg testified that Workman did not look like the man she had seen fleeing along East Park Street.

This kind of record, along with Marty Krompier's story and the doubts cast upon Allie Tannenbaum's veracity through the cross-examination of Ruth Sands, must have conveyed at least a suggestion of reasonable doubt to the jurors.

It was all in vain, however. Amid some high courtroom drama, the defense collapsed when Workman tried to establish an alibi for his whereabouts on that big night six years before.

As the trial went into its second week, Louis Cohen, owner of the Stuyvesant Funeral Home in New York, testified that he had employed Charlie Workman as a manager and car dispatcher—salary, $45 per—from 1933 to 1936. Cohen swore that the Bug had been diligently at work directing his hearses on their rounds—try to imagine a man more qualified for the job—when the prosecution contended that he was across the river on the errand that would make Arthur Flegenheimer a customer of some competing funeral home. And the witness wasn't just trusting to fragile memory. He had payroll records to prove it.

What defense lawyer could ask for more in a case of murder?

The trouble was that Bill O'Dwyer, over in his office in Brooklyn, was listening to a telephoned playback of that testimony from Frank Bals, his top detective, and he didn't like the sound or the smell of it. He told Captain Bals to have Cohen trailed when he left the witness stand and came back to Manhattan. "Let's see who he meets or talks to on the phone," O'Dwyer said.

Well, the funeral salesman must have talked to lots of people, especially over his bugged wires, because at 9:30 that very night he found himself in the cavernous Municipal Building in Brooklyn, ever so dark and forbidding, answering all kinds of sticky questions and telling quite a different story.

In this session, under the steel-edged interrogation of Frank Bals rather than the gentle guidance of Samuel Kessler, it turned out that Cohen had not employed Charlie Workman for anything like three years. He had employed him for two weeks, $90 worth, and it wasn't to dispatch the dead but to deal with the living in the person of some union troublemakers among the drivers. And how did he happen to employ a man like that with no direct experience in the funeral business except as a *supplier* of corpses? Well, Louis Cohen's brother-in-law had brought Mr. Workman down to the

Lower East Side mortuary to "straighten out" the labor thing. And who was Louis Cohen's brother-in-law? Why, it was Isidor Friedman, professionally known as Danny Fields. And had Danny Fields prevailed upon him to set the new man up with a business card—Charles Workman, Mgr., Stuyvesant Funeral Home—"for the sole purpose of providing an alibi and a cover" for the Murder Inc. gunman?

"That is correct," said a very unhappy Louis Cohen.

But that wasn't all. Just to nail the lid a little more securely on the defense coffin, Frank Bals proceeded to crack Max Katz, a Cohen driver waiting in the wings to corroborate the prefabricated alibi. The next step for Cohen himself, naturally, was Mr. O'Dwyer's inner sanctum on the fourth floor. The Bohola Boy, later elected Mayor of Sodom and Gomorrah but driven into the exquisitely corrupt sanctuary of Mexico (as President Truman's Ambassador, that is) when the Kefauver Crime Investigating Committee hearings in 1951 linked him a trifle too warmly with Don Francisco Costello and also kicked up some dust about Albert Anastasia escaping the Murder Inc. net, had a highly satisfactory chat with the hapless defense star.

It may be assumed that Bill O'Dwyer, since deceased, suggested to his uneasy visitor that the penalties for perjury were rather severe in New Jersey, as in New York. He may even have hinted that apart from any perjury rap across the river it could be most unhealthy for an honest undertaker on the island of Manhattan to get involved with the likes of a lifetime delinquent such as Charlie Workman.

In Newark the next morning, June 11, Bill Wachenfeld greeted Judge Daniel J. Brennan with a request to reopen the cross-examination of the defense witness Cohen. When the Judge granted it, Workman, the soul of correct courtroom behavior up to that moment, bounded out of his chair, livid with emotion.

"May I take the stand, Your Honor?" he called out. "Please let me take the stand."

"Not now," the Judge said.

Two guards wrestled the Bug back into his chair but as Cohen neared the stand he whirled toward him, calling out, "Mr. Cohen, Mr. Cohen, I don't want you to commit perjury." Restrained again, he shouted, "I'm all right. Let me alone. For God's sake, let me alone." Then he turned to his bewildered chief counsel and said, "Let me take the stand. What the fuck is the matter with you?"

The banging gavel silenced Workman at this point and Cohen, nervously turning a straw hat in his hands, took the stand and confessed that he had lied the day before. He said that his books had been falsified to show that three-year employment record for the defendant. So the Bug wasn't dispatching funeral cars in Manhattan on the night the four new corpses were being set up in Newark—or, in any event, he couldn't make that story stick.

The defense called for a recess.

Four hours later Sam Kessler came back into the courtroom and announced that his client wanted to enter a plea of *non vult.*

The lawyer was dejected. He knew the case almost certainly had been lost but was convinced that he had an excellent chance to upset it on appeal. Workman, for his part, with his emotion-wracked parents on hand in the conference room and backing him all the way, wanted to go for broke on the stand or gamble on a plea. Kessler could not in good conscience let the Bug submit himself to Wachenfeld's cross-examination; he knew that the worst possible witness for

Charlie Workman had to be Charlie Workman himself. While he never would say so, even to this day, it is a fair assumption that the lawyer, down deep, felt from the beginning that once the hard question was put to him—did you kill Dutch Schultz?—the defendant either would have to come up with a pure Academy Award performance in perjury or put himself in the electric chair. Ethically, of course, Kessler could not wittingly let Workman tell the big fib under oath in any event. And so the defense side came asunder.

Wachenfeld did not oppose the *non vult* plea once Workman conceded that he understood it was tantamount to a confession of guilt. Then Judge Brennan asked the defendant to rise.

The sentence was life at hard labor.

The Bug, in his 34th year and hardly at home in state prisons for all the nine arrests since his early teens, took it without flinching.

Catherine Workman, the woman who loved him, gasped.

William L. Vieser, an associate defense counsel, then gave the reporters a copy of an "order" which the defendant had addressed to Sam Kessler before the plea was switched. This is what it said:

> "I, Charles Workman, being of the opinion that any witness called in my defense will be intimidated and arrested by members of the District Attorney's office or police officials and not wishing members of my family and others to be subjected to humiliation on my account, do hereby order you as my counsel not to call any witnesses in my defense except myself. And I forbid you to call any other witnesses to the stand.

> "I further state if such witnesses are called I will openly state in court I do not want them to testify."

Removed to the prison floor, Workman was permitted a brief visit with his kid brother Abe, who threw his arms around him and wept uncontrollably. The detectives guarding the Bug heard him give this advice to Abe Workman: "Whatever you do, live honestly. If you make 20 cents a day, make it do you. If you can't make an honest living, make the government support you. Keep away from the gangs and don't be a wise guy. Take care of Mama and Papa and watch 'Itchy' (a younger brother). He needs watching."

The Bug's piece of wisdom about staying on the straight and narrow even if it meant leaning on the government for the rent money had a curious echo years later in Charlie Workman's own branch of society. Marty Krompier, of all people, was arrested in 1960 on a charge of fraudulently pocketing $1,269 in welfare payments in New York's Long Beach while he was earning a small living as a delivery man for a camera store.

After the sentencing of Workman, a Bronx detective who knew Emma Flegenheimer called her up to tell her that the man accused of murdering her son was going to prison for a long time.

"I'm so glad to hear about it," said the aging woman. "Thank God, thank God."

For her, the book on Arthur was closed at last.

"In nature there are neither rewards nor punishments—there are consequences."

—ROBERT INGERSOLL

EPILOGUE

BEFORE CHARLIE WORKMAN WENT INTO TRENTON STATE Prison, he put aside his classic no-comment stance for a few words in the Newark County Jail with Stephen P. Flarity, a Newark *News* reporter.

"Charlie," Flarity said, "will you tell what you had intended to say if you took the witness stand?"

"Ask Kessler," Workman replied.

"Did Reles and Tannenbaum tell the truth on the witness stand?"

"Why not ask them?"

"Charlie, were you in Newark on the night of October 23, 1935?"

"Steve," Workman replied, "it's all over now. If you come to see me in 15 years I might talk to you."

Time would not bear out the Bug's rosy assessment of what his life sentence really meant. While he was a model prisoner from the start, minding his own business, doing his work, he had no chance of coming out quite that fast. He would put in his first bid for freedom in 1956, as the law permitted after the first 15 years of a life term, but New Jersey had no charity in its heart for the outlander. Indeed, the annual Workman parole pleas were going to be turned down with much regularity from that point on. It was apparent that the Garden State, so badly sullied in the massacre at Newark two decades before, was intent on extracting the last full measure of punishment from the one man convicted in the murder of Dutch Schultz and his three cohorts.

Workman did his first eleven years in the maximum security prison at Trenton. His name turned up only casually during this stretch, but he wasn't quite going to be forgotten. He was only on the inside six months or so, in fact, when he was in the public prints again, and once more it was the fault of his primary nemesis—Abe Reles.

On November 12, 1941, still chirping along and supposedly the man who was going to enable Bill O'Dwyer to nail the untouchable Albert Anastasia in a murder case, Reles departed this vale of tears in a most mysterious plunge from his sixth-floor suite in Coney Island's Half Moon Hotel. The police said he died in an attempt to escape, and all the necessary accoutrements for that kind of foolhardy venture were produced. There were the usual strung-together bedsheets, secured with wire. And there was another length of wire enfolding the torso and attached to the radiator below the window sill out of which the bird had flown. When the wire snapped, the star witness of Murder Inc. fell five stories to an extension roof over the oceanfront hotel's kitchen.

It was all clear as the murky Atlantic itself, because Frank Bals, later boosted all the way to Seventh Deputy Police Commissioner when Bill O'Dwyer became Mayor, had no less than five of his aces on round-the-clock duty in the Half Moon with the long-memoried chatterbox who was going to stick Murder Inc.'s Lord High Executioner in the electric chair in the 1939 slaying of a party named Morris (Moish)

Diamond. Was it conceivable that the handpicked cops on the Reles detail, more men than there were guarding the President in the White House on that November day, all fell asleep at once? Was it conceivable that some master operative of the sorely beset hoodlum empire had made his way into Reles' room past the guard detail? Finally, was it even remotely conceivable that there was nothing suspicious about the whole thing and that Reles really was trying to shake off the comforts of the songbird's life and make his way back into a world that had to be unfriendly toward him at best? Considering all the quiet gangland lives the guy had messed up while turning pleasantly plump on the side of law enforcement, one might have concluded then that the only man in the world who had more enemies at the time was Adolf Hitler.

Burt Turkus, for one, did not believe that Reles had died in an attempt to escape. He still doesn't. "Abe Reles was thrown out of that window," he says today. "I never knew who did it but I know he was thrown out. I know he wasn't risking his life on a piece of bedsheet and some wire."

Joe Valachi, the next best underworld baritone after Reles, was more explicit. He said the police tossed the O'Dwyer informant out the window and "the boys" all knew about it at the time. "The boys," in the Valachi frame of reference, had to mean the Sicilian branch of the mobs, the ones who would have fretted the most over the specter of an Albert Anastasia caught up in the toils at long last.

Revived ten years later when Senator Kefauver and his colleagues started to poke around in the muck and mire of New York, Reles' strange exit finally received the attention of a special Kings County Grand Jury. The panel examined 86 witnesses and came up empty, finding no evidence of foul play when, in Bill O'Dwyer's words, "the perfect case" against Anastasia "went out the window with Abe Reles." But the jury nevertheless did come to a rather devastating conclusion in the matter of Mr. A., who eventually would meet his maker in the form of enemy Cosa Nostra guns in the street-floor barber shop of Manhattan's Park Sheraton Hotel on October 25, 1957. The presentment said, unequivocally, that the case against Mr. A. in the Diamond murder had not rested upon the broad Reles shoulders at all. "On the contrary, as a matter of law," the jury said, "he was only one of several accomplices. In view of the availability of the other accomplices, it follows that Reles was not even an essential witness. The prosecution of Anastasia required corroboration and Reles could not have supplied it."

Well, Reles *was* around to supply the corroboration they needed in Newark to make their case against Charlie Workman, and this was duly noted by the newspapers when the Coney Island swan dive occurred. No recorded paeans of joy issued from the Bug's cell in Trenton, of course, and he receded from the public prints again. He was back early the next year, however, when he wrote to Sam Kessler and instructed him to offer his services to the United States Navy. The prisoner said he wanted to enlist in a suicide fleet to hit Japan and avenge Pearl Harbor. He said he could bring along some fellow inmates who had served a total of 400 years and, like him, were willing to lay down their lives to wipe off the rest of their debt to society. While the brass hats turned it down, it was an engaging idea. One had to wonder what would have happened if this country had ever turned a band of hard-nosed cons led by the paramilitary Murder Inc.'s most decorated veteran against the Japanese. Probably a beef from Tokyo about how we weren't fighting fair.

Workman did not come in for any published notices again

until 1944—once more as a point of historical reference in the saga of the New York underworld. This time the spark —watch that word—was the death in Sing Sing's electric chair of Mendy Weiss, his Newark helpmate. On the lam for two years because he was one of those who came up in Tom Dewey's massive Lepke-Gurrah racket indictment, Weiss had been picked up by federal men in Kansas City in the spring of 1941 while Workman was awaiting trial. There was no move to ring him into the Schultz case, of course, since Dewey now had him locked into the Rosen murder with Lepke Buchalter and Louis Capone. When Weiss, 38, was put to death, the newspapers recalled what a fibber he had been back in 1935. How could he have said he had put six slugs into the Dutchman in the back room of the Palace Chop House when Arthur was in the toilet relieving himself at the time and Charlie Workman had to go in there and get him? It was a rather distasteful sidelight but worth noting when the State of New York finally pulled the switch on Mendy Weiss.

Three more years passed before the Bug made the papers again—this time in a 1947 medical bulletin announcing that he was dying from complications which had set in after an operation for gallstones. Catherine Workman rushed to the prison hospital with her brother-in-law, Abe, but the doctors had failed to take into account the patient's strong will and fine body, kept trim with regular handball workouts. Workman rallied and recovered nicely. Now he had some prison hemstitching to complement his only other scar, a remnant of a shoulder wound carelessly picked up somewhere along the high-tension road on the outside.

The Bug earned himself a transfer to the Rahway State Prison Farm, a more leisurely bastille, in 1952, and the ques-

New York *Post*

Charlie (The Bug) Workman, between two detectives, leaving Brooklyn Supreme Court in 1941 on his way to New Jersey to face trial in the murder of Dutch Schultz.

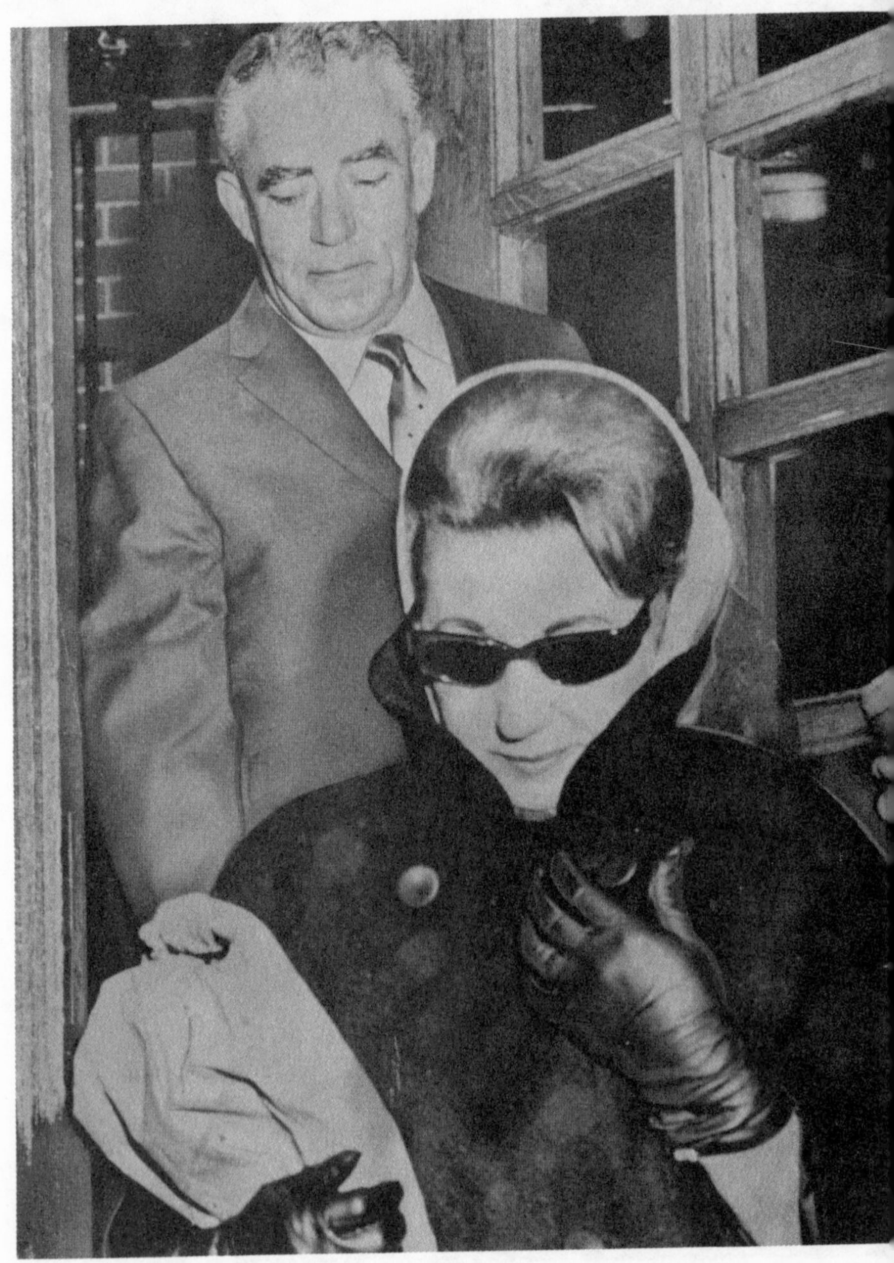

New York *Post*, Calvacca

Led by his wife, Catherine, Charlie Workman comes out of Trenton State Prison after 23 years behind bars. He's a salesman now—in the Garment Center.

tion was asked, would a guy like that be safe in there? No problem. "Nobody is going to bother him in here," said Acting Superintendent Stephen Francsak. "It is just like on the outside. The men look up to a man with his background." And so it was. No. 33334 handled his assigned tasks—on the yard gang, in the commissary, in the library—not only without incident but with so much diligence that toward the end he had become a trusty delegated to Rahway's truck entrance. He could have walked away but preferred to wait out the stonehearted Parole Board. "If I had a thousand inmates like him I wouldn't have to worry with this job," said Warden Warren Pinto. "He's just like an ordinary guy, not one of the 'big shots' who try to gain special favors. He never asks for anything." The prison psychologist had Workman listed as "a reasonably stable individual," and it turned out that he was a thrifty sort as well. The Warden said he had built up a handful of U.S. Savings Bonds out of his 18-cents-a-day prison pay.

The year 1964 rolled around before the Bug finally won his parole and was transferred back to Trenton to be processed out.

On March 10, he was up at 6:20 A.M., shaved, had oatmeal and coffee in the mess hall, and then turned in his prison grays for a Continental sharkskin suit—also gray—which had been sent in for him. The rest of the paperwork took another couple of hours and then, having picked up his savings and the $10 bill most state prisons lavish on their departing guests, he was led to the reception room into the waiting arms of his wife, who hadn't missed more than one or two Sunday visits in all those years.

A moment later, the couple emerged into a driving rain from the little prison door fronting on Trenton's Third Street, patrolled at the moment by four armed guards, one of them carrying a shotgun. Catherine Workman, wearing dark glasses, had a kerchief over her streaked gray hair. Her husband, hatless, was tanned and fit but looked nothing like the sleek and dark-visaged hoodlum who had come into that prison back in 1941. Now he was a stocky 54-year-old grandfather with steel gray hair who could have been mistaken for the corner grocer.

Plainly angry because there was a swarm of reporters and photographers on the sidewalk and he had hoped to slip out unnoticed, Workman helped his wife to a blue Thunderbird parked at the curb. His brother Abe, at the wheel, had a towel draped over the window on his side so that he could not be photographed close-up. Mrs. Workman got in alongside him and the Bug climbed into the back seat. The T-bird whisked away from the curb even before the rear door was closed, grazing a Sheriff's car as it headed for the New Jersey Turnpike.

Charlie Workman was going home at last—22 years and 9 months, or 8,307 days, after his dramatic courtroom turnabout. He would go to the offices of the New York State Parole Commission on lower Broadway in Manhattan. He would check himself in that day and thereafter report in periodically for the rest of his life—every week at first, then every month, now four times a year. After a while, this would represent a minimal inconvenience; the Parole Board moved in time to the very fringe of the Garment Center itself, and it was there, in his old stamping ground, that Charlie Workman would go to work, carrying a sample case instead of a shoulder holster. He would become a salesman, purveying notions—zippers and the like—to dress manufacturers. Mild-mannered and gentle, working beyond his years, he would do well. If you knew him and dared to ask about the old days, Charlie Workman would duck it. He would light a cigarette and tell you that if he knew then what he knew now he would have stayed away from that other life. He would tell you that he was a pretty lucky guy after all, because in the time of his long travail he was sustained by a pretty wonderful woman, Catherine Workman, still at his side. And now there were the grandchildren too. Charlie Workman would tell you that he had no complaints about the way things had turned out. He had something to savor at the end.

But he would never really be a free man again. He would always be the man who, in his own words, went into the shithouse and killed the Dutchman.

And paid the price.

INDEX